The Mind: Striving for Excellence

Dr. Anil Korade

DEDICATION

To my dearest wife, Dr. Manisha,
whose steadfast support and love are my greatest strength.
To my son, Shivansh,
whose laughter and innocence bring endless joy to my life.
And to my parents,
for their unwavering guidance, sacrifices, and encouragement that have
shaped who I am today.
This work stands as a testament to your love, inspiration, and belief in me.

CONTENTS

Unlocking the Power of the Mind

Have you ever wondered how your mind could become your greatest ally in achieving personal growth, resilience, and success? Imagine unlocking its hidden potential, turning obstacles into opportunities and realizing your fullest capabilities. *The Mind: Striving for Excellence* is a journey to discover the incredible power of your mental abilities.

In this book, we invite you to embark on an exploration of human thought, unravel the mysteries of consciousness, and discover practical techniques for applying these insights in daily life. Gain greater clarity, overcome stress, and thrive in every aspect of life. Whether you are striving for personal development, a deeper understanding of the mind, or a path to emotional well-being, this book offers transformative insights for you.

Together, we will explore, grow, and empower ourselves, realizing that the mind's potential knows no limits—it is time to unleash yours.

The mind is a vibrant, functional part of the body, filled with an incredible diversity of thoughts, emotions, memories, and perceptions. It forms a complex network of interconnected pathways where information flows seamlessly, decisions are made, and understanding is built. Imagine your mind as a dynamic ocean—its emotions are like waves moving against the shores of consciousness. Just as the ocean changes with the weather, our mental state can fluctuate, influenced by external stimuli and internal experiences. In moments of turmoil, we may feel overwhelmed, much like a stormy sea. Yet, amidst the chaos, there lies a serene garden of insights, blooming quietly and offering a break from daily struggles. In these moments of clarity, we find rejuvenation and the ability to navigate complexities with inner grace.

The mind constantly adapts and evolves in response to new information, experiences, and challenges—reshaping our sense of self over time. It is like a sculptor shaping clay, molding our identity through actions, choices, and interactions. Embarking on this transformative journey into the complexities of the human mind reveals boundless potential. Contrary to myths about only using a fraction of our brain's capacity, neuroscience shows that our brains are fully engaged in diverse tasks throughout the day. Our journey begins with a deep understanding of concepts like perception, cognition, emotion, and consciousness, offering us valuable insights into how we think, feel, and behave. Through self-reflection, we unravel hidden truths, confront limitations, and embrace new possibilities. By developing mindfulness, enhancing emotional intelligence, and cultivating a growth mindset, we can enhance every sphere of life—personal, professional, and emotional.

We begin by exploring the origins of human thought, delving into the evolutionary roots of cognition. Drawing from Darwinian Theory, we examine adaptive mechanisms that have shaped the way we think. Insights from psychology and philosophy, including concepts like dualism and physicalism, give us a comprehensive understanding of the mind. We explore mindsets and their profound impact on behavior, identifying strategies to nurture a growth-oriented perspective and achieve personal development.

Mindtech Unleashed Our exploration also covers the transformative impact of technology on cognition and behavior. From artificial intelligence to virtual reality and smartphone interventions, emerging technologies are revolutionizing how we perceive, think, and interact. We delve into the intersection between human intelligence and AI, discussing the potential implications of these advancements on consciousness and personal growth. These technologies, informed by neuroscience, offer new ways to optimize focus, memory, and overall mental performance.

Living an optimal life requires understanding how to manage stress, foster emotional intelligence, and harness grit for success. We examine altered states of consciousness that enhance creativity, and the powerful flow state that underpins peak performance. By fostering mind synergy—a harmonious integration of thoughts, emotions, and perceptions—we can create a unified, enriched mental state.

A Unified Approach To truly maximize our potential, we need to achieve mindsynchronization: a seamless synergy of all cognitive processes. Through the use of meditation, mindfulness practices, and emotional intelligence exercises, we align various facets of the mind to enhance flexibility, creativity, and problem-solving abilities. This approach fosters a sense of inner unity and resilience.

Our journey is one of continual learning and reflection. We pause to consider our progress, explore ethical challenges, and contemplate the societal implications of our evolving understanding of the mind. By integrating insights from psychology, neuroscience, philosophy, and technology, we not only understand ourselves better but also contribute to a broader societal evolution.

"The Mind: Striving for Excellence" is not just a book—it is a roadmap to unlock your potential and live a more fulfilling life. By diving into the depths of the mind, you will find powerful tools for personal growth, resilience, and well-being. Whether you want to enhance your creativity, deepen your relationships, or achieve personal excellence, this book will guide you on your journey. So, are you ready to open your mind, embrace self-discovery, and empower yourself to reach new heights? Your journey to excellence awaits—let the transformation begin.

1 EXPLORING DEPTH OF THE MIND

"The mind is like an iceberg, it floats with one-seventh of its bulk above water."- Sigmund Freud

In the exploration of the mind, a tapestry of questions unfolds, crossing through the fields of philosophy, neuroscience, and existential inquiry. The mind, a concept both fascinating and elusive, invites reflection that stretches beyond the limits of the visible and tangible world. Its elusive nature raises questions about its very essence. Unlike the brain, a physical organ that can be seen and touched, the mind is an intangible entity, encompassing thoughts, emotions, consciousness, and subjective experiences—a mosaic that profoundly shapes human existence.

Understanding the mind becomes increasingly complex when we try to separate it from the brain, which is responsible for observable neural activities and the execution of cognitive functions. While the brain operates through physical processes, the nature of the mind resists precise localization within this biological structure. The challenge lies not only in distinguishing the mind from the brain but also in examining the interplay between them. There remains an enduring mystery about which of the two takes the lead—whether the mind orchestrates the actions of the brain or if the brain serves as the primary conductor in this dance.

The relationship between the mind and the body has been a subject of philosophical debate for centuries, raising questions about the distinction between the physical vessel and the intangible entity it houses. While the brain manifests in physical form, the mind introduces another dimension—one that invites contemplation of how they interact. This interaction creates a complex, interconnected system that intertwines the processes of thinking, reasoning, and personal awareness. The mind encompasses a wide range of elements, including perceptions, memories, and the ability to make decisions. It is closely linked to the brain's activities but transcends purely physiological functions, embracing the deeply reflective dimensions of human experience.

With its far-reaching influence, the mind serves as the linchpin of individual behavior, shaping one's perception of the world. What might seem simple at first glance reveals itself to be a profound aspect of consciousness. The relationship between the mind and brain invites researchers to embark on a multidisciplinary journey, drawing on psychology, neuroscience, and other fields to gain a deeper understanding of cognition. Through these diverse perspectives, a more comprehensive understanding of the mind emerges, offering insights into the web of cognitive processes.

Consider a highly advanced computer—its hardware system consists of billions of circuits and processors, which process information, control physical tasks, and execute commands. Now, imagine this computer housed within the human skull. The hardware, in this analogy, represents the brain, which manages physical and cognitive functions. However, just as important is the software—the mind—which governs higher-level aspects of cognition, including self-awareness and creativity. This is where the mind comes into play, as it brings forth a distinct sense of self-awareness.

Picture an individual embarking on the journey of writing a book. In this creative endeavor, the brain orchestrates the motor functions necessary for typing, coordinating the firing of neurons, the movement of muscles, and the visual processing required to transfer thoughts into written words. Meanwhile, the mind acts as the source of inspiration, guiding the unique arrangement of ideas into a narrative. It draws from a reservoir of experiences, cultural influences, and emotions to craft a literary masterpiece. Just as the brain serves as a meticulous conductor overseeing the process, the mind emerges as the maestro, infusing creativity and meaning into the task.

Together, the brain and the mind exemplify a harmonious collaboration, where the tangible and the intangible work in unison to express the art of creation. This relationship mirrors the complexity of human existence itself, where cognition, creativity, and experience intertwine, leading us to continually ponder the profound nature of the mind.

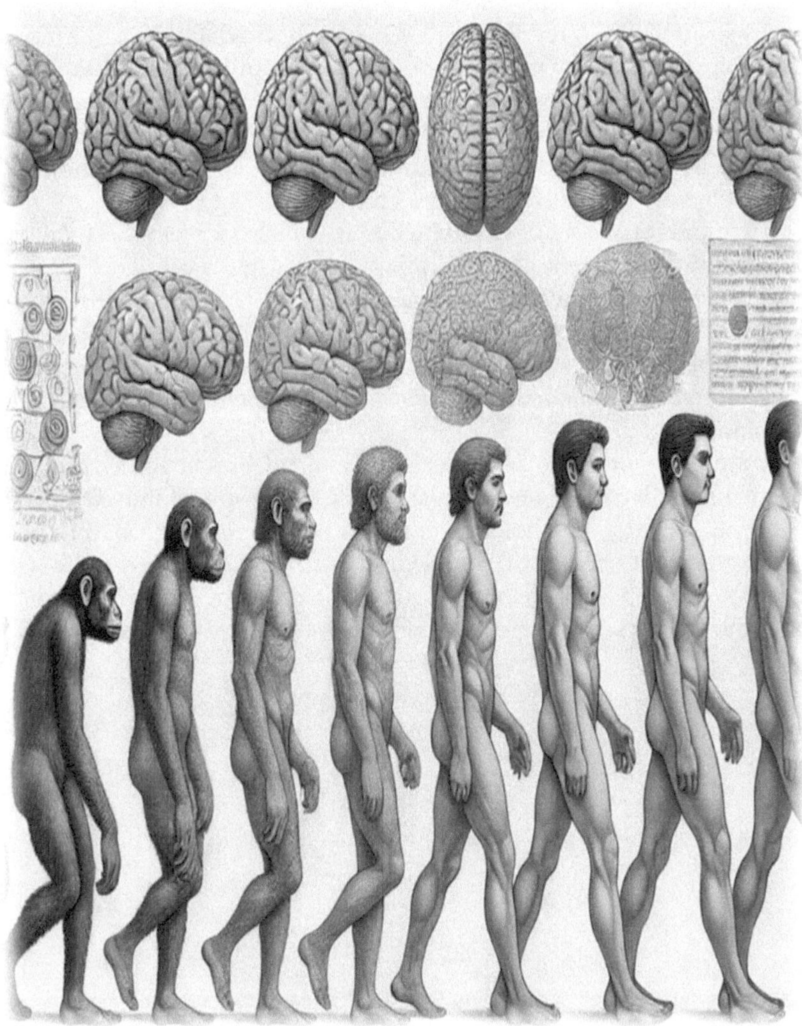

- **Evolution of the Mind**

"The mind is everything. What you think, become." - Buddha

The human mind is a truly remarkable product of evolution, shaped and refined over millions of years by the powerful forces of natural selection. To truly understand this extraordinary creation, we need to dive deep into its evolutionary origins. At the core of this journey lies the field of psychology, which explores how the mind's functions have been adapted and honed by evolution.

Our journey begins with Charles Darwin's groundbreaking work, which sparked an intellectual revolution. Darwin's ideas challenged the accepted beliefs of his time and transformed how we understand the complexities of life. As we delve into the origins of the mind, we explore the interaction between cognition and the environment—how the brain has developed mechanisms to tackle challenges, like avoiding predators and finding food, to increase our ancestors' chances of survival and reproduction.

This exploration does not stop with survival; it also looks at how culture has influenced our cognitive abilities, helping shape what it means to be human. Social interactions play a central role here, revealing how our brains evolved in response to relationships, communication, and cultural learning. These factors have woven together in a tapestry, where cooperation, symbolic thinking, and even language come together, each one adding richness to our understanding of the mind's evolution.

As we move through history, we find a blend of scientific evidence and philosophical reflection, which gives us insights into humanity's age-old struggle for survival. Psychology serves as a guiding light on this journey, uncovering layer after layer of knowledge. Each new discovery sheds light on the mind's development, reminding us of the unique human journey that defines who we are and how we understand ourselves in the vast story of life.

- **Architectural Emergence**

At the heart of our exploration is a profound quest to understand the origins and intricate design of the human mind—a marvel shaped over millennia by the challenges faced by our ancestors. This journey into the adaptive functions within our cognitive framework reveals responses finely tuned by the relentless pressures of survival and reproduction. Our pursuit of this cognitive architecture seeks to uncover how the mind evolved into its present complexity.

Drawing from the evolutionary insights of Steven Pinker, who emphasizes natural selection's role in developing cognitive abilities, and Daniel Dennett's philosophical views on consciousness as an emergent phenomenon, this journey takes us deep into the mind's design and purpose. Imagine embarking on this journey as an intrepid explorer, equipped with the tools of science, philosophy, and introspection.

We begin by examining fundamental cognitive processes—perception, memory, and decision-making—that may have conferred survival advantages on our ancestors, helping them navigate their environments effectively. As we explore further into the mind's labyrinth, we confront the enigmatic essence of consciousness itself.

In this exploration, consciousness emerges as a pivotal force, shaping human development in profound ways. This subjective awareness—our ability to perceive thoughts, sensations, and surroundings—linked early humans to their environment, helping them interpret, anticipate threats, and devise solutions, which provided a significant evolutionary edge.

Moreover, consciousness facilitated social cooperation and collaboration, essential elements of human evolution. By fostering empathy, perspective-taking, and the theory of mind, consciousness laid the groundwork for cooperative behavior and complex social structures. Through shared awareness, early humans formed close groups, passed on cultural knowledge, and advanced in language, culture, and technology.

Consciousness also paved the way for higher cognitive functions, including abstract reasoning, introspection, and self-awareness, driving the evolution of the mind toward greater complexity. These abilities enabled humans to reflect, imagine future scenarios, and engage in metacognition, sparking innovation and problem-solving.

An example of this cognitive evolution is our ability to recognize faces, crucial for social interaction, communication, and survival. Picture yourself tracing this skill back in time: early humans who could quickly distinguish between familiar faces (such as tribe members) and potential threats (like predators) had a survival advantage. This ability helped them form alliances, identify kin, and navigate social hierarchies. Primitive facial recognition skills, such as identifying two eyes, a nose, and a mouth, gradually evolved through natural selection, becoming more sophisticated over generations. As we delve deeper, we find specialized brain regions, such as the fusiform face area, that process facial features. Cultural factors also influence facial recognition; for example, individuals from cultures where eye contact is highly valued may develop different facial recognition skills than those from cultures where direct gaze is considered impolite.

In the midst of the mind's complexity, facial recognition stands out as a remarkable adaptation. This skill, essential for social cohesion, communication, and survival, is deeply woven into our species' evolutionary story. Imagine our ancient ancestors navigating their environments, where survival often depended on distinguishing friend from foe. Those with a keen sense of facial recognition enjoyed advantages in identifying group members, detecting threats, and building alliances.

Psychological and neuroscientific studies have revealed the neural mechanisms behind facial recognition, uncovering specialized brain areas, like the fusiform face area in the temporal lobe, dedicated to processing facial features and expressions. Advanced imaging techniques have provided insights into the intricate circuits responsible for encoding and interpreting facial information.

Philosophical inquiry also invites us to explore the deeper implications of facial recognition. Questions about intention and consciousness prompt reflection on how our perceptions of faces are shaped by cultural norms, personal experiences, and social dynamics. Contemplating these aspects helps us understand how facial recognition influences our interactions, communication, and understanding of others' mental states.

Through a synthesis of scientific research and philosophical reflection, we gain a nuanced view of facial recognition as an adaptation crafted by evolution. This mechanism illustrates the remarkable ingenuity of natural selection in shaping the human mind's intricate architecture. Furthermore, it highlights the interconnectedness of biological evolution, cognitive processes, and social behavior, revealing the complex tapestry of the human experience.

- **Challenges Faced by Ancestors**

In our journey through the foundations of evolutionary psychology, we encounter the formidable challenges that shaped the adaptive responses of our ancient ancestors. The struggle for survival, the complexities of social interaction, and the relentless quest for sustenance emerge as the crucibles that forged the capabilities of the human mind.

At the heart of our exploration is an understanding of the harsh realities faced by early humans in their daily fight for survival. Imagine these early humans traversing vast savannahs, where predators like lions lay hidden in the tall grasses. Those with an acute sensitivity to subtle signs of danger—such as the rustling of grass or the faint scent of a nearby carnivore—gained a significant advantage in the evolutionary race. This ability to detect and quickly react to potential threats was far from arbitrary; it played a vital role in survival.

Research in evolutionary psychology supports this idea, demonstrating that humans have developed mechanisms to recognize potential threats efficiently. Studies show a natural predisposition to notice and respond more rapidly to danger-related stimuli, such as images of snakes or spiders. This heightened sensitivity is believed to be an adaptive trait shaped by our ancestors' millennia-long coexistence with predators in their environments.

Consider the everyday scenario of walking through a dimly lit alley at night, where even individuals who have never encountered predator in such settings may feel sense unease or heightened alertness, instinctively scanning their surroundings for potential threats. This response, deeply rooted our evolutionary past, underscores adaptive nature cognitive architecture.

Beyond individual survival, our exploration extends to the intricate web of social dynamics that characterized ancestral communities. Through lens evolution, we discern complexities relationships, alliances, and conflicts defined early human societies. Imagine these communities facing formidable challenges such as hunting large game or defending against rival groups. In scenarios, effective cooperation among individuals within community emerged a prerequisite for survival success.

Richard Dawkins and others have proposed the social brain hypothesis, suggesting a link between complexity of human behavior size development brain. In ancestral communities, individuals endowed with larger, more developed brains were better equipped to navigate intricacies relationships, form alliances, cooperate effectively others.

Daniel Dennett's insights into cultural evolution further enrich our understanding of cooperation within these communities. He emphasizes how norms and practices, transmitted across generations, shape individuals' behavior influence the dynamics social groups. For instance, development rituals or traditions around cooperative activities, such as hunting communal gathering, could strengthen bonds promote among group members.

Consider a scenario where group of early humans embarks on hunting expedition to capture mammoth. Effective cooperation becomes indispensable for success, as individuals must coordinate their actions, communicate effectively, and share resources achieve common goal. Over time, cultural practices norms surrounding rituals may emerge, reinforcing fostering solidarity among community members.

The quest for sustenance emerges as another crucible that shaped adaptive responses of human mind throughout evolution. Foraging food was a primary activity survival, requiring individuals to utilize range cognitive abilities efficiently locate and acquire resources in diverse environments.

John Tooby and Leda Cosmides propose that the human mind is equipped with cognitive adaptations specifically evolved to solve complex problems associated foraging. These include skills such as spatial reasoning, pattern recognition, decision-making, memory retrieval—essential for navigating challenges of procuring food.

Imagine a group of early humans traversing the savannah landscape, utilizing spatial reasoning to navigate their surroundings and locate potential food sources such as berry bushes or waterholes. They develop keen patterns recognition identify edible fruits tracks game animals, allowing them anticipate where resources are likely be found.

When faced with multiple options for foraging, individuals must engage in decision-making, weighing the potential risks and rewards of different strategies. Memory retrieval becomes crucial remembering locations productive foraging sites types food that are safe to consume. Over time, through trial error, learn from past experiences adjust their behavior accordingly.

Through the evolutionary lens, we gain a profound understanding of mind as finely tuned tool sculpted by crucibles survival, social dynamics, and sustenance. adaptive functions encoded within our cognitive framework are not arbitrary but purposeful responses to challenges that defined ancestral environment. intricate processes natural selection, abilities have been meticulously honed over millennia, enabling us thrive in constantly changing world shaped pressures.

Embarking on our journey through the evolution of human mind, we are guided by beacon evolutionary psychology, offering profound insights into cognitive development. Within this discipline, acquisition language emerges as a fascinating phenomenon, deeply rooted in past and profoundly shaping social interactions cultural dynamics.

Language acquisition, as illuminated by evolutionary psychology, represents a complex interplay of biological predispositions and cultural influences. Imagine child growing up in bilingual household. From an early age, they are exposed to two distinct languages, each with its own set sounds, grammar rules, nuances. Through interactions caregivers exposure linguistic input, the gradually learns differentiate between languages acquire proficiency both.

Drawing from developmental psychology, we can observe how children progress through various stages of language acquisition. For instance, during the prelinguistic stage, infants engage in babbling and vocalizations, laying foundation future development. As they enter holophrastic begin to use single words convey complex meanings, such saying "juice" request a drink. This transition marks emergence symbolic thought use, critical milestone cognitive

In parallel, consider the role of cultural context shaping language acquisition. cultures where storytelling is valued, children are exposed to rich linguistic narratives from an early age, fostering their skills and comprehension abilities. Similarly, communities multilingualism prevalent, navigate between multiple languages effortlessly, adapting communication strategies different social contexts.

Through empirical research and philosophical reflection, we gain deeper insights into the mechanisms underlying language acquisition. For example, studies in neurolinguistics reveal neural substrates involved processing, highlighting brain's remarkable plasticity adaptability to linguistic input. Inquiries nature of consciousness prompt us ponder subjective experience acquisition, as children develop a sense self their interactions with others environment.

Ultimately, the evolution of language acquisition underscores adaptive nature human mind, finely tuned by millennia natural selection. It exemplifies how biological predispositions interact with cultural influences to shape our cognitive abilities and linguistic diversity.

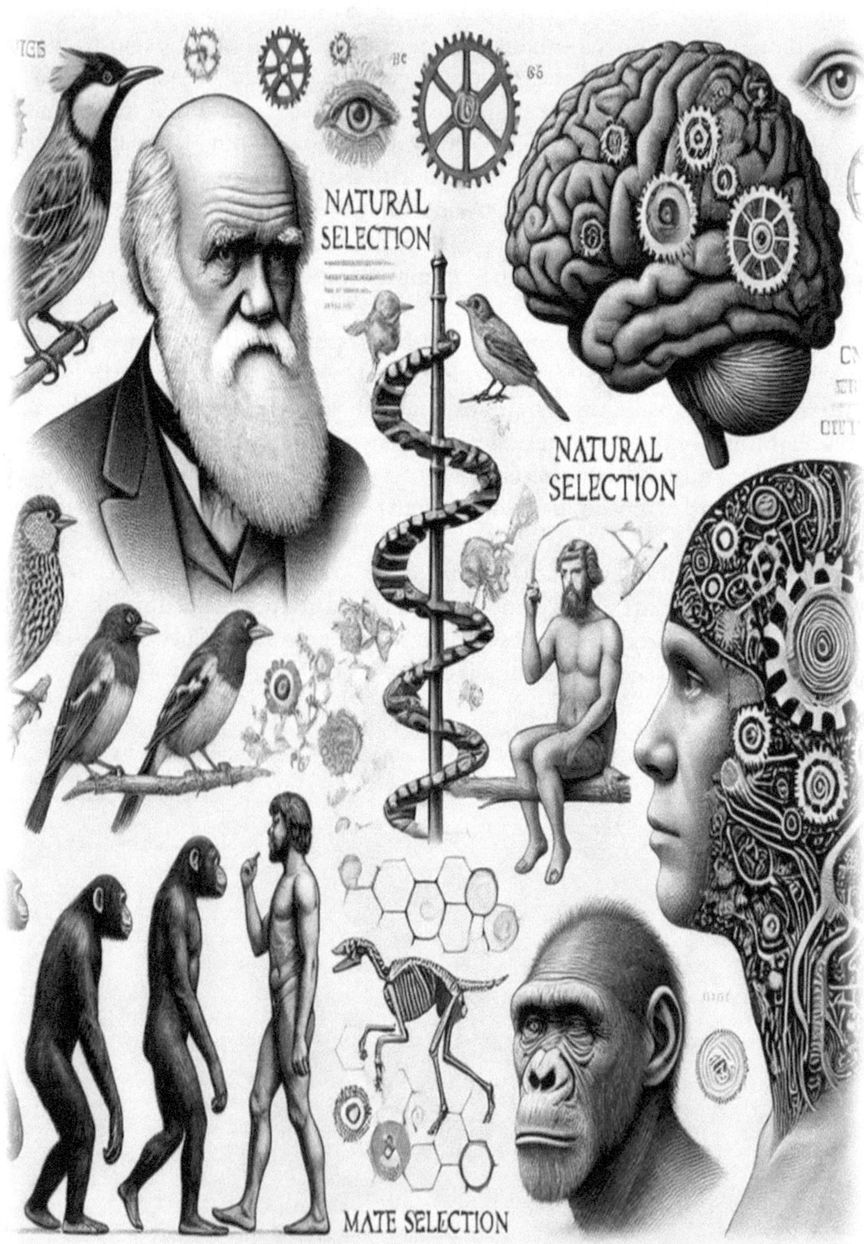

- **Darwinian Roots of Mind**

"Survival of the fittest" – Charles Darwin

Our journey into understanding the evolution of the human mind begins with a profound exploration of Charles Darwin's revolutionary ideas, which continue to shape the way we think about evolution today. Daniel Dennett referred to Darwin's theory as a "Dangerous Idea," because of how fundamentally it reshaped our understanding of the natural world, laying the groundwork for future scientific theories. Darwin's groundbreaking work, *On the Origin of Species* (1859), challenged existing beliefs by introducing the concept of natural selection. His ideas were revolutionary, shaking conventional notions of creation and explaining the diversity of life on Earth in a new way. Darwin's concept of natural selection offered a transformative lens not only for understanding the variety of species but also the complexity of the human mind.

One of the key pieces of Darwin's theory lies in his study of the finches of the Galápagos Islands. These islands, located off the coast of Ecuador, are home to many different species of finches. Darwin noticed that while these finches shared some common physical traits, they also had notable differences, particularly in their beak shapes. This observation led him to formulate the theory of natural selection. He proposed that variations within a species could provide certain individuals with advantages in their specific environments. For example, finches with long, slender beaks were better at eating insects, while those with shorter, stronger beaks could more easily crack open seeds. Over time, these advantageous traits were passed on to future generations, leading to the evolution of specialized species.

Darwin's ideas extended beyond the realm of biology to our understanding of the human mind. He recognized that humans, too, are subject to the forces of natural selection. Traits like intelligence, language, and social behavior, which were often attributed to divine design, could be understood as products of evolution. Daniel Dennett, in his book *Darwin's Dangerous Idea: Evolution and the Meanings of Life* (1995), argued that natural selection is not just a biological concept but a powerful idea that could help us understand different aspects of life, including philosophy and cognitive science.

Traditionally, many religious and philosophical beliefs suggested that abilities like language were unique gifts from a divine source, setting humans apart from all other species. However, Darwin and Dennett offered a different view—that these abilities evolved gradually, through natural processes, just like any other trait. For example, early hominids may have developed simple vocalizations and gestures to communicate. These forms of communication provided significant survival advantages, leading to the complex languages we use today.

The idea of natural selection reshaped how we think about the development of human traits, including language and consciousness. Rather than seeing these as mystical phenomena or as products of divine intervention, Dennett suggested that consciousness and other complex features of the human mind emerged as adaptive properties over millions of years of evolution.

Darwin's ideas also influenced our understanding of psychology. Evolutionary psychologists began to explore how certain cognitive functions and behaviors may have evolved to enhance survival and reproduction. This approach can be seen in the study of mate selection, for instance. Natural selection favors traits that improve the chances of reproduction, and this applies to psychological and behavioral characteristics as well as physical traits.

One concept that has emerged from this line of research is parental investment—the resources, such as time and energy, that parents invest in their offspring. In many species, including humans, females invest heavily in offspring due to pregnancy, lactation, and caregiving. As a result, women are often more selective when choosing mates, preferring partners who demonstrate high genetic quality or the ability to provide resources and protection. Conversely, males tend to compete for access to mates and are generally more willing to engage in short-term mating strategies. This difference in mating strategies between males and females is part of what is known as sexual selection theory.

For example, studies have shown that men tend to place a greater emphasis on physical attractiveness and youthfulness in their partners, as these traits are associated with fertility. On the other hand, women often prioritize qualities like social status, ambition, and resource availability—traits that suggest a partner can provide for their offspring. These mate preferences are not only shaped by biological factors but also influenced by culture and historical context, demonstrating how evolutionary and cultural forces together shape human behavior.

- **Evolutionary Adaptations**

Exploring how the human mind has adapted to handle challenges in our environment means looking at the groundbreaking work of researchers like Leda Cosmides and John Tooby. Their studies help us understand the cognitive tools that have evolved over time to improve our chances of survival in the complex world of predators, prey, and the ancient landscapes our ancestors lived in. Tooby, in particular, made major contributions to evolutionary psychology, showing us how our minds have developed to meet these challenges.

One important example of their research focuses on social exchange—the ways in which people cooperate and help each other while trying to avoid being taken advantage of. In the environments our ancestors lived in, cooperation was essential for survival and reproductive success. However, there were always some individuals who tried to benefit from others' efforts without doing their fair share. To address these challenges, humans developed mechanisms that allow us to detect and respond to cheating or unfair behavior.

Their research, using both experiments and theoretical models, has uncovered the mechanisms behind social exchange. One key finding is the "cheater detection mechanism"—a part of our mind that helps us spot when someone is breaking the rules. Imagine a small hunter-gatherer tribe where everyone agrees to share the meat from a successful hunt. If one person keeps taking more than their fair share, others in the group are likely to notice and feel emotions like anger or resentment. This ability to detect cheaters works quickly and almost automatically, which suggests it evolved as a useful survival tool.

Tooby and Cosmides also found that this mechanism for detecting cheating is influenced by cultural factors and context. For example, different societies might have different ways of dealing with risky situations, such as threats from predators, based on their traditions and social rules.

The research also sheds light on the cognitive tools we have evolved to deal with danger. For example, early humans living on the African savanna had to be constantly aware of predators like lions or leopards. As they moved through tall grasses or thick bushes in search of food, they learned to pay attention to subtle signs of danger, such as rustling leaves or distant growls. Their senses—sight and hearing in particular—became finely tuned to detect these cues, which the brain processed rapidly, putting them on high alert.

Over time, as they faced these dangers again and again, early humans got better at recognizing patterns in predator behavior. If someone in the group spotted a lion nearby, they would share that information, and everyone would adjust their route to stay safe. This knowledge, passed down and shared, helped them develop ways to avoid danger more effectively.

Humans also developed mental shortcuts, called heuristics, that helped them prioritize safety. For instance, it was often better to assume that a rustle in the grass meant danger and take action, rather than risk ignoring a real threat. These instincts favored caution, which helped our ancestors survive in an unpredictable world full of dangers.

2 UNDERSTANDING THE MIND

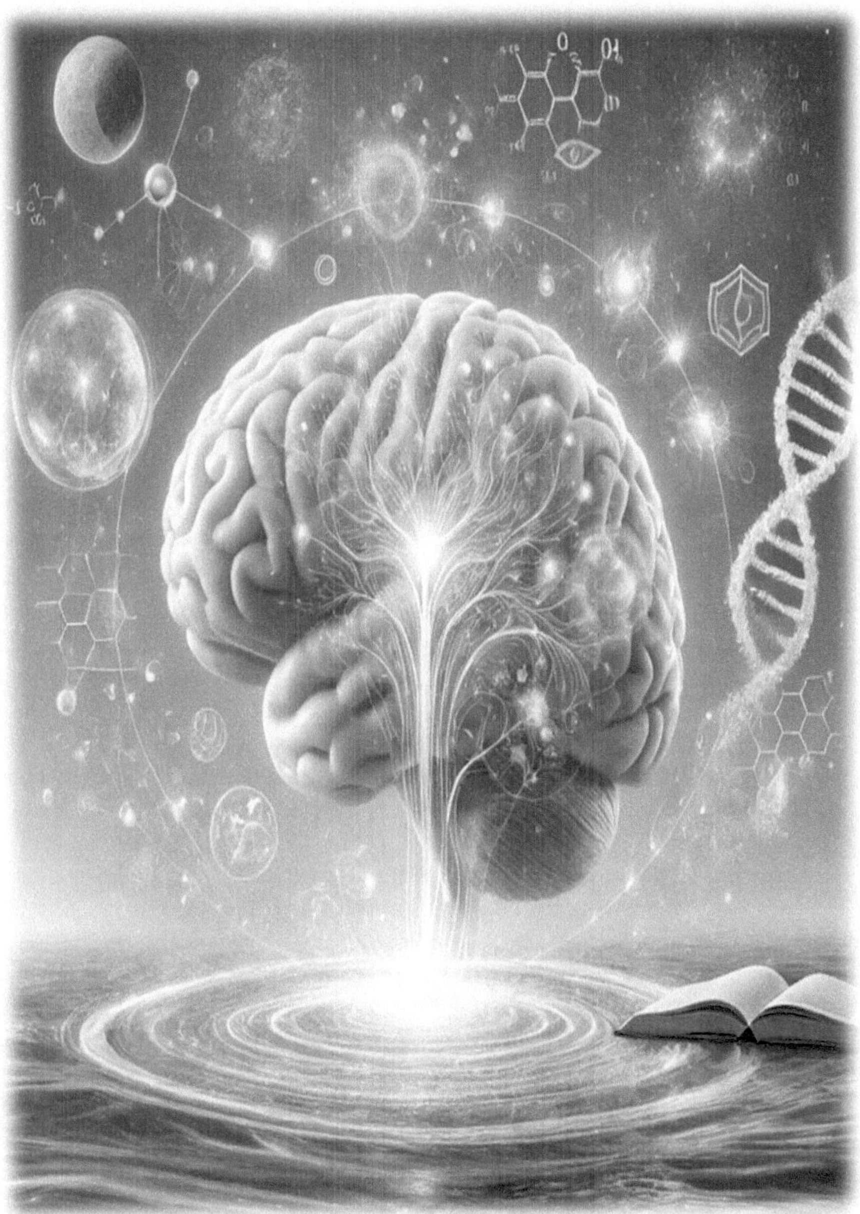

- **Cultural Evolution and Cognitive Development**

The convergence of cultural evolution and cognitive development signifies a dynamic interaction—a symbiotic relationship in which the adaptive capabilities of the human mind and the fluid nature of culture are deeply interconnected. This relationship extends beyond individual growth, shaping the collective intelligence of societies. Researchers from various fields have shed light on this captivating journey, revealing the complex interplay between cultural and cognitive development.

At the center of this journey is a strong connection between cultural growth and how our minds develop. Tomasello (1999) explains that as cultural practices change, they put pressure on our thinking processes, encouraging our minds to adapt. The human mind, influenced by its surroundings, adjusts and improves its abilities to meet the changing needs of society and culture.

Consider the development of farming practices in ancient India and how it influenced the way people thought and learned. In the early days of human settlements in the fertile plains of the Indus Valley, communities depended on hunting and gathering for survival. But as the population grew and resources became harder to find, people started experimenting with farming to ensure a steady supply of food. Over time, they learned advanced techniques to grow crops like wheat, barley, and rice. This cultural shift brought significant changes to society, from social structures and economies to new inventions.

According to Tomasello's theory, as cultural practices change, they put pressure on people's thinking, requiring them to adapt. In the case of agriculture, adopting new farming techniques meant people needed skills in planning, problem-solving, and working together. For instance, imagine a community where families worked together to grow rice. Each family member had a role, whether it was planting, taking care of the crops, harvesting, or storing the yield. Children grew up in this environment, actively participating and learning from their parents and elders about the details of farming. Through hands-on experience, they learned to observe, predict, and adapt to changes in their surroundings.

Farming also required tools like plows, irrigation systems, and storage facilities, which led to advancements in craftsmanship and engineering. These improvements further shaped the community. Over time, the ongoing interaction between culture and learning led to the development of specialized knowledge among farmers. People adapted and improved their skills to meet new challenges, leading to better productivity, efficiency, and sustainability in their farming practices.

Cultural evolution helps our minds grow by encouraging learning. As people interact with their surroundings, they pick up knowledge, skills, and social values. This process, highlighted by researchers like Bandura (1977), not only supports individual learning but also makes our minds flexible—able to adapt to different situations. In many rural villages across India, traditional skills are passed down from generation to generation, preserving knowledge built over centuries.

Take, for example, the craft of pottery-making, which is a respected art in Indian society. In a small village in Maharashtra, young children like Ravi grow up watching their parents and grandparents create beautiful pottery using old techniques. They observe and get involved, learning both the practical skills of shaping clay and the deeper meaning behind the craft—such as the importance of patience, precision, and respecting the earth. This kind of learning goes beyond techniques; it also involves understanding the values and norms connected to the craft. Ravi learns to respect the wisdom of his elders, value the bond with nature, and appreciate the beauty of handmade items.

Bandura's theory shows how such practices contribute to mental flexibility. By actively working on pottery, Ravi develops the ability to think and act differently, learning how to manage challenges and adapt to his community's needs. For example, as he grows older and moves to a new village, he might come across different artistic styles. Thanks to the flexibility he developed through his earlier experiences, he can incorporate these new styles into his work, expanding his skills and perspective. This process of learning also creates a sense of belonging with others who continue the craft, helping to preserve cultural heritage for future generations.

Language, a key part of cultural evolution, plays a powerful role in how our minds grow. Vygotsky (1978) shows that language is not just a tool for communication but also a support for our thinking. It helps pass down ideas, values, and knowledge, shaping the way we understand the world and enabling complex thinking.

Think about the tradition of storytelling in Indian families, where grandparents often share stories from ancient epics like the Mahabharata and Ramayana. These stories are not just entertaining—they carry cultural values, moral lessons, and history from one generation to the next. When children listen to these stories, they are not just absorbing information passively. Instead, they actively engage with the tales, ask questions, make connections, and learn deeper meanings. Through this storytelling process, language becomes a way to build thought, giving children a framework to understand complex ideas and societal values.

For instance, picture a young girl named Maya, sitting attentively as her grandmother recounts the teachings of Lord Krishna to Arjuna from the Bhagavad Gita. As the tale unfolds, touching on themes of duty, righteousness, and the essence of life, Maya's mind begins to grasp the deeper meanings of morality, spirituality, and the interconnectedness of all living things. These moments, filled with wisdom and reflection, gradually mold Maya's worldview, shaping the way she perceives life and guiding the choices she makes as she grows.

Language is the medium through which ideas and knowledge are passed down, creating a rich tapestry of experiences for individuals to draw upon as they navigate life. It not only helps transmit values but also supports higher-level thinking like critical analysis, problem-solving, and abstract reasoning. The discussions and debates sparked by these stories help children learn how to analyze, evaluate, and synthesize information, improving their thinking abilities. In this way, language becomes a transformative force in personal growth, shaping understanding and helping individuals develop advanced thinking skills, all within the context of their culture. Through the power of language, we can explore the depths of our heritage and grow on our journey of discovery.

The passing of cultural knowledge from one generation to the next leaves a lasting impact on how people think and understand the world. Sperber (1996) explains that evolution shapes not only the content of what we learn but also the ways in which we process information. The ideas shared across generations influence how individuals see, interpret, and respond to their surroundings.

In a traditional Indian household, cultural traditions are passed down through generations, enriching how people understand the world. Consider the celebration of festivals, a vital aspect of cultural tradition. During Diwali, the festival of lights, families come together to celebrate the victory of light over darkness and good over evil. Children hear stories from the Hindu epic Ramayana, which tells the tale of Lord Rama's return to his kingdom after defeating the demon king Ravana. These stories are not just entertaining; they teach moral values like righteousness, loyalty, and the importance of family bonds. By participating in the rituals and celebrations, children internalize these values and make them part of how they see the world.

For example, a young girl named Aisha listens with fascination as her grandmother tells the story of Lord Rama's unwavering commitment to dharma (righteousness) and his dedication to truth and justice. Inspired by these stories, Aisha learns that integrity and determination are essential virtues. As she grows older, she incorporates these lessons into her decisions and interactions with others. When she faces challenges in her personal or professional life, she draws on these teachings for guidance. Over time, the celebration of Diwali becomes part of the shared consciousness of society, deeply tied to values of morality, ethics, and spirituality.

The interaction between cultural traditions and how we think highlights the deep impact Indian culture has on shaping how individuals perceive, understand, and respond to their surroundings. Cultural contexts play a crucial role in shaping how people see the world. Hofstede's dimensions theory (1980) suggests that shared values influence behavior patterns. The beliefs, norms, and practices within a culture become key parts of a person's growth, affecting how they think and interact with others.

Consider two individuals, Priya and Aarav, who were raised in different parts of India—one in a traditional rural community in Rajasthan and the other in the bustling urban environment of Mumbai. Priya grew up in a close-knit village where values like family honor, respect for elders, and harmony are deeply rooted. From an early age, she participated in activities that emphasized communal bonds, collective decision-making, and mutual support. She learned the importance of maintaining community unity through shared traditions, gatherings, and cooperative work. As she navigated her environment, Priya internalized these norms, which taught her to value interdependence, cooperation, and community well-being. Her thinking is shaped by the beliefs of her culture, and she approaches life with empathy, relational harmony, and loyalty to her community.

In contrast, Aarav was raised in the diverse, fast-paced city of Mumbai, where ambition and innovation are celebrated. His environment emphasized individualism, entrepreneurship, personal goals, adaptability, and self-expression. Aarav grew up in a culture that encouraged independence, creativity, and the pursuit of one's dreams. This background helped him develop traits like autonomy, initiative, assertiveness, resilience, and adaptability.

Now, imagine both Priya and Aarav facing a challenge in their respective communities. Priya's upbringing, centered on community well-being, might lead her to use collaborative problem-solving, seeking consensus and cooperation to resolve conflicts. Aarav, on the other hand, might approach the situation by asserting his needs and preferences, taking proactive steps to solve the problem independently. This example shows how cultural context shapes the way individuals see the world and respond to challenges. Priya, rooted in a collectivist culture, and Aarav, influenced by individualism, have different approaches to interacting with others and solving problems based on their unique environments.

- **The Role of Social Learning**

Social learning plays a fundamental role in the interaction between cultural evolution and cognitive development, significantly shaping individuals' mental development within society. One of the most influential psychologists of the 20th century, Albert Bandura (1977), highlighted the powerful effects of learning, particularly through observational modeling. He emphasized that mechanisms such as imitation, modeling, and vicarious reinforcement serve as active pathways for individuals to not only acquire new skills but also absorb and internalize the cultural practices around them.

Observational learning, a key aspect of social learning, involves acquiring knowledge and skills by watching others. Bandura's (1977) research highlights the significant influence of this type of learning on cognitive development. Through careful observation, individuals can learn new behaviors, problem-solving strategies, and cultural norms without needing to experience them directly. This process enables the efficient transmission of knowledge in a societal context, aiding adaptation to the evolving demands of the environment.

For example, a child might closely observe their parent as they put a leash on the dog, hold the collar, and walk the dog along the sidewalk. The child also notices the verbal cues and body language the parent uses to communicate with the dog. Initially, the child may imitate these actions by using a toy animal, attaching a leash, and pretending to walk it around the house. This playful imitation helps reinforce their understanding of the observed behavior. As the child becomes more confident, they may express a desire to participate in the actual dog-walking routine. The parent can gradually introduce the child to the process by assigning simpler tasks, like holding the leash while the parent maintains control. Through repeated observation and guided practice, the child learns the necessary skills, such as keeping the right leash tension, navigating obstacles, and using commands to control the dog. Over time, this process refines the child's observational learning, helping them become a more independent dog walker.

Social modeling, another key aspect of learning, focuses on how role models influence cognitive processes. Bandura (1977) emphasizes that people often imitate the behaviors of those they admire or respect. These role models serve as examples, providing frameworks for behavior and thought patterns. This process not only helps individuals acquire specific skills but also encourages the internalization of cultural values, beliefs, and norms embodied by these models.

The Guru-Shishya tradition is a prime example. In this relationship, the Guru (teacher) imparts knowledge to the Shishya (student), extending beyond academic learning to instill deep respect and shared values. The Shishya carefully observes the Guru's behavior, including not only teaching techniques but also daily routines, mannerisms, and overall approach to life.

Through observation, the Shishya emulates the Guru's actions, gradually internalizing the values and beliefs they represent. For instance, a music teacher may not only teach specific techniques but also demonstrate discipline, dedication, and perseverance through their own practice routines. This form of modeling influences both skill development and character formation.

In classical art forms like Bharatanatyam, students learn complex steps and expressions by closely observing and practicing the movements demonstrated by their Guru. This process passes on not only the skills of the art form but also the associated cultural traditions, shaping the student's development and worldview.

The Guru-Shishya tradition ensures the continuity of knowledge and cultural practices across generations. Though this system has evolved over time, it remains relevant today. Many modern fields in India still incorporate mentorship and apprenticeships, where younger individuals learn by observing and practicing alongside experienced professionals, whether in craftsmanship, music, or business.

Imitation, a fundamental mechanism within social learning, serves as potent tool for the transmission of cultural practices. Bandura's (1977) work emphasizes that individuals, especially in context, imitate behaviors others to align with norms. This not only fosters spread cognitive skills but also perpetuates practices community. Imitation becomes vehicle through which individuals contribute continuity and evolution their society.

India's vibrant tapestry of classical dance forms like Bharatanatyam provides a captivating example how imitation acts as potent tool for cultural transmission. Bharatanatyam, highly stylized form, is traditionally learned through rigorous process imitation. Aspiring dancers, known Shishyas, meticulously observe their Guru (teacher) they gracefully execute intricate footwork, expressive hand gestures (mudras), and facial expressions. This goes beyond simply mimicking physical movements. Shishyas also internalize the Guru's artistic interpretation, emotional portrayal, adherence to underlying narratives embedded in dance. fosters deep understanding significance art form. imitative learning, steps, gestures, nuanced emotions are passed down from generation generation. vital mechanism preserving heritage integrity Bharatanatyam. While plays crucial role transmission, it's not rigid process. Over time, talented may introduce subtle variations performance, reflecting own interpretation creativity. balance between faithful individual expression allows form evolve maintaining its core essence. impact extends floor. dedication, discipline, perseverance displayed by Gurus become models Shishyas. sense pride reinforces values within

Vicarious reinforcement, a key element of Bandura's Social Learning Theory, refers to learning from observing the outcomes of others' actions. By watching how behaviors are rewarded or punished in their environment, individuals modify their own actions accordingly. In the context of cultural evolution, vicarious reinforcement plays a crucial role in maintaining and perpetuating societal practices. Positive consequences for adhering to cultural norms, or negative consequences for deviating from them, shape cognitive processes and reinforce social continuity.

Take, for example, a traditional society where respecting elders is a deeply rooted cultural value. In this setting, children observe how adults treat their elders with respect, following customs like bowing or offering assistance. If a child witnesses someone disrespecting an elder, and sees that person facing disapproval or social exclusion, they learn from this negative consequence. Conversely, when someone follows the norm and treats elders with respect, receiving praise and positive reinforcement from others, the child absorbs this as well.

In this scenario, by observing the consequences of others' actions, the child experiences vicarious reinforcement and adjusts their behavior accordingly. This reinforcement strengthens adherence to cultural norms, ensuring that these practices are passed down through generations.

- **Cultural Transmission and Cognitive Representations**

The transmission of cultural knowledge from one generation to the next has a profound impact on individuals' cognitive representations. Sperber's influential work emphasizes how this process not only transforms the content of information but also affects how it is processed within the human mind. Through real-world examples, we can see how culture shapes cognitive frameworks, offering valuable insights into the dynamic interaction between culture and cognition.

Consider the tradition of storytelling in indigenous communities. Stories passed down through generations convey not only historical events and values but also shape mental frameworks. For instance, in Native American tribes, values such as heroism, resilience, and respect are woven into these stories. As community members internalize these narratives, they integrate them into their worldview and decision-making processes. This reflects the broader influence of cultural narratives and symbols transmitted across generations.

Another example can be found in religious rituals. In Hindu culture, practices like puja (worship), aarti (offering light), and prasad (food offering) are deeply ingrained traditions. By participating in these rituals, individuals uphold and reinforce beliefs associated with spirituality, community bonding, and reverence for divinity. These rituals provide individuals with tools for interpreting their surroundings and analyzing their experiences.

In business contexts, cultural norms also influence cognitive processes. In India, where collectivism is a dominant value, decisions often prioritize group consensus and long-term relationships over individual interests. As a result, strategies that emphasize collaboration, empathy, and holistic thinking emerge, reflecting the deeply embedded cultural frameworks. The transmission of ideas across generations occurs through various mediums, including oral traditions, written texts, and social practices.

For example, the passing of culinary traditions in Indian households involves sharing recipes for traditional dishes, along with the associated techniques and meanings, which strengthen familial bonds. The younger generation not only learns the steps involved in cooking but also internalizes the heritage and identity associated with the cuisine.

The interplay between cultural transmission and cognitive representations can be observed in real-life scenarios where cultural values influence individual thinking. In India, the concept of "Guru-Shishya Parampara" (teacher-disciple tradition) has been embedded in society for centuries. In this tradition, knowledge and wisdom are passed down from gurus (teachers) to shishyas (disciples) through direct mentorship and oral transmission. The emphasis on reverence for the guru and the pursuit of knowledge shapes the cognitive frameworks of those involved. Disciples internalize not only the teachings but also the values of respect, humility, and dedication to learning that their gurus embody.

Similarly, the influence of cultural context on cognitive development is evident in gender roles within Indian society. Historically, India has been characterized by a patriarchal social structure, with distinct expectations for men and women. These gendered norms, instilled from an early age, shape individuals' perceptions and behaviors throughout their lives. For example, boys may be encouraged to display assertiveness and leadership qualities, while girls may be socialized to prioritize nurturing and caretaking roles. These deeply rooted norms affect individuals' decision-making processes and their roles in society.

The caste system, although officially abolished, continues to influence social hierarchies and interactions in parts of India. Individuals belonging to higher castes may feel entitled or superior, while those from lower castes often develop a sense of subservience and deference. These differences in behavior and perception are shaped by the caste-based structures that have been passed down through generations.

Cultural beliefs, norms, and practices are integral to cognitive development, shaping individuals from a young age. For instance, the celebration of festivals like Diwali instills a sense of community, spirituality, and tradition in children. Through collective celebrations, rituals, and familial bonds, children develop perspectives and attitudes that reflect their cultural upbringing.

The interplay between cultural transmission and cognitive development extends to everyday values such as hospitality. The Indian norm of "Atithi Devo Bhava" (guests are equivalent to gods) emphasizes the importance of hospitality and respect for guests. This cultural value guides individuals in welcoming guests warmly, offering food and refreshments, and ensuring their comfort during their stay. Such values contribute to the creation of a harmonious and inclusive environment.

In rural, agrarian communities, problem-solving approaches are influenced by agriculture, the primary livelihood. These communities develop strategies shaped by resilience, resourcefulness, and cooperation to address challenges such as unpredictable weather, crop failures, or pests. Conversely, in urban settings, problem-solving may rely on modern technologies and collaborative methods that reflect global trends and technological advancements. These diverse paradigms highlight the adaptive nature of cultural frameworks.

The interaction between cultural context and cognitive development is a dynamic, reciprocal process. As individuals immerse themselves in the values, norms, and practices of their culture, their development becomes closely intertwined with the surrounding context. Hofstede's Dimensions Theory offers a framework for understanding how cultural values influence cognitive patterns, shaping not only individual cognition but also social interactions and problem-solving within diverse societies.

- **Social Brain Hypothesis**

The social brain hypothesis, a concept from neuroscience and evolutionary psychology, suggests that the large size of the human brain is primarily due to the complexity of the social interactions and relationships humans engage in. This theory posits that the demands of living in social groups have driven the evolution of larger brains, particularly in primates, including humans.

The social brain hypothesis was first proposed by British anthropologist and evolutionary psychologist Robin Dunbar. Dunbar argued that the size of an individual's neocortex, a part of the brain associated with higher cognitive functions, is correlated with the size of their social group. Specifically, he suggested that there is a limit to the number of stable relationships one can maintain, known as Dunbar's number, which for humans is commonly estimated to be around 150 individuals.

Dunbar's hypothesis suggests that the challenges and rewards of navigating complex social structures—such as maintaining relationships, understanding others' intentions, forming alliances, and cooperating—have driven the expansion of the human brain over time. Advanced cognitive abilities are necessary to manage the dynamics of group living, and a larger brain provides the capacity for this kind of social processing.

Numerous studies have explored this hypothesis, examining the correlation between brain size, particularly the neocortex, and group size across different primate species. Research has shown positive correlations between neocortical size and social group size in primates, supporting the idea that social complexity may be a driving force behind brain evolution. One of Dunbar's key contributions to this field is his work titled "Neocortex as a Constraint on Group Size in Primates" (1992), in which he presents evidence linking neocortex size to social group size in primates. Additionally, research by Shultz and Dunbar titled "Encephalization is Not a Universal Macroevolutionary Phenomenon in Mammals but is Associated with Sociality" (2006) examines the relationship between the encephalization quotient (a measure of brain size relative to body size) and social behavior in mammals.

While the social brain hypothesis has gained considerable support, it is important to acknowledge that other factors, such as ecological and environmental pressures, also contribute to brain evolution. Nevertheless, the hypothesis remains a prominent and influential concept in psychology, providing a framework for understanding the evolution of human cognition in the context of social complexity.

- **Harmony and Unified Knowledge**

Wilson's idea of *consilience* promotes the idea that knowledge from different fields should come together, encouraging collaboration between disciplines and combining evidence from various sources. When applied to understanding the evolution of the mind, this idea encourages scientists to bring insights from fields like biology, psychology, anthropology, and neuroscience to gain a more complete picture. The study of the mind is complex and requires a combination of perspectives to truly understand how the human mind has evolved over time.

From a biological perspective, the focus is on understanding the genetic and neurobiological foundations of how the mind works. With advancements in genetics, researchers can now study the biological roots of cognitive traits more precisely. By looking at how genes are passed down and how they vary, scientists aim to discover how certain abilities are inherited. For example, studies have identified specific genetic markers that are linked to intelligence, memory, and other mental functions. These findings provide insight into how these traits have evolved and shaped the human mind. At the same time, researchers use advanced brain-imaging techniques such as functional magnetic resonance imaging (fMRI) and electroencephalography (EEG) to explore how different parts of the brain work. These tools allow scientists to see which areas of the brain are active during tasks like memory recall, decision-making, and sensory processing, helping them better understand how the brain supports these functions.

Psychology complements biology by focusing on how mental processes and behaviors have evolved. Evolutionary psychology looks at how cognitive functions like memory, perception, and problem-solving have changed over time to help humans survive. By studying both humans and animals, researchers try to uncover universal patterns in how the mind works. For instance, research on how animals navigate through different environments has shown that they have innate strategies for survival. Psychology also examines how cognitive abilities develop over the course of a human's life, from childhood to old age. This research helps explain how people adapt to challenges at different stages of life. When biology and psychology are combined, scientists can gain a deeper understanding of how genes, brain functions, and environmental factors work together to shape the human mind.

Anthropology contributes to this understanding by studying how culture and society influence the mind and its evolution. Anthropologists explore the ways in which societal structures, rituals, and cultural practices shape cognitive development. By observing different cultures, anthropologists learn how cultural norms and values influence how people think. For example, storytelling, art, and music are not only expressions of cognitive abilities but also ways in which these abilities develop. Cultural artifacts, such as tools or artwork, give us a glimpse into the cognitive diversity of past societies. Religious ceremonies and rituals also play a significant role in shaping the mind, as they help individuals connect with their community and form a sense of identity. Participating in these rituals has been shown to enhance cognitive skills like attention, memory, and emotional control.

One of the strengths of anthropology is its ability to compare different cultures and find both similarities and differences in how cognition develops. Cross-cultural studies show how various factors, such as child-rearing practices and education, influence cognitive development in different societies. *Consilience* encourages researchers to integrate findings from anthropology with biological and psychological data to get a fuller picture of how the mind evolves. By combining insights from genetics, neurobiology, and anthropology, scientists can understand how cultural practices and genetic elements interact to shape brain functions and cognitive processes, emphasizing the close relationship between culture and cognition.

India offers a valuable example of how cultural diversity influences cognitive development. Different regions of the country have their own traditions, practices, and social structures, and anthropological research has shown how these differences shape mental development. In rural areas, religious festivals and traditional rituals play a key role in shaping how people think and behave. These events, which often involve storytelling, music, and dance, transmit cultural values while also stimulating cognitive processes like memory and attention. Participating in such rituals helps individuals develop a sense of belonging and identity.

In urban areas, where traditional and modern lifestyles often mix, people engage in a variety of cultural activities like art exhibitions and theater performances. These experiences foster creativity and critical thinking, helping individuals develop skills in problem-solving and aesthetic appreciation. Cross-cultural research in India also explores how factors like economic status, education, and access to resources affect cognitive development. For example, children in rural areas may rely on non-formal ways of learning, such as observing others or practicing hands-on skills. These learning methods help them develop practical abilities, which are essential in agricultural communities. On the other hand, children in urban settings, who have access to better education and technology, are often taught literacy, numeracy, and logical reasoning, preparing them for careers in technology, finance, and other modern industries. Integrating these findings with biological and psychological research helps scientists better understand how environment and cognition work together to shape mental development in different settings.

Cognitive neuroscience connects biology and psychology by studying the brain processes that underlie thinking and behavior. Using tools like functional neuroimaging, researchers can map out which parts of the brain are responsible for processes like memory, language, and decision-making. For instance, one study in India used fMRI to examine how bilingual individuals encode memories. The research showed that different areas of the brain were activated depending on the language being used, highlighting the complex relationship between language and memory.

Genetics also plays an important role in understanding how cognitive traits are passed down through generations. Advances in genetic research have allowed scientists to identify specific genes linked to intelligence and memory.

For example, researchers in India conducted a study on the genetic basis of mathematical ability, discovering several genes that are associated with strong numerical skills. This research provides valuable insights into the genetic factors that influence cognitive abilities and their evolutionary significance. *Consilience* calls for the integration of genetic and neurobiological data to gain a deeper understanding of the forces shaping the human mind.

Beyond biological and psychological research, cultural practices also play a role in the evolution of cognition. Linguistic anthropology, for instance, explores how language has evolved and shaped cognitive abilities. In rural Indian communities, researchers have documented the development of sign languages among deaf populations, showing how humans adapt to create communication systems in different cultural settings. Other cultural practices, such as tool-making and artistic expression, also provide insights into the evolution of the mind. Archaeological findings, such as cave paintings, reveal the social and cognitive behaviors of early humans.

By integrating linguistic, archaeological, and anthropological findings, *consilience* encourages a holistic exploration of how culture has shaped the evolution of the mind. This interdisciplinary approach allows researchers to gain a fuller understanding of human cognition and its development, emphasizing the interconnectedness of biology, culture, and environment.

- **Cognitive Abilities and Mate Choice in Intersexual Selection**

Intelligence is a multifaceted cognitive trait that can be highly valued in mate choice. High may signal genetic fitness, suggesting individuals possess adaptive and problem-solving capabilities crucial for survival reproduction. often associated with the ability to navigate complex environments, make informed decisions, respond effectively challenges. Research suggests abilities related are heritable some extent, subconsciously seek partners traits enhance intellectual diversity of their offspring. This aligns concept "good genes" hypothesis, where choose mates indicating advantages

Imagine an individual attending a social event where they meet potential romantic partners. encounter someone who demonstrates high intelligence through various indicators such as advanced education, critical thinking skills, and intellectual curiosity. The is drawn to partner's intelligence, finding it attractive valuable. appreciate ability engage in stimulating conversations, contribute insightful perspectives, demonstrate prowess domains. seen desirable trait that signals adaptability, problem-solving abilities, genetic advantages for their offspring. ancestral environments, would have conferred survival reproductive benefits. Individuals with higher may been better able navigate complex dynamics, find food shelter, protect themselves offspring from threats. Selecting mates increased likelihood of inheriting advantageous traits enhance chances success. Research suggests has component heritable some extent. Therefore, subconsciously seek partners increase favorable cognitive traits. This aligns concept "good genes" hypothesis, choose indicating offspring, intelligence. By choosing partner also diversity Children born parents complementary strengths inherit broader range enhancing adaptability skills diverse environments. addition evolutionary associated relationship success modern societies. Couples similar levels tend more satisfying stable relationships, can intellectually share common interests, support each other's personal professional growth.

Problem-solving skills are essential cognitive abilities that contribute to an individual's capacity navigate various life challenges. In the context of mate choice, individuals may be drawn partners who demonstrate effective abilities. This can particularly relevant ancestral environments where adaptability and resourcefulness were crucial for survival. selection mates with strong enhance overall fitness offspring by providing them a combination genetic traits adaptability, resilience, ability thrive changing environments.

Imagine an individual evaluating potential romantic partners at a social gathering. They encounter someone who demonstrates strong problem-solving skills in variety of situations, such as resolving logistical challenges, finding creative solutions to problems, and effectively managing stressful circumstances. The is drawn partner's abilities, them attractive valuable. appreciate capacity approach challenges with proactive mindset, identifying practical taking decisive action when needed. This level competence resourcefulness that appealing mate.In ancestral environments, adaptability were crucial for survival. Individuals possessed better equipped overcome obstacles, find food shelter, navigate unpredictable Selecting mates these adaptive abilities would have enhanced likelihood survival reproductive success both their offspring. From evolutionary standpoint, choosing partner may enhance overall fitness combination genetic traits adaptability, resilience, effective passed down parents provides offspring greater thrive changing environments throughout lives. relationship, can collaborate address shared achieve common goals. work together financial difficulties, manage conflicts, obstacles arise relationship. collaborative enhances stability satisfaction contributing its long-term success. also facilitate parental cooperation support within family unit. are adept demands child-rearing, needs children, provide nurturing supportive environment grow

Creativity involves the ability to think outside conventional boundaries, fostering innovation and adaptability. In realm of mate choice, can be attractive as it may signify an individual's capacity introduce novel ideas, perspectives, solutions into relationship. Partners with creative traits bring diversity flexibility family dynamics, potentially contributing overall success adaptability social unit. From evolutionary perspective, could enhance likelihood offspring thriving diverse unpredictable environments.

Imagine a scenario where an individual is evaluating potential romantic partners. They encounter someone who highly skilled in artistic expression, such as painting, music, or writing. This creative talent serves signal of the individual's capacity for thinking outside conventional boundaries and introducing novelty into relationship. may be drawn to partner's creativity, seeing it attractive quality that adds depth richness their interactions. appreciate ability bring fresh perspectives, ideas, solutions shared experiences. long-term relationship family setting, creativity can enrich dynamics by new activities, hobbies, traditions. example, organize art projects, writing exercises, musical performances joy excitement life. mate choice also adaptability parenting. individuals more flexible parenting approaches, willing explore innovative methods child-rearing adapt unique needs interests children. foster supportive nurturing environment offspring thrive.

Consider another scenario where an individual is considering potential partners for a committed relationship. They meet someone who demonstrates strong entrepreneurial spirit, constantly generating innovative ideas and pursuing new ventures. This creativity can be highly attractive in the realm of mate choice. partner's signals willingness to think outside box take calculated risks pursuit goals. mindset beneficial navigating challenges uncertainties life, demonstrating adaptability resilience face adversity. family context, may contribute financial stability well-being household. generate additional income streams, explore career opportunities, or launch ventures that create value future generations. From evolutionary perspective, choosing with enhance likelihood offspring thriving diverse unpredictable environments. ability innovate adapt changing circumstances provide competitive advantage securing resources survival reproduction.

Cognitive traits related to communication, including verbal fluency, eloquence, and social perceptiveness, play a role in mate choice. Effective communication is crucial for establishing maintaining relationships. Individuals with strong skills may be better equipped navigate interactions, resolve conflicts, build meaningful connections. From an evolutionary standpoint, selecting partners could contribute the successful coordination of parental efforts cooperation within groups, ultimately benefiting overall reproductive success involved. intricate dance choice, abilities such as intelligence, problem-solving skills, creativity, serve signals genetic fitness, adaptability, competence. selection mates based on these reflects strategy aimed at enhancing survival offspring dynamic ever-changing environment.

Imagine an individual attending a social gathering where they encounter potential romantic partners. engage in conversations with different individuals and observe their verbal communication skills. notice one person who is articulate, expressive, adept at conveying thoughts feelings clarity precision. The drawn to partner's effective skills, finding them attractive engaging. appreciate ability of partner articulate ideas, express emotions, meaningful conversations, which fosters sense connection rapport. relationship, crucial for navigating interactions, resolving conflicts, expressing affection. Partners strong skills can communicate needs desires openly, listen empathetically each other's perspectives, collaboratively find solutions challenges that arise. facilitate building connections emotional intimacy between Through open honest communication, couples deepen understanding other, strengthen bond, cultivate supportive nurturing relationship environment.

Consider another scenario where an individual is evaluating potential partners based on their social perceptiveness and conflict resolution skills. They observe someone who demonstrates a keen understanding of dynamics, accurately reading nonverbal cues responding empathetically to others' emotions. The attracted partner's perceptiveness, recognizing it as valuable trait in navigating interpersonal relationships. appreciate ability understand empathize with perspectives, fostering sense trust, empathy, mutual respect. romantic relationship, essential for effectively resolving conflicts addressing disagreements. are socially perceptive can recognize early signs tension, communicate assertively yet empathetically, collaborate finding mutually satisfactory resolutions conflicts. From evolutionary standpoint, selecting strong skills contributes successful coordination parental efforts cooperation within groups. Effective communication enhance couples work together harmoniously, support each other child-rearing responsibilities, foster cohesive family unit.

- **Symbolic Thinking and the Evolution of Language**

Symbolic thinking is the ability to use symbols, such as words, images, or gestures, to represent objects, actions, and ideas, allowing humans to think in abstract ways. This cognitive skill is essential to human thought and is closely linked to the development of language.

Symbolic thinking enables humans to go beyond direct experiences and engage in complex processes, like problem-solving, planning, and creating cultural artifacts. For example, neuroscientific research, using brain imaging techniques, has identified that the prefrontal cortex plays a key role in tasks that require symbolic thinking. When reading a book, we rely on symbolic thinking, as each word represents a particular object, concept, or action. This allows readers to mentally create scenes, characters, and events based on the words they read. We use this cognitive ability to understand and connect ideas, interpret an author's message, and navigate complex literary themes.

Reading a book also requires planning and problem-solving skills, as readers must follow the story, keep track of characters, and anticipate how the plot may develop. Books themselves are cultural creations that use symbols to convey thoughts, experiences, and imagination across generations. Functional magnetic resonance imaging (fMRI) studies have shown that reading comprehension and problem-solving both activate the prefrontal cortex, further illustrating the role of symbolic thinking in these activities.

The evolution of language is deeply connected to the development of symbolic systems. Early humans likely communicated using gestures, sounds, and simple drawings, which helped them work together, plan, and pass on knowledge to future generations. Over time, these basic communication methods evolved into the complex languages we have today.

There are different theories about how language began. The Gesture-First Hypothesis suggests that early humans primarily used gestures before developing spoken language, while the Vocalization-First Hypothesis argues that vocal sounds were central to early communication. Imagine a group of early humans on a hunting trip. They might use gestures like pointing or hand signals to share information about the location of prey or dangers nearby, enhancing their cooperation and increasing their chances of a successful hunt. As they got closer to their prey, they might also use vocal sounds like grunts or calls to coordinate their actions from a distance. In reality, both gestures and vocalizations were likely used together, creating a flexible and effective communication system. This system laid the foundation for language, which became increasingly complex and capable of expressing a wide range of ideas, emotions, and intentions.

Noam Chomsky's theory of Universal Grammar suggests that humans are born with an innate ability to acquire language. According to this theory, the brain has built-in structures that help with learning languages, and symbolic thinking plays a fundamental role in this process. Developmental psychology research has shown that symbolic thinking in children often appears before and develops alongside language skills.

For example, when a child plays with toy animals and uses their imagination to assign them roles in a story, this type of pretend play is a form of symbolic thinking. The child is using symbols (the toys) to represent abstract ideas (characters or actions). This ability to connect objects with symbolic meanings helps lay the groundwork for language development.

Symbolic thinking also involves understanding that one object can represent another. A child may pretend a block of wood is a phone or a cardboard box is a spaceship. This ability to see symbolic relationships reflects early cognitive development and helps prepare children to learn language. As children grow, they begin to use words to represent objects, actions, and ideas, applying their symbolic thinking to language. Through imaginative play, children practice expressing their thoughts and desires verbally, creating a natural environment for language learning.

Studies have shown that children who engage more frequently in complex pretend play tend to have better language skills. Pretend play encourages creativity and provides children with opportunities to practice using symbols, which helps develop their vocabulary and understanding of language. Long-term studies suggest that children who demonstrate strong symbolic thinking skills in early childhood are more likely to perform well in reading and language tasks later in life, highlighting the importance of symbolic thinking as a foundation for language development.

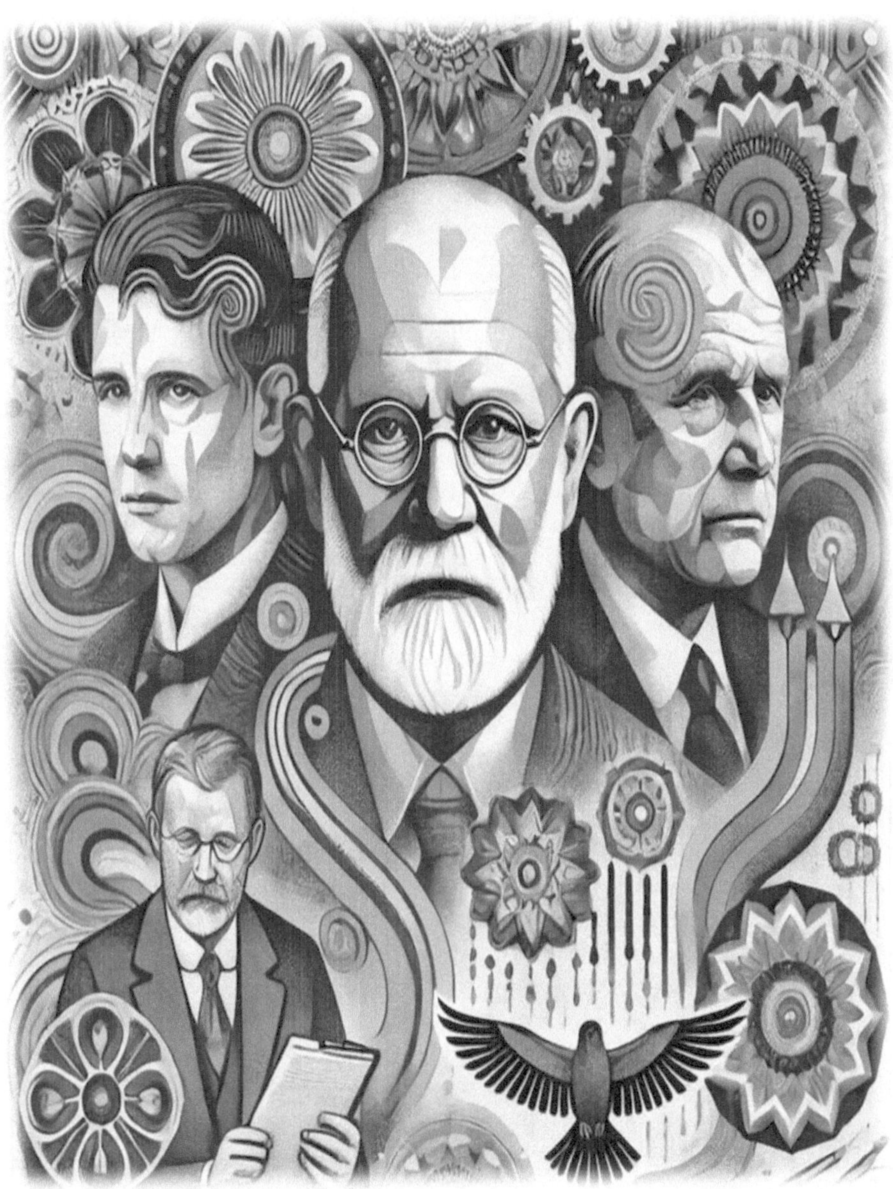

Psychological Perspective

The behavioral approach, pioneered by Ivan Pavlov and B.F. Skinner, offers valuable insights into how human behavior is shaped by conditioning. This approach emphasizes the role of external stimuli and reinforcement mechanisms in influencing actions, demonstrating how behavior can be learned and modified based on environmental factors.

Pavlov's Contributions

Ivan Pavlov's work on classical conditioning revealed how neutral stimuli could become associated with reflexive responses through repeated pairings. In his well-known experiment with dogs, Pavlov observed that the animals naturally salivated when presented with food—a natural reflex known as an unconditioned response. He then paired this presentation of food with the sound of a ringing bell. After repeated pairings, the dogs began to salivate at the sound of the bell alone, even when food was not present. This process, known as classical conditioning, demonstrated how associations between stimuli and responses can lead to learned behavior.

This concept of classical conditioning is widely applied in advertising and marketing. Advertisers use these techniques to create positive associations with products or brands in consumers' minds. For example, a commercial for a soft drink may feature images of people enjoying a sunny day at the beach, accompanied by lively music. The joyful expressions of the characters as they sip the drink link the product with feelings of relaxation and happiness. Over time, through repeated exposure, viewers begin to associate the product with those positive emotions, similar to how Pavlov's dogs associated the bell with food. Eventually, the sight or mention of the soft drink may evoke feelings of leisure and enjoyment in consumers, making them more likely to purchase it.

Skinner's Theory

B.F. Skinner, another key figure in behavioral psychology, introduced the concept of operant conditioning, which focuses on how behavior is influenced by its consequences. In this model, behaviors are shaped by reinforcement and punishment. Reinforcement refers to any stimulus that increases the likelihood of a behavior being repeated, while punishment decreases the probability of the behavior occurring again.

In everyday life, these principles are frequently applied. For instance, in a household setting, parents may use positive reinforcement to encourage responsible behavior in their children. Imagine a child being assigned chores such as cleaning their room or helping with laundry. When the child completes these tasks, the parent responds with praise and perhaps a small reward, like a favorite snack or extra playtime. This pattern of positive reinforcement helps the child associate completing chores with enjoyable outcomes, fostering a sense of satisfaction and accomplishment. Over time, the child becomes motivated to take on responsibilities willingly, not out of obligation but from an understanding that their efforts are valued.

On the flip side, operant conditioning can also be used to discourage negative behaviors, such as temper tantrums. When a child throws a tantrum, the parent might apply a mild form of punishment, such as temporarily taking away a favorite toy or limiting screen time. The child begins to learn that undesirable behavior results in unpleasant consequences. Consistent application of these consequences over time helps the child associate tantrums with negative outcomes, which reduces the likelihood of future outbursts. As the child develops, they may internalize this connection, leading to improved emotional regulation and more constructive ways of expressing their needs.

Operant Conditioning in Social Relationships

Operant conditioning principles extend beyond family dynamics and play a significant role in shaping interpersonal relationships. People often use reinforcement strategies to strengthen social bonds and encourage desirable behaviors within relationships. For example, if a friend offers support during a difficult time, the recipient may respond with gratitude and affection, reinforcing the friend's helpful behavior. This positive reinforcement strengthens the relationship, increasing the likelihood of continued support in the future.

Conversely, punishment may be used in relationships to discourage undesirable behaviors. For instance, if a friend consistently shows up late to social events, others in the group might express disapproval or withdraw attention as a form of mild punishment. By withholding positive reinforcement or applying social consequences, they communicate the value of punctuality and the importance of adhering to shared expectations within the relationship. This approach encourages the individual to adjust their behavior in order to maintain social harmony and acceptance.

Sigmund Freud's theory of psychosexual development

Sigmund Freud's theory of psychosexual development suggests that an individual's personality is shaped through a series of stages, each centered on a particular erogenous zone. These stages—oral, anal, phallic, latency, and genital—highlight how conflicts between instinctual drives and societal expectations influence a person's behavior and traits throughout their life.

The journey begins at birth with the oral stage, which lasts until about 18 months of age. During this stage, an infant explores the world primarily through their mouth. Sucking, biting, and tasting provide sensory pleasure and comfort. Caregiving during this time plays a crucial role in shaping future behaviors. If a baby receives nurturing and consistent care, they are likely to develop a sense of trust and security, laying the foundation for healthy relationships. However, if the child experiences neglect or inconsistency, they may grow up feeling insecure, which can manifest in behaviors like overeating or smoking in adulthood.

The next stage is the anal stage, which occurs between 18 months and 3 years. Here, the focus shifts to control over bodily functions, especially during toilet training. How parents guide their child through this stage significantly influences the child's sense of autonomy and self-control. If the child is subjected to harsh or overly strict training, they may develop feelings of shame and doubt, which could lead to problems with authority or excessive rigidity later in life. In contrast, a child whose parents offer patient guidance is more likely to develop a healthy sense of independence and self-regulation.

Following the anal stage is the phallic stage, which takes place from around 3 to 6 years of age. During this stage, children become more curious about their bodies and begin to explore their gender identity. This phase involves the development of unconscious desires and internal conflicts, often centered around their parents. For example, a young boy might feel rivalry toward his father for his mother's attention, while a girl may experience conflicting feelings of admiration and envy toward her mother. Successfully navigating these struggles helps shape the child's sense of self and affects their future interpersonal relationships.

The latency stage follows, spanning from about 6 years old until puberty. During this time, psychosexual focus is less prominent, and children direct their energy toward social, academic, and creative pursuits. This period provides an opportunity for children to develop skills that will be crucial during adolescence and adulthood. For example, engaging in activities like sports, academics, or hobbies helps children develop competence, preparing them for future challenges and successes.

Finally, the genital stage begins at puberty and continues into adulthood. During this stage, sexual desires reawaken, and individuals focus on intimate relationships. Adolescents face challenges related to self-discovery, romantic attraction, and identity exploration. Successfully resolving earlier conflicts allows them to form healthy, fulfilling relationships. For instance, an adolescent's first experiences with romantic relationships may involve navigating trust, commitment, and self-expression, all of which are influenced by how well earlier stages were resolved.

To illustrate these stages, consider the example of Aditya. As an infant in the oral stage, Aditya finds comfort in nursing and exploring his surroundings by putting objects in his mouth. His caregivers provide nurturing and consistent care, which helps him develop emotional trust. As he reaches toddlerhood and enters the anal stage, Aditya's parents guide him patiently through toilet training, which fosters his independence and self-confidence. In the phallic stage, Aditya becomes curious about his body and gender, and his caregivers provide a supportive environment for him to explore and ask questions, contributing to his healthy self-awareness.

During the latency stage, Aditya becomes absorbed in school, friendships, and extracurricular activities. His caregivers encourage his intellectual and social growth, helping him build a sense of competence. As Aditya enters adolescence and the genital stage, he navigates romantic relationships with the support of his family, who foster open discussions about relationships and personal values. This guidance helps Aditya develop respect, empathy, and a balanced approach to intimacy.

Freud's theory of psychosexual development provides insight into how early experiences and conflicts can shape an individual's personality and behavior. Each stage builds upon the previous one, contributing to a lifelong journey of growth and self-discovery.

Erik Erikson's Theory of Psychosocial Development

Unlike Freud, who concentrated largely on early childhood, Erik Erikson expanded our understanding of human development with his theory of psychosocial development, which spans the entire lifespan. Erikson's theory is composed of eight distinct stages, each defined by a unique challenge or crisis that individuals must navigate. These stages emphasize the interaction between biological maturation and social experiences, thereby shaping personality in a dynamic interplay between the self and the surrounding environment.

The first stage, Trust vs. Mistrust, occurs during infancy. During this foundational period, infants learn to trust or mistrust their caregivers depending on the consistency, reliability, and responsiveness of care they receive. When caregivers provide loving, attentive care, infants develop a secure attachment and a fundamental trust in the world around them. Conversely, when caregivers are inconsistent or neglectful, infants may struggle with mistrust, viewing the world as unpredictable and unreliable. This stage forms the basis for future relationships, impacting how individuals perceive others and whether they feel the world is a safe place.

The second stage, Autonomy vs. Shame and Doubt, takes place during toddlerhood. In this period, children begin asserting their independence, exploring their ability to control their actions and make decisions. Activities like toilet training and choosing what to wear serve as opportunities for toddlers to develop autonomy. When caregivers offer supportive guidance without over-controlling, children cultivate a sense of confidence in their abilities. On the other hand, overly critical or controlling behavior from caregivers can lead to feelings of shame and doubt, making children unsure of their capacity to navigate the world.

The third stage, Initiative vs. Guilt, unfolds during early childhood, as children start to assert themselves more socially and explore their environment through imaginative play. Encouragement from caregivers and teachers helps children develop a sense of initiative, fostering confidence in their ability to take risks, plan activities, and express themselves. However, when children face excessive criticism or punishment for their exploratory behavior, they may experience guilt, feeling hesitant to initiate activities or express their creativity. At this stage, the balance between freedom and guidance is crucial for nurturing a child's sense of purpose.

As children grow into Middle Childhood, they enter the fourth stage: Industry vs. Inferiority. During this period, they develop competence through learning, social interactions, and achievements in school and other activities. Success in academic pursuits, social relationships, or extracurricular activities fosters a sense of industry, enabling children to feel capable and effective. However, when children face repeated failures or receive constant criticism, they may struggle with feelings of inferiority. This stage is essential for cultivating self-esteem and confidence in one's ability to contribute meaningfully to society.

During Adolescence, individuals face the fifth stage: Identity vs. Role Confusion. This stage is marked by a search for personal identity and the exploration of values, beliefs, and goals. Adolescents seek to answer the question, "Who am I?" and develop a clear sense of self by exploring different roles, relationships, and social groups. When supported in their exploration, adolescents are more likely to establish a cohesive identity. Conversely, those who face pressure to conform or are discouraged from exploring their individuality may experience role confusion, struggling to understand their place in the world.

The sixth stage, Intimacy vs. Isolation, occurs during Young Adulthood. In this stage, individuals seek to form close, meaningful relationships, whether romantic or platonic. Successful navigation of this stage results in the capacity to build relationships characterized by intimacy, trust, and mutual respect. Those who fear rejection or struggle to open up emotionally may experience isolation, leading to loneliness and a sense of detachment from others. This stage is crucial for fostering deep connections that provide emotional support and fulfillment throughout adulthood.

In Middle Adulthood, individuals encounter the seventh stage: Generativity vs. Stagnation. At this point in life, the focus shifts to contributing to society and nurturing the next generation, either through parenting, mentoring, or community involvement. Generativity brings a sense of purpose and fulfillment, allowing individuals to feel that they are making a positive impact. Conversely, those who do not find meaningful ways to contribute may experience stagnation, feeling disconnected or unproductive, which can lead to feelings of emptiness or self-absorption.

Finally, in Late Adulthood, individuals reach the eighth stage: Ego Integrity vs. Despair. This stage involves reflecting on one's life and evaluating whether it was well-lived. Those who can look back with a sense of satisfaction, recognizing the choices they made and the relationships they built, achieve ego integrity, resulting in feelings of wisdom and contentment. In contrast, individuals who dwell on regrets and missed opportunities may experience despair, feeling disconnected and fearful as they approach the end of their lives. This final stage is about finding peace and accepting the journey one has taken.

Erikson's theory of psychosocial development provides a comprehensive framework for understanding how individuals evolve throughout life. Each stage presents its own challenges, but through the successful navigation of these crises, individuals develop strengths that contribute to a well-rounded and resilient personality. The journey from infancy to late adulthood is thus marked by growth and transformation, shaped by the interplay of personal and social factors.

Example: Arjun's Psychosocial Development

Consider Arjun through Erikson's psychosocial stages. As an infant, Arjun is surrounded by his parents' loving care, developing trust as they consistently meet his needs. In toddlerhood, his parents guide him patiently through toilet training, helping him gain autonomy and confidence. As a preschooler, they encourage his imagination, allowing him to take initiative in creative play. In school, Arjun's diligence and determination shine, and his parents' support helps him develop competence.

During adolescence, Arjun questions his identity, navigating relationships and values with his parents' encouragement. Their guidance helps him form a strong sense of self. As a young adult, Arjun builds deep connections with friends and loved ones, enriched by his family's nurturing. In middle adulthood, Arjun contributes to his community and family, finding fulfillment in mentoring others and leaving a positive legacy. Finally, in late adulthood, Arjun reflects on his life with satisfaction, surrounded by loved ones, embracing the wisdom and experiences of a life well-lived.

gratitude humility. embraces final chapter dignity serenity, behind generations come.

Carl Jung's Concept of the Collective Unconscious

Carl Jung's concept of the collective unconscious represents a significant contribution to psychology, offering profound insights into deeper layers human consciousness and interconnectedness experiences.

Jung proposed that alongside an individual's personal unconscious (which contains repressed or forgotten memories, thoughts, and emotions), there exists a collective shared by all human beings. Unlike the unconscious, which is unique to each individual, universal inherited. It innate psychological elements are common humanity, regardless of culture upbringing.

Within the collective unconscious, Jung posited existence of archetypes, which are universal symbols, motifs, or patterns that manifest in myths, stories, dreams, and religious symbols across different cultures time periods. These archetypes represent fundamental aspects human experience, such as hero, mother, shadow, wise old man. According to Jung, inherited, pre-existing structures unconscious shape thought patterns, behaviors, emotions.

Jung suggested that the collective unconscious influences individual psychology in profound ways. Archetypes from manifest dreams, fantasies, and creative endeavors, providing individuals with symbolic representations of universal themes experiences. By tapping into unconscious, may gain insights their own psyches, find meaning experiences, connect broader aspects human condition.

Jung's concept of the collective unconscious suggests that certain symbols, myths, and motifs are universally present in human culture because they emerge from shared psychological experiences. These universal elements reflect common themes dilemmas faced by humanity throughout history. However, specific cultural expressions archetypes may vary, influenced unique contexts which arise.

Jung believed that the process of individuation, or journey towards self-realization and wholeness, involves integrating aspects collective unconscious into one's conscious awareness. By recognizing engaging with archetypal symbols motifs, individuals can achieve greater self-awareness, personal growth, psychological integration.

Jung's Collective Unconscious and Heroic Narratives across Cultures

Jung's concept of the collective unconscious has sparked considerable debate within the field of psychology. Critics argue that there is a lack of empirical evidence supporting its existence, and they point to the subjective nature of interpreting symbols and archetypes. Additionally, some scholars have criticized Jung for essentializing and universalizing human experience, thus overlooking cultural and individual differences.

The Hindu epic "Ramayana" is one of the most revered texts in Indian literature, portraying Lord Rama as the central figure who embodies righteousness, virtue, and dharma (duty). Rama's journey begins when he is exiled from his kingdom of Ayodhya due to a promise made by his father, King Dasharatha, to his stepmother Kaikeyi. Despite being the rightful heir to the throne, Rama willingly accepts his exile and embarks on a journey into the forest. The plot of the "Ramayana" revolves around Rama's quest to rescue his beloved wife, Sita, who has been abducted by the demon Ravana. His unwavering devotion to Sita drives him to confront numerous challenges and adversities in his pursuit of her freedom.

Throughout his journey, Rama faces various tests of character that assess his commitment to righteousness. He demonstrates qualities such as integrity, compassion, and selflessness, even in the face of temptation and adversity. His ultimate triumph comes when he defeats Ravana, the symbol of evil and injustice. With the help of loyal allies—including the monkey warrior Hanuman and an army led by Sugriva—Rama confronts Ravana in a climactic battle and emerges victorious, rescuing Sita and restoring order. At every step, Rama remains steadfast in upholding dharma, or righteous duty. His actions exemplify the principles of honor, justice, and sacrifice, inspiring generations of devotees to emulate his example and uphold their own duties and responsibilities in life. The story resonates with audiences across cultures because of its universal themes of love, devotion, and the eternal struggle between good and evil. It symbolizes a timeless quest for truth and spiritual liberation that transcends individual circumstances and cultural boundaries.

In Greek mythology, Hercules is celebrated as a legendary hero whose exploits and trials have been passed down through tales and legends for generations. Hercules, the son of Zeus—the king of the gods—and Alcmene, a mortal woman, possesses extraordinary strength and prowess due to his divine lineage, marking him as a figure destined for greatness.

Hercules' most famous feats are the Twelve Labors, a series of seemingly impossible tasks assigned to him as penance for his past misdeeds. These labors were given to him by King Eurystheus of Tiryns as a means for Hercules to atone for inadvertently causing the deaths of his wife and children in a fit of madness induced by the goddess Hera, who resented Hercules due to his divine parentage.

The Twelve Labors take Hercules on a perilous journey across the ancient world, where he faces monstrous beasts, cunning adversaries, and supernatural challenges. From slaying the Nemean Lion and defeating the Hydra to capturing the Golden Hind and retrieving the Apples of the Hesperides, each labor tests Hercules' strength, courage, and cunning.

Through these trials and tribulations, Hercules learns valuable lessons about humility, perseverance, and redemption. Despite facing seemingly insurmountable obstacles, he perseveres with determination and courage, ultimately proving himself worthy of redemption and divine favor. Hercules' journey represents more than just a series of heroic feats; it embodies timeless themes of strength, courage, and the triumph of the human spirit over adversity. His story has inspired countless works of art, literature, and culture throughout history, symbolizing the indomitable nature of the human will and the capacity for redemption and transformation.

The myth of Hercules follows the classic narrative structure of the hero's journey, as outlined by Joseph Campbell. Hercules embarks on a quest filled with challenges and trials, undergoes personal growth and transformation, and ultimately emerges victorious, fulfilling his destiny and earning a place among the gods.

Humanistic Psychology and the Teachings of Swami Vivekananda

Humanistic psychology, led by Abraham Maslow and Carl Rogers, marked a significant shift in understanding human behavior and motivation. Unlike traditional approaches that often emphasize pathology and dysfunction, humanistic theories highlight the innate potential for growth and self-actualization within individuals. These theories stress the importance of subjective experiences, personal agency, and the pursuit of fulfillment in shaping one's life.

Humanistic psychology proposes that every individual has an inherent drive toward growth, fulfillment, and self-realization. This perspective stands in contrast to deterministic views that emphasize external influences or unconscious forces as the primary drivers of behavior. Instead, humanistic theorists believe that individuals possess the capacity to consciously strive for their full potential, transcend limitations, and lead meaningful lives. This focus on personal thoughts, emotions, and perceptions sets it apart from behaviorism, which centers on observable behaviors, and psychoanalysis, which delves into unconscious drives. Humanistic psychology emphasizes the importance of individuals' interpretations of their experiences in motivating their actions.

Central to this approach is the concept of personal agency—the ability to make autonomous choices and exert control over one's life. Humanistic theorists highlight the role of personal responsibility, freedom, and self-determination in driving growth and fulfillment. They propose that individuals have unique psychological needs that must be met to achieve well-being. Maslow's hierarchy of needs, for example, outlines a progression of needs ranging from basic physiological requirements to higher-order needs like self-transcendence. According to Maslow, satisfying these needs in a progressive manner contributes to a sense of fulfillment.

Humanistic psychology takes a holistic approach to personal development, emphasizing the integration of mind, body, and spirit. Rather than reducing human experience to isolated components, it acknowledges the interconnectedness of various aspects of existence and advocates for understanding individuals as whole beings.

Swami Vivekananda, a prominent figure in Indian spirituality and philosophy, exemplifies the principles of the humanistic approach, particularly through his advocacy for personal growth, self-realization, and individual empowerment. He firmly believed in the inherent potential for greatness within every person and emphasized that each individual possesses divine qualities and the capacity for self-realization. Vivekananda's teachings encouraged people to recognize their inner strength, cultivate their talents, and strive for excellence in all areas of life.

Central to his philosophy was the idea of self-discovery and self-fulfillment. He urged individuals to explore their innermost being, understand their true nature, and realize their inherent divinity. He highlighted the importance of introspection, meditation, and spiritual practices as pathways to self-realization and fulfillment.

Vivekananda championed the ideas of personal agency and empowerment, advocating for individuals to take control of their lives and destinies. He rejected notions of fatalism and passivity, urging people to assert their willpower, overcome obstacles, and shape their own futures. His message of self-reliance and empowerment inspired countless individuals to pursue their aspirations with confidence and determination.

Despite his emphasis on individual growth and self-realization, Vivekananda also stressed the importance of compassion and service to others. He believed that true fulfillment comes not only from personal achievement but also from selfless service to humanity. His teachings encouraged people to cultivate a spirit of empathy, compassion, and altruism, contributing to the welfare of society through acts of kindness, generosity, and social responsibility.

Vivekananda was a staunch advocate for religious harmony, unity, and tolerance. He celebrated the diversity of cultural and religious traditions, recognizing the inherent dignity and worth of every individual, regardless of their background or beliefs. His message of universal brotherhood and inclusivity resonated deeply with people around the world, inspiring a spirit of unity and cooperation across diverse communities.

Albert Bandura's Social Learning Theory and Its Application in Various Contexts

Albert Bandura's social learning theory provides a comprehensive framework that integrates both cognitive and behavioral perspectives to explain human behavior. At the core of Bandura's theory is the concept of observational learning, where individuals acquire new behaviors and skills by observing and imitating others. Through his experiments, Bandura demonstrated that people can learn not only through direct reinforcement but also by observing the actions of others and their outcomes. This process of imitation allows individuals to learn without directly experiencing rewards or punishments themselves.

Bandura emphasized the crucial role of models in shaping behavior. These models serve as sources of information and guidance, influencing individuals through their actions, attitudes, and the outcomes they achieve. Bandura highlighted that the social context plays a significant role in determining the effectiveness of modeling—people are more likely to imitate behaviors modeled by individuals they perceive as similar to themselves or possessing desirable traits.

The theory also underscores the importance of cognitive processes, such as attention, retention, and motivation, in facilitating observational learning. Individuals must pay attention to the model's behavior and its consequences, retain the observed information in memory, and be motivated to reproduce the behavior. Factors such as perceived relevance, outcome expectancy, and self-efficacy influence an individual's motivation to imitate the behaviors they observe.

A central tenet of Bandura's theory is the concept of reciprocal determinism, which suggests that behavior is influenced by the dynamic interplay between individual characteristics, behaviors, and environmental factors. Individuals not only learn from their environment but also actively shape and modify it through their actions, highlighting the constant interaction between internal and external influences on human behavior.

Bandura's social learning theory has practical applications across various fields, such as education, therapy, and socialization. Educators can utilize modeling and observational techniques to facilitate skill acquisition and promote behavioral change among students. Therapists may employ role-playing exercises to help clients learn new coping strategies and social skills. Parents and caregivers, by serving as positive role models, can create supportive environments that foster healthy development in children.

Celebrity endorsements in advertising provide a vivid example of Bandura's social learning theory at work, particularly in the realm of consumer behavior. Advertising campaigns often leverage celebrities as models to endorse products or services, capitalizing on the admiration and influence these figures hold over their fan base. For example, a famous athlete endorsing a sports brand's shoes or apparel serves as a powerful model for consumer behavior.

Consumers, especially those who admire the celebrity, engage in observational learning as they observe the endorser using or promoting the product in advertisements. According to Bandura's theory, individuals are more likely to imitate behaviors demonstrated by admired figures, especially when those behaviors are associated with desirable outcomes or status. In the context of endorsements, consumers may emulate purchasing behavior to align themselves with the values or lifestyle of their favorite celebrities.

The effectiveness of celebrity endorsements hinges on the social context and the product being endorsed. Consumers are more inclined to imitate behaviors modeled by individuals they perceive as similar to themselves or possessing traits they admire. For example, an athlete endorsing sports products may resonate with consumers interested in fitness and sports-related activities.

Bandura also emphasized the role of perceived relevance and outcome expectancy in motivating individuals to imitate behaviors. When consumers view a celebrity endorser as credible and trustworthy, they are more likely to believe that using the endorsed product will lead to favorable outcomes, such as improved performance or enhanced social status. This belief fuels the motivation to emulate the behavior modeled by the endorser.

Ultimately, celebrity endorsements influence consumer behavior and purchasing decisions by tapping into the principles of observational learning and imitation. Consumers who admire the celebrity endorser are more likely to purchase the endorsed product, believing it will align them with the perceived lifestyle, values, or aspirations of the celebrity. This demonstrates how Bandura's social learning theory explains the mechanisms underlying the impact of endorsements on behavior.

Parenting styles have a profound impact on child behavior, a phenomenon vividly explained by Albert Bandura's social learning theory. Consider a family where parents exhibit contrasting parenting styles: one parent adopts a nurturing and empathetic approach, while the other displays authoritarian and hostile behavior. The children in this family observe and internalize the behaviors modeled by their parents, ultimately shaping their social development.

The nurturing parent demonstrates kindness, empathy, and respect toward others, including family members, friends, and strangers. For example, this parent offers assistance to neighbors, listens attentively, and employs constructive problem-solving strategies during conflicts. The children observe and imitate these positive behaviors, incorporating acts of kindness, empathy, and respect into their social interactions.

On the other hand, the authoritarian parent may exhibit aggressive or punitive behaviors, such as yelling, criticizing, or using physical punishment as discipline. In response to disobedience or defiance, this parent may resort to harsh punishment, creating a tense atmosphere within the household. The children observe these interactions and may internalize the aggressive behaviors, replicating them in their interactions with peers or siblings.

Over time, these contrasting parenting styles profoundly influence the behavior and social development of the children. Those exposed to positive practices are more likely to exhibit prosocial behaviors, such as empathy, cooperation, and respect for others. In contrast, children exposed to negative practices may display aggressive or hostile behaviors and struggle with emotional regulation. This example highlights the critical role of parenting styles in shaping child behavior and socialization. By understanding the principles of observational learning outlined in Bandura's theory, parents can consciously model positive behaviors and attitudes, fostering an environment that promotes healthy emotional development in their children.

The Bollywood film "Dangal" is based on the true story of wrestler Mahavir Singh Phogat and his daughters, Geeta and Babita Kumari. The movie portrays Mahavir's journey as an authoritative parent who defies societal norms to train his daughters to become world-class wrestlers. Set in Haryana, India, the film begins with Mahavir's disappointment at not being able to fulfill his own dream of winning a gold medal in wrestling for his country. Determined to realize his aspirations through his children, he decides to train his daughters in wrestling, despite criticism and opposition from the community. Mahavir adopts an authoritative parenting style characterized by high expectations, discipline, and unwavering support for his daughters' athletic endeavors. He sets strict training regimens and pushes them to excel in the sport, instilling in them a sense of determination and perseverance.

Despite initial reluctance, Geeta and Babita gradually embrace their father's rigorous training and begin to excel in wrestling. Under Mahavir's guidance and encouragement, they overcome numerous obstacles, including societal prejudice and gender stereotypes, ultimately becoming champion wrestlers.

"Dangal" exemplifies the positive outcomes of authoritative parenting in nurturing children's talents and fostering success. Mahavir's approach empowers his daughters to defy societal expectations, pursue their passions, and achieve greatness in the male-dominated sport of wrestling. Through his unwavering support and disciplined training, Mahavir cultivates a strong sense of self-confidence and determination in Geeta and Babita. They learn valuable life lessons such as resilience, perseverance, and the importance of hard work, which ultimately propel them to international acclaim.

The film underscores the transformative power of parental guidance and belief in shaping children's destinies. Mahavir's authoritative parenting style not only molds his daughters into champion athletes but also instills in them values like courage, integrity, and tenacity that serve as the foundation for their remarkable achievements.

"Taare Zameen Par" is another poignant Bollywood film that beautifully illustrates the impact of parenting styles on child behavior and development. The story revolves around eight-year-old Ishaan Awasthi, a creative and spirited boy who struggles with dyslexia. His parents, particularly his father, exhibit an authoritarian style, focusing solely on academic achievement and discipline. As Ishaan grapples with learning difficulties and feelings of inadequacy, his parents fail to understand his unique needs and talents. They pressure him to excel academically, dismissing his artistic pursuits as distractions. Feeling misunderstood and overwhelmed, Ishaan's self-esteem plummets, and he becomes withdrawn and despondent.

Everything changes when his parents decide to send him to a boarding school, hoping that strict discipline will improve his performance. At the boarding school, Ishaan encounters Ram Shankar Nikumbh, an unconventional art teacher who recognizes his dyslexia and nurtures his artistic talents. Under Nikumbh's compassionate guidance and patient mentoring, Ishaan begins to blossom. He discovers newfound confidence in his abilities and learns to embrace his differences. Through creative expression, Ishaan finds his voice and overcomes his challenges.

The film highlights the profound impact of parenting styles on a child's emotional well-being. Ishaan's parents' authoritarian approach stifles his creativity and emotional growth, leading to feelings of alienation and despair. However, Nikumbh's supportive and empathetic style empowers Ishaan to embrace his true self and thrive despite his challenges. "Taare Zameen Par" serves as a powerful reminder of the importance of understanding and nurturing children's individual strengths and needs. By adopting an authoritative and empathetic approach, parents and educators can create an environment that fosters a child's holistic development and allows them to shine brightly, like stars on earth.

• The Mind-Body Debate: Dualism vs. Physicalism

The debate surrounding the nature of the mind and its relationship to the body has fascinated philosophers for centuries. At the core of this discussion are two opposing perspectives: dualism and physicalism. Dualists argue for the existence of distinct mental and physical entities, while physicalists maintain that mental phenomena can be fully explained by physical processes. This essay will explore the historical roots, key arguments, contemporary relevance, and enduring significance of this philosophical debate.

Dualism has its origins in ancient philosophical traditions, with notable proponents such as Plato and René Descartes. Plato's theory of Forms proposed the existence of an immaterial realm where abstract entities, including the soul, exist independently of the physical world. Descartes, in his seminal work "Meditations on First Philosophy," famously articulated dualism by proposing a non-physical mind or soul that interacts with the material body through the pineal gland. On the other hand, physicalism gained prominence with the rise of modern science and the development of neurobiology. Thinkers like Thomas Hobbes argued that mental states could be reduced to physical processes, rooted in the movements of particles. This perspective became more refined as neuroscience advanced, with contemporary philosophers like Patricia Churchland advocating for a neuroscientific understanding of the mind, where consciousness is viewed as an emergent property of the brain's neural activity.

Dualism, a philosophical stance with deep historical roots, posits the existence of two distinct entities: the mind and the body. This perspective challenges the notion that mental phenomena can be fully explained by physical processes alone, suggesting instead that the mind possesses qualities that are irreducible to matter. One of the central tenets of dualism is the argument for the inseparability of mental and physical states. Dualists contend that mental states exhibit properties that cannot simply be reduced to physical phenomena. They often point to subjective experiences, consciousness, and the sense of self as prime examples of these unique attributes. Such experiences, like pain or pleasure, are inherently personal and private, existing within the realm of individual consciousness. Dualists argue that these experiences cannot be fully accounted for by examining the brain alone. While neuroscientists may identify correlations between specific brain activity patterns and mental states, dualists maintain that these correlations do not equate to a complete explanation. There remains a gap between objective measurements of brain activity and subjective, first-person experiences. Furthermore, dualists emphasize the ineffable nature of consciousness itself, which encompasses not only sensory perceptions but also thoughts, emotions, and self-awareness. No amount of neuroscientific explanation can capture the full richness and depth of human experience. Even if scientists were to map out every neural pathway and synaptic connection in the brain, it would still fall short of explaining what it means to be conscious. A related challenge posed by dualism is the problem of interaction between the non-physical mind and the physical body. René Descartes famously proposed that the pineal gland served as the link between the immaterial mind and the material body. However, critics argue that this idea lacks empirical support and violates principles of causality. The notion that a non-physical entity could causally influence physical events raises difficult questions about how such interactions could occur without violating the laws of physics. Despite these criticisms, dualism offers a compelling perspective on the mind-body relationship, emphasizing the uniqueness and irreducibility of the mind, which invites us to reconsider our assumptions about the nature of consciousness.

Physicalism stands in stark contrast to dualism, positing that mental phenomena are ultimately reducible to physical processes within the brain. This philosophical stance advocates for a unified scientific framework in which the complexities of the mind can be understood through the lens of empirical evidence and naturalistic principles. One of the core arguments put forth by physicalists is the principle of the unity of science. Physicalists assert that adopting a dualist perspective introduces unnecessary metaphysical entities, complicating our understanding of the natural world. By adhering to a monistic view of reality, they argue for a seamless integration of different realms within scientific inquiry. Central to the physicalist perspective is a wealth of neuroscientific evidence supporting the idea that mental states have a basis in physical processes. Advances in neuroscience have provided compelling insights into the workings of the brain, revealing intricate neural networks underlying cognition, emotion, and consciousness. Studies on brain activity, utilizing techniques such as functional magnetic resonance imaging (fMRI) and electroencephalography (EEG), have yielded valuable data on the neural correlates of various mental phenomena. Researchers have identified specific regions and patterns of neuronal activity associated with functions like perception, memory, and decision-making. These findings offer a tangible material substrate for mental processes, lending support to the physicalist view. Moreover, the concept of emergence provides a framework for understanding how complex mental states arise from the interactions of simpler elements. Consciousness, for instance, is seen as an emergent property resulting from the interplay of neurons and synaptic connections. While consciousness may appear to be a distinct and irreducible phenomenon, physicalists contend that it can be explained in terms of neurobiological processes. Physicalism also appeals to Occam's Razor, the principle of parsimony, which favors simpler explanations over unnecessarily complex ones. By grounding their principles in empirical evidence, physicalists offer a more parsimonious explanation compared to dualism. Rather than postulating the existence of non-physical substances, they advocate for a reductionist approach that seeks to explain mental phenomena in terms of underlying mechanisms. Furthermore, physicalism aligns with the methodology of naturalism, which emphasizes the importance of studying the world through observation and experimentation. By prioritizing evidence grounded in the physical world, physicalists maintain a commitment to rigor and objectivity in their exploration of the mind.

The ongoing debate between dualism and physicalism remains a vibrant topic in contemporary philosophy of mind, stimulating profound inquiries into the nature of consciousness and human cognition. In today's age, where scientific advancements continually reshape our understanding of the brain, this debate holds significant implications for various fields, including psychology, neuroscience, and artificial intelligence. Neuroscientific research stands at the forefront of challenging traditional dualist views by providing insights into the neural correlates of mental phenomena. Through techniques such as neuroimaging and electrophysiology, scientists have made remarkable strides in mapping the brain's activity during cognitive processes. These findings have led to a deeper understanding of how the physical structures and functions of the brain relate to subjective experiences, effectively undermining the notion of an immaterial mind distinct from the body. However, despite this progress, the "hard problem" of consciousness remains a formidable challenge. The hard problem, famously articulated by philosopher David Chalmers, centers on the subjective aspects of consciousness that seem resistant to reductionist explanations. While neuroscience can identify correlations between brain activity and conscious experience, it struggles to explain why certain patterns of neural activity give rise to specific conscious states. This philosophical inquiry underscores the limitations of a purely physicalist approach and highlights the need for interdisciplinary dialogue between neuroscience, philosophy, and other fields. Moreover, the implications of the dualism-physicalism debate extend far beyond academia, permeating practical domains such as mental health treatment, brain-computer interfaces, and artificial intelligence. Understanding the nuanced mind-body relationship is crucial for developing effective interventions for psychological disorders and enhancing well-being. Brain-computer interfaces, which allow direct communication between the brain and external devices, rely on insights from neuroscience to bridge the gap between human cognition and technological applications. Furthermore, the development of artificial intelligence raises questions about the possibility of creating synthetic minds. While physicalism provides a framework for understanding computational cognition, it also prompts ethical considerations regarding the rights and responsibilities of artificial agents. As society grapples with these complex issues, philosophers, scientists, and ethicists must work together to navigate the societal challenges posed by advancing technologies. The debate between dualism and physicalism represents a fundamental inquiry into the nature of human existence. While dualism offers an intuitive explanation of the mind's uniqueness, physicalism grounds its arguments in empirical evidence and scientific rigor. As our understanding of the brain and consciousness continues to evolve, the exploration of these complexities will shape not only philosophical discourse but also the future of our society.

- **Consciousness**

The exploration of consciousness has fascinated philosophers, scientists, and thinkers across different fields and historical eras. This chapter delves into the intricate debate on consciousness, focusing on essential themes like qualia, neural correlates, and the mind-body problem.

At the heart of discussions on consciousness lies the concept of qualia, which refers to the subjective, first-person experiences that accompany mental states. Philosophers such as Thomas Nagel have highlighted the profound implications of qualia, emphasizing their ineffable nature and their role in shaping our understanding of consciousness. Qualia represent the raw, qualitative aspects of sensations, perceptions, emotions, and other phenomena that are inherently personal and private. They resist objective description and cannot be reduced to physical or functional processes. Examples include the redness of a rose, the taste of chocolate, or the feeling of sadness. In his influential essay, "What Is It Like to Be a Bat?", Nagel argues that consciousness cannot be fully understood through objective, third-person descriptions alone. He asserts that even with complete knowledge of a bat's brain, we would still lack an understanding of what it is like to experience the world as a bat. This irreducible aspect is what Nagel describes as the "subjective character of experience" or the "what it is like" quality of being. The ineffability of these experiences—the inability to adequately convey them to others—poses a significant challenge to traditional scientific approaches that emphasize observation and measurement. Recognizing qualia suggests that consciousness involves more than just information processing or neural activity; it includes a subjective perspective that cannot be captured solely by analyzing the brain.

Neuroscientific perspectives offer valuable insights into the relationship between the brain and consciousness. Contrary to views that see consciousness as transcending physical phenomena, proponents of the neuroscientific approach argue that consciousness can be understood through the study of brain activity. Theories proposed by researchers like Christof Koch and Giulio Tononi emphasize the neural correlates of consciousness and the mechanisms that generate conscious awareness. These theories are based on the idea that conscious experiences, including perceptions and emotions, are closely linked to the activity of neurons and neural networks. Advances in neuroscience have allowed researchers to observe and manipulate brain activity with increasing precision. Koch has contributed to the Integrated Information Theory (IIT), which suggests that consciousness arises from the functioning of neural circuits where information is processed in complex ways. According to IIT, consciousness is associated with high levels of integrated information, meaning that specific patterns of brain connectivity give rise to conscious experiences. From this perspective, consciousness is not a property of individual neurons but emerges from the collective activity of interconnected networks. Tononi's work focuses on the concept of "phi," which represents the level of integrated information within a system. Systems with a high value of phi are thought to exhibit maximal integration and differentiation of information, leading to conscious experience. Through computational models and empirical studies, neuroscientists aim to identify the neural mechanisms underlying consciousness. They use techniques such as neuroimaging, electrophysiology, and computational modeling to map conscious experiences to specific patterns of brain activity. While neuroscience provides promising insights into the basis of consciousness, it remains a complex field. Researchers hope to unravel the mysteries of consciousness by integrating findings from neuroscience, psychology, and philosophy. Continued technological advancements and interdisciplinary collaboration hold significant potential for enhancing our understanding of consciousness and its neural foundations.

The study of consciousness is inherently multidisciplinary, drawing on insights from philosophy, psychology, neuroscience, and cognitive science to unravel the mysteries of subjective experience and the mind-body relationship. This chapter highlights the interdisciplinary nature of consciousness research, focusing on collaborative efforts and ongoing reflections that advance our understanding. Philosophy provides the foundation for consciousness research by offering conceptual frameworks and posing fundamental questions about the nature of consciousness. Philosophical inquiries into qualia, intentionality, and the mind-body problem lay the groundwork for interdisciplinary dialogue and critical reflection on the implications of consciousness for reality and human experience. Psychology provides valuable insights into the cognitive processes underlying consciousness, exploring phenomena such as attention, perception, memory, and self-awareness. Experimental psychology uses empirical methods to investigate the mechanisms that give rise to conscious awareness, shedding light on the relationship between neural activity and subjective experience. Psychological research informs consciousness studies across domains such as child development, psychopathology, and altered states of consciousness.

Neuroscience provides a biological basis for understanding the intricate networks of neurons and circuits that underlie consciousness. Advances in neuroimaging techniques, such as functional magnetic resonance imaging (fMRI) and electroencephalography (EEG), allow researchers to observe brain activity in real time and correlate specific patterns of neural activation with conscious experiences. Neuroscientific findings provide insights into the neural correlates of consciousness and inform theoretical models that explain how awareness emerges from brain activity. Cognitive science integrates knowledge from linguistics, anthropology, and computer science to explore cognition and consciousness. Computational models and artificial intelligence (AI) contribute to our understanding of cognitive processes by simulating the emergence of conscious systems. Computational modeling bridges the gap between experimental data and theoretical frameworks, promoting interdisciplinary collaboration and refining theories of consciousness. Despite progress in the field, significant challenges remain regarding the nature of subjective experience and the "hard problem" of consciousness. Philosopher David Chalmers has articulated the hard problem as the difficulty in explaining why certain patterns of neural activity give rise to specific conscious states. This challenge underscores the limitations of a purely physicalist approach and highlights the need for interdisciplinary dialogue between neuroscience, philosophy, and other fields.

Future directions in consciousness research may involve integrating cross-disciplinary findings, addressing ethical considerations, and examining the role of consciousness in shaping human behavior and society. The study of consciousness remains a vibrant field of inquiry that draws on diverse disciplines to address its complexities. Philosophical, psychological, and neuroscientific perspectives converge to illuminate the mechanisms underlying conscious experience. Through collaborative efforts, researchers aim to advance our understanding of consciousness and its role in human existence. The debate surrounding consciousness encompasses a rich tapestry of perspectives, from philosophical examinations of qualia to neuroscientific investigations of neural correlates. While differing viewpoints exist, the study of consciousness continues to inspire deep reflection on this enigmatic aspect of the human mind.

- **Perspective from Non- Western Philosophy**

The discourse on the nature of the mind has largely been shaped by Western philosophical traditions, but non-Western philosophies offer invaluable alternative perspectives that deepen our understanding of consciousness, selfhood, and cognition. From ancient Eastern wisdom to indigenous belief systems, these diverse traditions provide unique insights into the mysteries of the human psyche. Hindu philosophy, particularly within the Advaita Vedanta school, explores the self through the concept of Atman. Atman, often translated as the true self or soul, is considered identical to Brahman, the ultimate reality or cosmic consciousness. This perspective challenges the notion of an individual, distinct self, emphasizing instead the interconnectedness of all beings within a unified whole. Atman is not viewed as a separate entity but as the essence of one's being, transcending the limitations of the ego and the material world. According to Vedanta, an individual's sense of self (ego) is a product of ignorance (avidya) that obscures their true nature. Through practices like meditation, self-inquiry (atma-vichara), and the study of sacred texts (shravana), individuals aim to overcome this ignorance and realize their pure, unchanging essence.

Meditation is central to this pursuit, providing a means to quiet the mind and turn inward to explore consciousness. By calming the fluctuations of the mind (chitta vritti), practitioners seek to experience their underlying unity with Brahman. Sustained meditation practice enables individuals to transcend identification with the ego and recognize the interconnectedness of all beings. Self-inquiry is another essential practice, where individuals systematically examine the nature of the self. By questioning the validity of their perceptions, thoughts, and emotions, practitioners discern the distinction between the transient and the eternal. This inquiry leads to the realization of the self beyond temporary experiences. The sacred scriptures of Hinduism, particularly the Upanishads and the Bhagavad Gita, offer guidance for seekers on this path. These texts explore the nature of consciousness and provide teachings and parables to help individuals achieve self-realization. The realization of Atman is not merely intellectual but experiential, involving the direct perception of one's true nature. This realization transforms perception, allowing individuals to recognize the non-dual nature of existence. With the dissolution of the ego, an expansive awareness of interconnectedness arises, transcending the boundaries of personal identity.

Buddhist philosophy, with its foundational teaching of Anatta (non-self), offers a radical departure from the idea of a permanent, unchanging soul common in many other religious traditions. Instead of a fixed, substantial self, Buddhism views the self as a conditioned phenomenon—a composite of ever-changing elements influenced by causes and conditions. This idea is encapsulated in the doctrine of Dependent Origination (Paticca-samuppada), which explains how all phenomena arise dependently. The self, like everything else, arises from various factors, including physical and mental aggregates, sensory experiences, and environmental influences. Mindfulness and Vipassana meditation are fundamental practices in Buddhism that develop insight into the nature of reality. Through mindfulness, practitioners cultivate awareness of sensations, thoughts, and perceptions as they arise and pass away in the present moment. This practice allows individuals to observe the impermanence and insubstantial nature of phenomena, leading to a deeper understanding of the non-self. Vipassana, or insight meditation, complements mindfulness by encouraging systematic investigation into the characteristics of existence—impermanence (Anicca), unsatisfactoriness (Dukkha), and non-self (Anatta). By observing the impermanence and insubstantiality of all things, practitioners gradually dismantle the illusion of a fixed, independent self. This shift in perspective challenges attachment to the ego and self-referential experiences. As individuals come to see themselves as dynamic processes embedded in an interconnected web of causes and conditions, they are freed from suffering caused by attachment, aversion, and ignorance, ultimately leading to the cessation of suffering (Nirvana). Buddhist philosophy emphasizes the fluidity of identity and the illusory nature of selfhood, cultivating insight into Anatta and transcending self-centered perspectives to attain a liberated state of being. This realization not only transforms one's inner state but also provides practical guidance for living a life characterized by wisdom, compassion, and freedom from suffering.

Indigenous philosophies from various cultures around the world offer profound insights into the nature of mind, consciousness, and self, often grounded in a deep connection to the natural world. These traditions provide alternative perspectives that challenge Western dualistic frameworks, offering holistic understandings that emphasize interconnectedness with all life forms and the environment. In many Native American traditions, the concept of spirit or soul is central to understanding human experience. Unlike Cartesian dualism, which posits a separation between mind and body, these traditions perceive the self as inseparable from the broader web of life. This perspective emphasizes the interconnectedness of all beings and recognizes the inherent relationship between humans and nature. This connection is not merely theoretical but is deeply embedded in cultural practices, rituals, and ways of being. For example, indigenous peoples engage in ceremonies to honor the land, water, and other living beings, acknowledging their role as stewards of the Earth. In these traditions, the self is not limited to individual identity but extends to collective consciousness and ancestral connections. In many indigenous cultures, ancestors are revered and considered integral to the community's wisdom. This perspective challenges the emphasis on individualism and highlights the importance of community, lineage, and intergenerational knowledge transmission. Indigenous philosophies also emphasize a holistic approach to well-being, encompassing physical, mental, emotional, and spiritual dimensions. Rather than viewing the mind as separate from the body or environment, these traditions recognize the interplay of all aspects of existence. This approach underscores the importance of balance, harmony, and reciprocity in maintaining well-being—both within oneself and in relation to the natural world. Furthermore, these traditions emphasize relationality in all interactions. Concepts such as kinship, respect, and reciprocity guide social relations and ethical conduct. This relational worldview fosters a sense of responsibility towards others and encourages practices of stewardship, sustainability, and mutual care.

Cross-cultural dialogue and comparative philosophy constitute essential avenues for exploring the profound diversity of thought and for enriching our collective intellectual heritage. Scholars in this field draw upon the accumulated wisdom of Eastern and non-Western philosophies, thereby expanding the horizons of philosophical inquiry. One of the primary aims is to bridge the intellectual chasm between disparate traditions and conceptual frameworks. Through such dialogue, scholars endeavor to surmount ethnocentrism and cultural biases, acknowledging the validity and complexity of diverse perspectives on fundamental questions of existence, reality, and consciousness.

Philosophers engaged in cross-cultural discourse approach these inquiries with both openness and humility, cognizant of the fact that no single tradition can claim an exclusive monopoly on truth. Instead, they advocate for a pluralistic ethos, appreciating the contributions of multiple perspectives. Embracing the concept of interconnectedness, cross-cultural philosophy presents a unique lens through which to understand the nature of consciousness. By integrating a multiplicity of discourses, it enriches our understanding in ways that transcend the dominant paradigms of separation and dualism. Traditions such as Hinduism, Buddhism, Taoism, and Confucianism offer profound insights into questions of selfhood and the nature of reality.

Through practices such as meditation, mindfulness, and self-inquiry, these traditions offer practical methodologies for transcending the limitations of the egoic self and embracing a broader, more inclusive mode of inquiry. Such practices cultivate a deeper appreciation for the multiplicity inherent in human conceptions of existence. Cross-cultural dialogue also creates fertile opportunities for collaboration and interdisciplinary exchange, fostering a dynamic intellectual landscape conducive to learning and growth. Furthermore, these dialogues hold significant implications for addressing contemporary global challenges, emphasizing cooperation and mutual understanding.

The principles of interdependence present in Hinduism, Buddhism, and Taoism offer valuable perspectives that can support initiatives promoting social justice, environmental care, and global harmony. In Hinduism, particularly within the Advaita Vedanta tradition, there is an emphasis on the unity between Atman (the true self) and Brahman (the ultimate reality), which challenges the notion of individual separation and highlights a shared essence among all beings. Similarly, Buddhism's concept of Anatta, or "non-self," dismisses the idea of a fixed, unchanging identity, instead portraying the self as ever changing and shaped by conditions. Taoism also upholds a view of interconnectedness, advocating respect for all forms of life through a profound appreciation of the harmony within the natural world. Together, these philosophies underscore a sense of interconnected existence that aligns well with modern efforts to foster a more inclusive and ecologically responsible global society

- **Free will and determination**

The debate about free will and determinism is one of the oldest and most important topics in philosophy. It asks whether people's actions are the result of their own choices or if they are controlled by factors that have already been decided. This discussion touches on deep questions about human freedom, responsibility, and how we make decisions.

Determinism is the idea that everything, including human actions, happens because of specific causes and laws of nature. It suggests that the universe works like a chain of events, where each event is linked to the one before it. According to to determinists, if someone could understand every detail about the universe right now and know its natural laws, they could predict exactly what would happen in the future.

From a deterministic point of view, human actions are shaped by many factors, such as genetics, upbringing, culture, environment, and social conditions. These elements combine to influence decisions and behaviors.

Supporters of determinism often point to science for evidence. For example, classical physics shows that the motion of large objects can be predicted, while quantum physics introduces some uncertainty at very small levels. However, even in quantum physics, experts debate whether this uncertainty is real or just the result of things we don't fully understand yet. Neuroscience also plays a role by showing how the brain's processes control decision-making, suggesting that human actions might simply be physical reactions, not free choices.

This view raises ethical questions. If our actions are caused by things beyond our control, can we really be held responsible for them? Are ideas like praise, blame, and punishment fair if people have no real choice in what they do? Critics of determinism argue that it takes away the meaning of responsibility and autonomy. They believe that without free will—the ability to truly choose—people aren't responsible for their actions, and the idea of moral accountability falls apart.

On the other hand, supporters of free will believe that people have the ability to make choices independently, even when influenced by outside factors. They argue that humans can think, reflect, and decide for themselves, shaping their own lives. At the heart of this belief is the idea of autonomy, or self-governance, where people are active participants in their decisions instead of being controlled by outside forces. Free will allows individuals to weigh different options and make choices that fit their values and goals.

An important part of free will is deliberation, or the process of thinking through decisions before acting. This ability to reflect on choices gives people control over their actions and helps them work toward their goals. Many philosophers believe free will is essential for moral responsibility. Without it, people would just be reacting to outside forces, not making real choices, and it wouldn't make sense to hold them accountable.

However, free will also faces challenges. Some skeptics argue that what feels like free will is actually an illusion, influenced by factors like genetics, upbringing, and subconscious thoughts. Advances in neuroscience add to the debate by showing how brain activity influences decisions, leading some to question how much control we really have.

The debate between free will and determinism remains an important topic, with big implications for freedom, responsibility, and ethics. It raises questions like: If our actions are controlled by outside forces, can we be held responsible? Can we truly blame or praise people for actions shaped by unconscious influences? Philosophers have offered different answers to these tough questions, showing a variety of ways to think about human choice and control.

Some thinkers, called compatibilists, believe that free will and determinism can work together. They argue that free will doesn't mean complete independence from all influences but rather the ability to act without being forced by outside constraints. From this view, people can still have moral responsibility within a deterministic world. Others, known as hard determinists, believe that determinism leaves no room for real free will, meaning people can't truly be held accountable for their actions.

In the end, the question of whether humans have true free will remains unresolved and fascinating. Science has given us new insights into how decisions are made, but the nature of human freedom and responsibility continues to spark debate. This topic remains a central part of philosophical inquiry, as thinkers and scientists alike try to understand what it means to choose and be responsible for our actions.

- **Thought vs thinking**

The difference between **thinking** and **thought** is an important idea in philosophy and psychology, helping us understand how we think and process information. While the terms are often used as if they mean the same thing, they actually refer to different parts of how the mind works. Both are crucial for how we understand the world, solve problems, make decisions, and act intelligently.

Thinking is an active mental process. It includes everything from understanding what we see and hear to solving problems and making decisions. Thinking is what allows us to connect with the world around us and interpret what we experience.

At its simplest, thinking helps us make sense of information from our senses, like sights, sounds, and smells. For example, recognizing a familiar voice or enjoying a meal involves thinking processes that turn sensory information into meaningful experiences.

One key part of thinking is **reasoning**, which helps us draw conclusions and make logical decisions. When we reason, we use facts and ideas to solve problems or evaluate arguments. Whether you're solving a math problem or deciding if an argument makes sense, reasoning helps you think clearly and effectively.

Problem-solving is another part of thinking. It's about figuring out solutions to challenges or finding ways to reach goals. Problem-solving includes breaking down issues, analyzing situations, and coming up with creative ideas to address them. Whether you're putting together a puzzle or tackling real-life problems, this shows how thinking helps us adapt and overcome obstacles.

Decision-making is also a part of thinking. It's the process of looking at different options and choosing the best one. This involves thinking about risks and benefits, considering long-term effects, and setting priorities. From picking what to eat for dinner to deciding on a career, decision-making is a daily activity that relies on thinking.

Thought, on the other hand, is more about the ideas and concepts that come from thinking. These include mental images, words, and symbols that help us understand and organize information. Thoughts help us create categories, compare things, and find relationships between objects or events.

In short, **thinking** is the active process of using your mind to solve problems, make decisions, and understand the world, while **thoughts** are the results of those mental efforts. Both work together to help us make sense of life and give meaning to our experiences.

Researchers have developed ways to study thinking. Two important models are **computational cognition** and **embodied cognition**, introduced by experts like Marvin Minsky, George Lakoff, and Mark Johnson.

Computational models compare the mind to a computer, describing thinking as processing information step by step, like running a program. These models suggest that the brain uses symbols and patterns to plan, reason, and solve problems.

By studying how thinking works, we can better understand the mind and improve areas like psychology, neuroscience, and artificial intelligence. This exploration helps us unlock how humans think and how we might create smarter systems in the future.

- **Embodied cognition**

Embodied cognition proposes that thinking is inherently connected to bodily experiences and interactions with the environment. This framework suggests that cognition is rooted in the body and influenced by physical and social contexts. It emphasizes how sensory-motor experiences shape thought, indicating that interacting with our environment is key to deriving meaning. From this perspective, thinking is affected by cultural norms, social interactions, and environmental factors, involving simulations of these elements in decision-making.

While computational and embodied cognition present different approaches, some researchers recognize the value of integrating both. A hybrid model acknowledges the complementary roles of symbolic representation and sensorimotor interaction, offering a deeper understanding of cognition—whether it involves abstract thought or physical engagement.

The environment plays a crucial role in shaping thought. It provides context for cognitive processes, including physical surroundings, social settings, and institutional influences. The environment determines which stimuli are most relevant, what actions are possible, and how we interpret events. As social beings, humans continually interact with others through communication, collaboration, and negotiation, providing opportunities for learning and shared understanding.

Culture also significantly influences thinking. It shapes our beliefs, attitudes, and worldviews, which in turn affect how we perceive and interpret experiences. Cultural differences manifest in language, behavior, and thought processes. Cultural schemas guide how we understand our environment, direct attention, and inform problem-solving.

Experience is another key factor in shaping thought. We draw on accumulated knowledge and memories to guide current cognitive processes. Experiential learning involves gaining knowledge through direct experience, trial and error, and reflection. Our past experiences serve as valuable resources for problem-solving, allowing us to apply what we have learned to new situations.

Environmental affordances refer to the opportunities for action provided by the environment. The layout, resources, and constraints of our surroundings influence how we perceive, plan, and act. Thinking is thus an adaptive process involving the interaction between internal cognitive processes and external environments.

Understanding how we think and learn is central to cognitive science. By distinguishing between different aspects of mental activity, philosophers and psychologists have gained insights into the nature of intelligence. Differentiating thinking from thought helps explain the underlying mechanisms of reasoning, decision-making, and problem-solving. Thought, in contrast, is the outcome of thinking—the ideas, solutions, and interpretations we generate.

Reasoning is the process of drawing logical conclusions and making inferences to solve problems or answer questions, while thought represents the outcome—interpretations and insights we create. This distinction drives ongoing research in cognitive science, artificial intelligence, linguistics, and philosophy as scholars seek to understand the mechanisms underlying human thought.

Scientists explore these complexities through theoretical models and empirical research, contributing to philosophical and psychological discussions about cognition, agency, autonomy, and responsibility. Future research may yield more accurate models of cognition, advancements in AI, and solutions to societal challenges involving mental health, education, and human-computer interaction.

Embodied cognition challenges traditional views by emphasizing the inseparable relationship between mind, body, and environment. This perspective posits that behaviors are not solely products of internal mental representations or computational processes but are deeply intertwined with bodily experiences, sensorimotor interactions, and environmental contexts.

Two core concepts within embodied cognition are simulation and environmental affordances. Simulation refers to the process in which individuals mentally recreate sensory-motor experiences to understand or represent abstract ideas. When people read about an activity like running, their brains may activate neural circuits associated with actual movement, allowing them to experience it mentally as if they were performing the activity. This mental simulation helps understand and represent the action by drawing on past sensory-motor experiences.

Environmental affordances refer to opportunities for interaction provided by the environment that influence perception, thinking, and decision-making. For example, an object that feels heavy may be perceived as more valuable compared to a lighter one, demonstrating how physical sensation shapes judgment and decision-making. Perception and action are tightly coupled—how we perceive the world is intimately tied to how we interact with it.

Language comprehension and social empathy are also influenced by embodied cognition. Words related to actions can elicit corresponding neural responses, facilitating comprehension. For instance, reading about a physical action can activate similar brain regions as if one were performing that action. Empathy, too, is facilitated through embodied simulation, where we simulate others' emotions, helping us respond appropriately to social cues.

Embodied cognition provides nuanced insights into human cognition, including language comprehension, social understanding, and decision-making. It highlights the importance of considering the embodied nature of thought when studying the complexities of the mind.

Embodied cognition is a multidisciplinary field drawing on insights from psychology, neuroscience, philosophy, robotics, and other disciplines. Researchers aim to develop theoretical models and empirical studies that elucidate how bodily experiences, sensorimotor interactions, and environmental contexts shape cognitive processes. This interdisciplinary approach provides a rich understanding of the complexities of human cognition.

Psychology plays a central role by investigating how cognition is influenced by experiences. Psychologists use behavioral studies to explore phenomena like simulation, language comprehension, social cognition, emotion processing, problem-solving, and decision-making within an embodied framework. They conduct experiments to investigate how sensations like warmth or weight influence perception and judgment.

Neuroscience offers valuable insights into the neural mechanisms underlying embodied cognition. Techniques like fMRI, EEG, and transcranial magnetic stimulation (TMS) help researchers understand how cognitive processes are represented in the brain. For instance, studies of mirror neurons—neurons that fire both when an individual performs an action and when they observe another performing the same action—shed light on the role of simulation in imitation and social understanding.

Philosophy contributes by providing conceptual frameworks for understanding embodied experience and its implications for cognition. Philosophers examine questions related to the mind-body relationship, consciousness, and embodiment, exploring how bodily experience shapes cognition and challenging traditional distinctions between mind and body.

Robotics intersects with embodied cognition by applying its principles to the design and development of intelligent systems. Roboticists draw inspiration from biological systems to create robots that can perceive, interact with, and adapt to their environments in a human-like manner. These robots are equipped with sensors and actuators, allowing them to learn through sensory-motor interactions similar to humans.

The multidisciplinary nature of embodied cognition integrates insights from diverse fields, enriching our understanding of human behavior and cognition. Collaboration across disciplines can pave the way for innovative approaches to enhancing human-machine interaction, developing rehabilitation techniques, and creating new educational interventions.

- **Language and its role in Thought**

Language, often seen as a vehicle for communication, is also a profound influencer of thought processes. Throughout history, philosophers, linguists, and cognitive scientists have been captivated by the relationship between language and thought. This dynamic interplay has been explored through various theories, with the Sapir-Whorf hypothesis standing out prominently. This hypothesis, named after linguists Edward Sapir and Benjamin Lee Whorf, presents a fascinating idea known as linguistic relativity. It suggests that the structure and vocabulary of a language play a crucial role in shaping how its speakers perceive and conceptualize the world around them. At its core, the hypothesis posits that different languages encode unique distinctions and conceptual categories. In other words, the tools available to speakers of a particular language influence not only how they communicate but also how they understand and interpret reality.

One key implication is that specific vocabularies can shape individuals' perceptual abilities. For instance, having a rich array of color terms can affect a speaker's ability to distinguish shades of color. Research shows that speakers of languages with more specific color terms are indeed better at differentiating subtle hues compared to those with fewer terms. In English, we have distinct words like "blue," "green," and "red." However, Russian distinguishes between light blue ("goluboy") and dark blue ("siniy"), enabling Russian speakers to discern color variations more quickly than English speakers. This finer categorization affects how individuals perceive and categorize colors.

Moreover, linguistic categories shape perception and conceptualization. The way time is conceptualized in language is an example. English predominantly uses ego-moving metaphors for time, such as "the future lies ahead" and "the past is behind." In contrast, Mandarin Chinese uses time-moving metaphors like "next month comes down" and "previous month goes up." These differences impact how speakers plan events and highlight language's influence on cognition.

Languages like Turkish and Quechua possess grammatical markers called evidentials, which indicate the source of information—whether it comes from personal experience, inference, or hearsay. In Turkish, suffixes added to verbs convey whether information is based on direct observation or inference. For example, "görmüşüm" means "I saw it myself," while "duymuşum" means "I heard it." These features shape attitudes towards knowledge and certainty, emphasizing the reliability of information and influencing how statements are judged.

Gendered language can also shape perception. Languages like Spanish and German assign gender to nouns and pronouns. For instance, "la luna" (the moon) in Spanish is feminine, while "el sol" (the sun) is masculine. Such a system subtly influences perceptions of gender roles and stereotypes, with studies showing that gendered pronouns reinforce associations and affect gender-related concepts within cultures.

While linguistic relativity has garnered significant interest, it has also faced criticism. Some scholars argue that the influence of language on thought may be more indirect than originally proposed, and there is ongoing debate regarding whether language shapes thought or merely reflects pre-existing patterns. Despite this, the hypothesis continues to offer a compelling framework for understanding the relationship between language and perception. By examining how language influences cognitive processes, it encourages us to reconsider the interaction between culture, language, and thought.

Language influences categorization by providing a framework for organizing and labeling experiences, enabling people to group objects, ideas, and concepts into meaningful categories. For example, words like "chair," "table," and "sofa" help facilitate the conceptualization and differentiation of types of furniture. Moreover, language plays a significant role in reasoning and problem-solving. It provides the structures and conventions needed to construct arguments, formulate hypotheses, and evaluate evidence. Language also affects stereotypes, impacting social judgments and behaviors. By serving as a tool for externalizing and sharing thoughts, language fosters social interaction, cooperation, and cultural transmission. It allows individuals to communicate intentions, beliefs, emotions, and desires, establishing shared meanings and coordinating collective actions. In this way, language is central to human cognition and essential to social adaptation.

- **Perception and epistemology**

Exploring the complex dynamics between perception and epistemology reveals how sensory experiences profoundly shape our comprehension of reality and our acquisition of knowledge. Perception is the process by which individuals gather information about their surroundings through the senses, including sight, hearing, touch, taste, and smell. It involves interpreting and organizing sensory input to create a coherent understanding of the environment, serving as the primary means by which people interact with and make sense of the world. Through perception, we can distinguish between different sensory inputs, recognize objects and patterns, and navigate our environment effectively.

Epistemology, the branch of philosophy concerned with the nature, sources, and limitations of knowledge, seeks to understand how knowledge is acquired, justified, and evaluated. Epistemologists delve into questions like: What is knowledge? How do we come to know the world? What criteria justify beliefs? These inquiries examine the conditions under which beliefs can be considered justified or warranted. Philosophers like Descartes and Locke have questioned the reliability of perception, challenging the notion that indubitable truths can be derived solely from experience. Central to these investigations is distinguishing between perceptual experiences that accurately represent the world and those that are illusory or deceptive, such as optical illusions or hallucinations. Philosophical theories—from direct realism to representationalism—seek to reconcile the subjective nature of perception with the pursuit of objective knowledge.

Cognitive penetration refers to the phenomenon in which higher-level cognitive processes, such as beliefs, expectations, and desires, influence lower-level perceptual experiences. This concept challenges the traditional view of perception as a purely bottom-up process driven solely by sensory input, highlighting instead the bidirectional interaction between cognition and perception. Cognitive penetration acknowledges that perceptual experiences are shaped not only by sensory information but also by prior knowledge and mental states.

For instance, individuals with a fear of spiders (arachnophobia) may perceive harmless spiders as larger or more threatening compared to those without such fears. This demonstrates how emotional factors can bias perception toward stimuli consistent with pre-existing beliefs or fears. Cognitive penetration has been studied across various domains, including vision, audition, and taste perception. For example, studies have shown that expectations about flavor can influence the perceived taste of food and beverages.

Neuroimaging studies provide insights into the mechanisms underlying cognitive penetration, revealing that attention and expectation can influence activity in early sensory areas of the brain. This neural evidence supports the idea that cognitive states impact sensory processing, shaping perceptual experiences. One key question in this field is the extent to which cognitive penetration distorts perception. While it may enhance the ability to interpret sensory input in certain contexts, it can also lead to biases and errors when mental states misinterpret or misrepresent available information.

Understanding cognitive penetration is crucial for unraveling the complexities of human perception and its implications for epistemology and the philosophy of mind. Cognitive penetration challenges traditional views of perception as a passive, veridical process, raising questions about the reliability of perception and our ability to access objective reality. Philosophers debate the epistemological consequences of cognitive penetration, exploring how it shapes knowledge and influences our pursuit of truth.

3 MINDSET

In the complex fabric of human cognition, mindset plays a crucial role, threading its influence through personal growth and success. As we delve into the "Foundations of Mindset," it becomes clear that mindset is more than a psychological idea—it is a powerful force that shapes how we see the world, influences our reactions to challenges, and directs the path our lives take. Essentially, mindset serves as the lens through which we view and interpret our experiences. This introduction serves as a gateway into the concept of fixed and growth mindsets—a journey that explores how beliefs about learning, abilities, and challenges shape professional development. The term "mindset," coined by psychologist Carol S. Dweck, refers to the set of attitudes we hold about our abilities and the nature of intelligence. Within this framework, two primary types of mindsets emerge: fixed and growth.

A fixed mindset operates on the belief that intelligence and abilities are innate and unchangeable. Individuals with a fixed mindset often perceive challenges as threats to their inherent capabilities, leading to a desire to appear competent at all costs. As a result, they may avoid difficult tasks to maintain the illusion of competence, viewing setbacks as indicators of failure.

In contrast, a growth mindset thrives on the belief that abilities can be developed through dedication, hard work, and resilience. People with a growth mindset embrace opportunities for growth, see effort as a path to mastery, and treat obstacles as stepping stones to future success. This mindset fosters a love for learning and resilience, which helps individuals reach their full potential. The roots of these mindsets extend back to formative years, shaped by experiences, feedback, and societal influences. Early interactions with caregivers, educators, and peers contribute to the development of these foundational beliefs, which often persist into adulthood.

As we navigate the "Mindsync" landscape, understanding the intricacies of mindset becomes crucial—not only for professional growth but also for embracing the principles of "Mindsync," where mind and technology converge for optimal outcomes. This introduction sets the stage for the transformative interplay between technology and mindset, emphasizing the power of harmony between the two.

This chapter invites you to reflect on your beliefs, challenge your assumptions, and move toward resilience and limitless potential within an expansive framework defined by an unwavering conviction in the ability to grow and improve. We delve into the complexities of a fixed mindset, examining the rigidity of perspectives and behaviors that may hinder advancement.

A fixed mindset is like a mosaic of traits seen as innate and unchangeable, qualities that are resistant to transformation. This mindset builds mental barriers that prevent growth, often shaping how one interprets effort and setbacks. At its core is a deep-seated belief that abilities are static, which can determine an individual's capacity for growth. For example, a child who excels at piano effortlessly might be consistently praised for their natural talent, leading them to internalize their ability as an unchangeable trait. On the other hand, a student struggling with a challenging subject might believe they are inherently incapable in that area, creating significant mental barriers that steer them away from situations that could reveal their perceived limitations.

Picture an employee known for their analytical skills. When faced with a project that requires advanced data analysis, they might shy away, fearing exposure of their inadequacies. Rather than viewing challenges as an opportunity for growth, they often see them as threats to their competence. For instance, someone used to excelling in exams with little effort may view the need for additional study as a sign of incompetence, disregarding the importance of persistence and diligence in academic success.

A critical aspect of a fixed mindset is how setbacks are perceived—often seen as confirmation of inherent limitations rather than an integral part of the learning process. Imagine an aspiring entrepreneur experiencing a setback in a business venture; instead of seeing it as an opportunity to learn and adapt, they might see it as evidence of their inability to succeed.

In the complex landscape of a fixed mindset, perceptions of challenges are often distorted. Those with a fixed mindset tend to see challenges not as opportunities for growth but as direct threats to their sense of competence. This cognitive distortion shapes how they respond, often triggering a defensive stance aimed at preserving their perceived image of innate intelligence. For instance, imagine a student who has consistently excelled in mathematics with little effort. When confronted with a difficult math problem, this individual may interpret the challenge not as a chance to expand their understanding but as a potential blow to their self-image as a "naturally gifted" mathematician. The perceived threat to their competence can provoke feelings of anxiety, reluctance, or avoidance, creating a barrier to embracing the learning opportunity the problem presents.

In a professional setting, consider an employee known for their technological skills who encounters a new software platform. Rather than viewing it as an opportunity to acquire a valuable new skill, the individual may perceive it as a threat to their expertise. This reaction can manifest as reluctance to engage with the technology or outright resistance to learning, hindering both personal growth and adaptability. The influence of a fixed mindset extends beyond academic or professional realms into personal life as well. Someone who has always been praised for their artistic talent might avoid trying a new art form for fear that they won't excel immediately, thus undermining their perceived abilities.

The effort, in this context, becomes a double-edged sword. Rather than being seen as part of the path to mastery, a fixed mindset distorts the principle of effort, interpreting it as a sign of incompetence or a revelation of one's limitations, rather than a commendable step toward improvement. If someone has coasted through their endeavors without needing significant effort, the idea of investing substantial work into a new challenge becomes entangled with the belief that persistence is a sign of inherent inadequacy. The fear of exposing perceived weaknesses becomes a powerful deterrent, leading to avoidance or shortcuts that undermine the very processes designed to foster learning and growth.

In a leadership role, for example, when a project demands intensive skill development, acknowledging one's current limitations might be seen as an admission of inadequacy. Effort, which should be recognized as an investment in improvement, is instead viewed as a symbol of vulnerability in a fixed mindset. The comfort zone becomes a refuge where competence can be maintained, often at the expense of genuine advancement. This mindset obstructs not only personal progress but also distorts the value of diligent effort, fostering an environment where setbacks and failures are viewed not as integral parts of growth but as reflections of personal inadequacy.

In this fixed mindset framework, setbacks take on a particularly formidable nature. Instead of being seen as stepping stones to development, they are interpreted as evidence of an individual's inherent limitations, further reinforcing the distorted view of effort and challenge. A student who has always excelled with ease may struggle to navigate a difficult subject or exam, interpreting their struggle not as a natural part of the learning process but as a failure of their innate abilities. This mindset impedes their ability to effectively cope with challenges, undermining the resilience needed for future success.

Through real-world examples, we can see how a fixed mindset subtly influences decision-making, attitudes toward risk, and overall well-being. For instance, consider a professional who is presented with the opportunity to lead a cross-functional project. Despite possessing the necessary skills, the fear of failure or not meeting perceived standards may lead this individual to decline the opportunity in order to preserve an image of inherent competence. Similarly, in personal finance, a fixed mindset can limit risk tolerance. Someone with this mindset might avoid investment opportunities that require a learning curve or come with the possibility of temporary setbacks, opting instead for traditional, low-risk options that safeguard their perception of financial competence.

A fixed mindset can have a deep impact on both personal and professional growth, often creating barriers that hinder individuals from realizing their full potential. When such a mindset becomes entrenched, it can influence decisions and behaviors across various life domains. For instance, in education, students with a fixed mindset may avoid challenging subjects, fearing that struggle or failure could reflect poorly on their intelligence. This reluctance can stifle intellectual curiosity and limit the development of a broad skill set, ultimately narrowing their educational growth.

In professional settings, a fixed mindset may prevent individuals from taking on new responsibilities or pursuing roles that require learning new skills. The fear of failure and the desire to appear competent can become significant obstacles, limiting personal advancement and diminishing contributions to the organization. Additionally, the pressure to project innate ability can take a toll on emotional well-being, leading to heightened stress and anxiety. Those who operate with a fixed mindset often experience feelings of judgment and criticism, which can erode self-esteem and resilience. Over time, these emotional burdens can become long-term hindrances to growth and development.

- **The Path from Fixed to Growth Mindset**

"Adaptation is the bridge between the challenges we face and the growth we achieve."

The consequences of a fixed mindset are far-reaching, influencing systems, individual trajectories, well-being, and overall progress. Recognizing and actively addressing these consequences is crucial for fostering a culture that embraces resilience and growth across all spheres of life.

As our exploration of the fixed mindset draws to a close, we are reminded of the challenges posed by such ingrained beliefs. However, in line with the philosophy of Mindsync, we extend empathy and understanding toward those with a fixed mindset. Acknowledging its presence is the first step in forging a transformative path beyond rigid dichotomies.

The journey from a fixed to a growth mindset calls on individuals to move beyond the boundaries of inflexibility. This transformation harmonizes various cognitive facets, encouraging individuals to embrace the complexities of the human mind. Growth and resilience come not from avoiding challenges but from engaging with them. By extending empathy toward the fixed mindset, we recognize the intricacies woven into the fabric of human cognition. Rather than viewing the fixed mindset as a hindrance, we can see it as an integral facet of the human mind's intricate tapestry.

This recognition invites us to understand our cognitive landscape as diverse and layered, with both light and shadow. The path from rigidity to growth calls for a nuanced understanding, encouraging introspection and a willingness to explore our own cognitive patterns. It is an affirmation that while the mind may at times feel fixed, it is also fluid, adaptable, and capable of expansive growth.

The journey of mindset evolution does not seek to erase the fixed mindset but rather invites individuals to engage with it as part of a grand cognitive evolution. It is an ode to the human capacity for transcendence, reminding us that the path to harmony is not a straight line but a rich, dynamic tapestry woven with threads of self-awareness, acceptance, and continuous growth

- **The Growth Mindset**

In a world of rapid change, the ability to adapt, learn, and confront challenges is essential. A fixed mindset—one that perceives intelligence and abilities as fixed traits—can act as a significant barrier to personal and professional growth. In contrast, the growth mindset embodies a transformative perspective, viewing abilities as expandable through commitment and perseverance. This chapter examines the fundamental principles of the growth mindset, underscoring the importance of embracing learning opportunities, understanding effort as a pathway to mastery, and cultivating resilience by viewing setbacks as integral steps in the journey to success.

Central to the growth mindset is the belief that challenges offer invaluable opportunities for learning. While a fixed mindset may regard obstacles as daunting and even insurmountable, those with a growth-oriented outlook perceive difficulties as moments of potential growth, encouraging a proactive approach to problem-solving and deeper comprehension of complex ideas. For instance, when faced with a challenging math problem, a student with a fixed mindset may feel discouraged and avoid it, whereas a growth-minded student might approach it with curiosity, ultimately expanding their skills. Here, obstacles transform into catalysts for continuous development.

In the professional sphere, a growth mindset reframes complex tasks as gateways to skill expansion. Imagine a project manager confronted with a demanding assignment. By perceiving this task as an opportunity to broaden their capabilities and refine strategies, they develop a genuine enthusiasm for the challenge, creating a cycle of continuous improvement—a quality invaluable in today's dynamic work environments.

A key tenet of the growth mindset is recognizing effort as an essential component of mastery. Unlike a fixed mindset that attributes success solely to natural talent, a growth mindset acknowledges the power of sustained effort in skill development. Consider an aspiring musician learning a new instrument. Where initial struggles may deter someone with a fixed mindset, the growth-oriented individual appreciates each practice session as a critical step toward mastery, transforming effort into a fulfilling and essential part of their journey.

In the workplace, this appreciation of effort translates to employees taking on challenges enthusiastically, recognizing that skill refinement and knowledge acquisition are investments in their own growth. This attitude fosters a work culture that values and celebrates learning and improvement, infusing enthusiasm into even the most challenging tasks.

A cornerstone of the growth mindset is the capacity to view failures as essential components of success. Rather than being disheartened by setbacks, individuals with a growth mindset harness these experiences for self-reflection and personal growth. Take, for example, an entrepreneur who faces a setback in their business venture. Instead of interpreting this as a definitive failure, they see it as an opportunity to refine their approach, identify areas for growth, and build resilience. Such experiences enhance their adaptability, allowing them to approach future challenges with a refined perspective and renewed determination.

Personal growth is also marked by the ability to transform setbacks into learning opportunities. Consider an individual striving for physical fitness who encounters challenges in their pursuit of a healthier lifestyle. Instead of viewing setbacks as failures, they adapt their approach, draw lessons from their experiences, and refine their regimen. Each setback thus becomes a meaningful step toward long-term well-being.

The growth mindset's power lies in recognizing setbacks as integral to the journey to success. Cultivating this forward-looking perspective not only fosters personal growth but also positively impacts those around us. In a world characterized by continuous change, the growth mindset serves as a guiding light, leading individuals along a path of lifelong learning and self-improvement.

Mindset development begins early, shaped by interactions with caregivers, educators, and societal influences. Each plays a critical role in molding our attitudes toward challenges and learning. Caregivers, for example, lay the foundation by encouraging children to value persistence and resilience over immediate results. When they praise a child's effort in learning to walk rather than simply focusing on achievement, they nurture a belief in the importance of perseverance.

Educators also play an instrumental role in mindset development. By emphasizing effort, learning strategies, and growth over raw talent or grades, teachers create an environment in which challenges are seen as opportunities. Constructive feedback that acknowledges progress and suggests areas for growth fosters a sense of continuous improvement and instills a love of learning.

Society at large further influences mindset formation. In cultures that prioritize grades and academic accolades, individuals may come to believe that success is defined by innate intelligence. In contrast, societies that celebrate diverse skills, resilience, and adaptability tend to foster a mindset that embraces challenges and personal growth.

This collective influence creates an ecosystem where mindsets are either growth-oriented or fixed. Recognizing the critical role of these early experiences, caregivers, educators, and broader societal influences share a responsibility to cultivate environments that encourage curiosity and adaptability. By celebrating learning and embracing diverse perspectives, we foster individuals with a deep sense of purpose, resilience, and the capacity for lifelong growth.

This holistic approach to human development establishes a harmonious framework for continuous growth. The attitudes instilled in childhood form a foundation that guides responses to life's inevitable setbacks, challenges, and uncertainties. In educational and professional environments, a culture that encourages a growth mindset promotes innovation, aids in tackling complex challenges, and nurtures collaborative, supportive spaces.

The impact of a growth mindset extends beyond the individual, affecting relationships and community dynamics. Those who embrace growth are better equipped to navigate complex social landscapes, developing skills such as conflict resolution, problem-solving, and empathetic communication that benefit both personal and collective development. Ultimately, a growth mindset becomes woven into the social fabric, influencing cultural norms and fostering a supportive environment for all.

Consider communities that prioritize critical thinking and problem-solving. Such communities serve as incubators for individuals who excel academically and contribute meaningfully to broader socio-economic spheres. The influence of a growth mindset radiates beyond personal success, shaping cultural attitudes and approaches to challenges. A society rooted in growth and resilience becomes a beacon of progress, encouraging its members to embrace change and transform obstacles into stepping stones for collective advancement.

Inspiring Real-Life Examples **of Growth Mindset**

Dr. APJ Abdul Kalam: The People's President

Born in 1931 in Rameswaram, Tamil Nadu, Dr. APJ Abdul Kalam came from a humble background. Despite facing financial constraints and limited access to educational resources, he possessed an insatiable thirst for knowledge and a deep passion for science and technology. Kalam's early years were marked by perseverance and determination. He excelled academically despite the challenges he faced, earning degrees in aerospace engineering and eventually obtaining a Ph.D. from the Madras Institute of Technology.

Throughout his career, Dr. Kalam encountered numerous obstacles and setbacks. Despite facing rejection and criticism, he remained steadfast in his commitment to making meaningful contributions to society through his work. A breakthrough came when he joined the Indian Space Research Organisation (ISRO) in 1963. He played a pivotal role in India's space program, spearheading projects and initiatives that helped propel the country into the ranks of space-faring nations.

However, Dr. Kalam's journey was not without its share of challenges. He faced setbacks, including the failure of India's first satellite launch vehicle in 1979. Yet, rather than being deterred by these setbacks, he embraced them as opportunities for growth and learning. His growth mindset enabled him to rise above adversity and continue striving for excellence. Dr. Kalam was deeply committed to transforming India into a developed nation by leveraging technology as a tool for social and economic progress.

In 2002, Dr. Kalam was elected as the 11th President of India, becoming known as the "People's President" for his humility, compassion, and dedication to serving the nation. During his tenure, he continued to inspire millions with his vision of a prosperous and inclusive India. Dr. Kalam's journey is a powerful example of resilience, determination, and the transformative power of education. His life story inspires us to overcome obstacles, embrace challenges, and strive for excellence in pursuit of our dreams.

Mary Kom: Overcoming Barriers in Boxing

Mary Kom, born Mangte Chungneijang Kom on March 1, 1983, in Manipur, India, faced numerous challenges on her path to becoming one of the most successful female boxers in the world. Growing up in a remote village, Mary was introduced to boxing at a young age. Despite facing resistance from her conservative community, she pursued her passion for the sport with unwavering determination.

In the early stages of her career, Mary Kom encountered skepticism and doubts about her abilities as a female boxer. Competing in a male-dominated field, many believed that women were not physically capable of excelling at the highest levels. However, Mary refused to be discouraged by societal expectations or gender stereotypes. She embraced a growth mindset, viewing each challenge as an opportunity for self-improvement.

Mary Kom's breakthrough came when she won a silver medal at the 2001 World Amateur Championships, marking the beginning of her meteoric rise.

Despite facing setbacks, including financial difficulties and injuries, Mary persevered, training rigorously and pushing herself to new heights. One of her crowning achievements came in the 2012 London Olympics, where she won a bronze medal in the women's flyweight category, becoming the first Indian woman boxer to win an Olympic medal.

In the years since her Olympic triumph, Mary Kom has continued to inspire millions with her resilience, perseverance, and indomitable spirit. Her numerous medals at World Championships and Asian Games have solidified her legacy as one of the greatest female boxers of all time. Mary Kom's story exemplifies the transformative power of determination and self-belief, inspiring us to overcome adversity, break barriers, and pursue our dreams with unyielding commitment.

- **Welcoming Opportunities**

The concept of the growth mindset, popularized by psychologist Carol Dweck, emphasizes the belief that intelligence and abilities can be cultivated through dedication, effort, and perseverance. In contrast to a fixed mindset, where individuals see their talents as static traits, those with a growth mindset embrace challenges, view setbacks as opportunities for growth, and persist in the face of obstacles. This chapter explores the practical application of the growth mindset across various domains, highlighting its transformative effects on individuals and organizations.

The journey toward cultivating a growth mindset begins with self-awareness and a willingness to challenge ingrained beliefs about one's abilities. It involves recognizing the power of mindset in shaping behaviors, attitudes, and ultimately outcomes. Through introspection and reflection, individuals can identify areas where they may hold limiting beliefs and consciously work to shift to a growth-oriented perspective.

A growth mindset values challenges as opportunities for learning and development. Instead of avoiding difficult tasks out of fear of failure, individuals with a growth mindset approach them with curiosity and enthusiasm, understanding that struggles are not reflections of inherent limitations but are natural steps on the path to mastery. By reframing these experiences, they cultivate resilience and perseverance in the face of adversity. Failures are seen as inevitable in any pursuit, but instead of dwelling on them or succumbing to self-doubt, individuals analyze what went wrong, extract valuable lessons, and adjust their approach. Every failure becomes a stepping stone to improvement, reinforcing that progress is achievable through effort and persistence.

A hallmark of the growth mindset is the proactive seeking of feedback and the embrace of continuous improvement. Rather than fearing criticism, individuals view it as valuable input and actively seek constructive feedback from peers, mentors, and supervisors, leveraging it to refine skills, overcome weaknesses, and achieve higher performance.

The benefits of a growth mindset extend beyond individual development to organizational success. Companies that foster a culture of learning, experimentation, and innovation are better equipped to adapt to change and thrive in dynamic environments. Leaders play a crucial role in promoting a growth mindset within their teams by encouraging risk-taking, celebrating progress, and providing opportunities for skill development and career advancement.

Real-World Examples of the Growth Mindset in Action
Sachin Tendulkar: A Testament to Growth

Sachin Tendulkar, one of cricket's most iconic figures, was born in Mumbai, India, in 1973. His fascination with cricket began at a young age, but his journey to greatness was far from easy. Despite displaying exceptional talent, Tendulkar faced doubts and skepticism due to his diminutive stature. Many questioned whether he had the physical attributes necessary to excel in the highly competitive world of international cricket. However, Tendulkar refused to be defined by others' perceptions or limited by the physical challenges he faced.

From the outset, Tendulkar demonstrated an insatiable hunger for improvement and an unyielding determination to succeed. Rather than allowing limitations to deter him, he embraced a growth mindset—the belief that abilities and intelligence can be developed through dedication and hard work. Throughout his formative years, he honed his skills tirelessly, spending countless hours practicing his batting technique and refining his game. He sought guidance from experienced coaches and mentors, continuously absorbing their insights to elevate his performance.

Tendulkar's relentless pursuit of excellence was driven by a deep belief in the power of hard work and perseverance. Throughout his cricketing career, he encountered numerous setbacks, including injuries, periods of poor form, and criticism from fans and pundits. Rather than allowing these challenges to demoralize him, he saw them as opportunities to learn and grow. Each setback fueled his determination to push himself further. His unwavering commitment to self-improvement and his ability to bounce back became defining traits of his illustrious career.

As Tendulkar's career progressed, his accomplishments became legendary. He shattered records, including runs scored in both Test and One-Day cricket, as well as centuries in international matches. Beyond his statistical prowess, Tendulkar's impact transcended boundaries—he became a symbol of perseverance, humility, and sportsmanship, inspiring millions. His journey serves as a testament to the power of determination, resilience, and self-belief, illustrating the transformative potential of adopting a growth mindset.

Albert Einstein: Embracing Growth through Intellectual Curiosity

Albert Einstein's transformation from a fixed to a growth mindset is a powerful narrative that embodies intellectual evolution and the pursuit of knowledge. Born into a middle-class Jewish family in Ulm, Germany, in 1879, Einstein exhibited an insatiable curiosity from an early age. However, his disdain for rigid educational structures often placed him at odds with traditional schooling, which prioritized rote memorization over critical thinking and creativity.

Despite challenges within the formal education system, Einstein remained undeterred. He devoured books on science, mathematics, and philosophy, immersing himself in a world of ideas and exploration. These experiences instilled in him a deep-seated belief in the power of independent inquiry.

Einstein's breakthrough came in 1905 when he published a seminal paper on the photoelectric effect and introduced the concept of special relativity. This revolutionary theory challenged the long-standing Newtonian framework, proposing that space and time are interconnected and form a single entity known as spacetime. The implications of his work fundamentally altered our understanding of the universe and laid the foundation for modern physics.

Despite his groundbreaking achievements, Einstein continued to push the boundaries of scientific inquiry, exploring new frontiers and grappling with the complexities of quantum mechanics. His willingness to embrace uncertainty and challenge conventional wisdom epitomized the principles of a growth mindset. He viewed setbacks not as obstacles but as opportunities for learning and growth, continuously expanding the horizons of human knowledge.

Einstein's legacy lies not only in his scientific contributions but also in his ability to inspire generations of thinkers, dreamers, and innovators. His story reminds us that true greatness is not defined by the absence of failure but by the courage to rise above challenges and continue the pursuit of enlightenment.

The Power of Perseverance: Satish's Mindset Transformation on the Path to Civil Services"

In the culturally rich and challenging academic environment of Pune, Satish, a talented and hardworking young man from a rural village in Maharashtra, set his sights on one of India's most prestigious goals—the UPSC examination. Known in his village for his sharp intellect and relentless dedication, Satish had always excelled in his studies, driven by a strong work ethic and a deep commitment to his dreams. With aspirations to serve his community through civil services, he left his village, ready to conquer the challenges ahead. However, despite his talent and determination, the demanding UPSC exam presented a series of unexpected obstacles.

In his first and second attempts, despite his hard work and thorough preparation, Satish faced failure. Each setback hit him hard, and as doubts crept in, his confidence began to falter. The extensive syllabus, competitive environment, and language barrier—especially with English—became formidable challenges. With every unsuccessful attempt, the vision of joining the civil services seemed more distant, and Satish began to question whether his goal was achievable.

But just as he was close to giving up, the support of his colleagues, teachers, and family became his anchor. Recognizing his potential, his peers shared study techniques and strategies, helping him refine his approach. His teachers, aware of his determination, encouraged him to view his struggles as part of the journey, reminding him that resilience was essential to eventual success. His family, proud of his dedication, continued to stand by him, offering unwavering belief in his abilities.

Gradually, Satish's mindset shifted. He began to see each failure not as an end but as a stepping stone, an opportunity to learn and grow. Breaking his preparation into smaller, achievable goals, he celebrated each small victory, building his resilience and self-assurance. His hard work and talent, bolstered by the encouragement of those around him, reignited his passion and gave him the strength to persevere.

In his third attempt, Satish finally achieved his goal, clearing the UPSC exam and realizing his dream of joining the civil services. His journey became a testament to the power of persistence, resilience, and a growth mindset. Satish's story illustrates that with dedication, self-belief, and the right support, even multiple setbacks can lead to ultimate success.

- **Bridging Perspectives for Cognitive Harmony**

The fixed mindset, often seen as restrictive, is not merely about rigidity; it can also be a vital source of stability and confidence. In the cognitive landscape, individuals with a fixed mindset find assurance in their established abilities. Imagine a skilled professional who has honed a particular craft through years of practice—this mastery becomes a foundation, a stable anchor from which further growth can take place.

Mindsync philosophy encourages viewing this stability not as a constraint but as a strong base from which to confidently pursue growth. A key strength of the fixed mindset lies in fostering self-assurance; when individuals believe in their abilities, they approach tasks with a sense of certainty, motivated to engage positively with new challenges.

Meanwhile, the growth mindset serves as a dynamic complement, inspiring individuals to explore new possibilities through adaptability and a commitment to improvement. Picture an entrepreneur entering a rapidly changing market—the ability to learn and adapt here becomes crucial. Mindsync invites us to celebrate the drive for growth while recognizing the essential role stability plays in encouraging us to push boundaries and tackle challenges.

Adaptability, a cornerstone of the growth mindset, is essential for navigating today's complexities. Individuals with a growth-oriented perspective see challenges as learning opportunities and willingly embrace change, using it as a catalyst for personal and professional growth. In today's fast-evolving world, this adaptability enables them to stay relevant, develop new skills, and keep pace with shifts in their field.

In the broader framework of cognitive development, Mindsync encourages appreciation of the balance between stability and adaptability. The fixed mindset offers a foundation of confidence, while the growth mindset introduces flexibility and innovation. Together, these mindsets create a harmonious blend that extends beyond limitations and drives holistic growth.

Rather than positioning fixed and growth mindsets as opposites, Mindsync envisions them as complementary aspects of cognition. Stability provides a solid base for growth, while adaptability opens new paths forward. This nuanced view forms the essence of a balanced cognitive framework, where individuals can anchor in their strengths while reaching toward new horizons.

As we conclude this exploration, Mindsync challenges us to transcend the simple division between fixed and growth mindsets. Cognitive harmony lies in understanding these mindsets as interconnected facets of the human experience. Mindsync urges us to appreciate their interplay, fostering self-reflection and resilience. It calls on us to integrate the benefits of both, crafting a life approach that draws on stability while embracing growth and adaptability.

This journey from fixed to growth mindset, from perceived limits to expansive potential, celebrates human resilience, adaptability, and the pursuit of lifelong learning. It is an invitation to participate in a grand cognitive symphony—a harmony built on self-awareness, acceptance, and an enduring commitment to growth.

4 MINDTECH UNLEASHED

In the rapidly evolving landscape of the digital age, humanity stands at the threshold of a transformative epoch, marked by the seamless integration of mind and technology. This immersive journey, aptly titled "Exploring Horizon: Unleashing the Potential of Mindtech," embarks on a multidimensional odyssey into the frontiers of groundbreaking technologies that are reshaping human cognition, artificial intelligence, and the synergistic relationship between humans and machines.

As we stand at the edge of this new frontier, the convergence of technological breakthroughs is dismantling barriers once considered insurmountable. Our exploration delves deep into these vast technological horizons, highlighting emerging trends like quantum computing, nanotechnology, and the burgeoning Internet of Things (IoT). Understanding these dynamic landscapes is essential to effectively harness their power and potential.

A central focus of our journey is the intricate interplay between artificial intelligence and human cognition. We explore the synergies that emerge when machines augment human intellect, from revolutionizing medical diagnostics to fostering innovation in creative fields. This exploration extends into the realm of Virtual Reality (VR), which has moved beyond gaming to redefine learning, work, and our perception of the world.

In the midst of the omnipresence of smartphones, a critical examination of their impact is crucial. We seek to understand whether these pocket-sized marvels are enhancing our cognitive well-being—through mental health apps and cognitive training tools—or if they are inadvertently impeding it, contributing to issues like screen addiction.

The concept of "data mining" emerges as a captivating aspect of this journey, where analyzing data from social media, GPS, and sensors provides unprecedented insights into human behavior. However, this is not solely a technical endeavor; it brings profound ethical considerations, privacy concerns, and societal implications when leveraging personal data for understanding behavior.

At the core of this journey lies artificial intelligence, the driving force behind many recent advancements. We seek to demystify the potentials embedded within AI—through algorithms and learning datasets—in domains like healthcare, finance, and autonomous systems. This exploration transcends mere technological inquiry; it also considers the nuanced ethical, social, and philosophical dimensions intertwined with these advancements.

As we venture into "Mindtech Unleashed," we are compelled to reflect on our responsibilities in this digital age. This exploration serves as a reminder of the imperative need for a harmonious and mindful integration of technology— one that benefits individuals, societies, and the collective human experience.

- **Tech Horizons**

The rapid pace of technological progress has thrust society into a whirlwind of innovation, creating a continuously evolving landscape filled with ongoing advancements. This chapter begin with an extensive exploration of various technological frontiers, spanning from cutting-edge fields like quantum computing and nanotechnology to the seamless integration of the Internet of Things (IoT) into our daily routines. Understanding these frontiers is not just an academic pursuit; it is essential for businesses and individuals aiming to navigate the challenges and opportunities of a rapidly changing digital era.

- **Quantum Computing**

Quantum computers have the remarkable ability to exist in multiple states simultaneously due to the principle of superposition. Imagine flipping a coin and having it land on both heads and tails at the same time—this is what allows quantum computers to perform a vast number of calculations simultaneously, offering exponential speed-ups for certain types of problems. Moreover, quantum entanglement enables particles to become so interconnected that the state of one particle instantly affects the state of another, regardless of the distance between them. This phenomenon has the potential to revolutionize information processing, opening entirely new possibilities in computation.

Take, for example, a busy professional who relies on a smartphone to manage daily tasks, communicate with colleagues, and stay informed. A common aspect of their routine is planning the commute to work. Classical computers use navigation apps with algorithms to calculate the fastest route based on distance, traffic, and road closures. However, these apps may not always provide the optimal route, especially in congested urban areas during peak hours.

Enter quantum computing, specifically designed to solve complex optimization problems. By harnessing the immense computational power of quantum algorithms, a quantum-powered navigation app could explore a much larger number of possible routes simultaneously and identify the most efficient path in real-time. This app could consider factors beyond just distance—such as driver preferences, congestion hotspots, environmental conditions, and weather—offering more personalized and adaptive routes that reduce travel time, fuel consumption, and environmental impact. By dynamically optimizing for accidents, roadwork, and other unpredictable changes, quantum computing could significantly improve commuting experiences, making them more efficient and less stressful.

Similarly, quantum computing promises to transform drug discovery. For a pharmaceutical company developing new medications for complex diseases like cancer, the traditional drug discovery process—screening millions of compounds to identify potential candidates—can be incredibly time-consuming and costly. With the power of quantum computing, researchers could simulate molecular interactions with unprecedented accuracy, predicting how different compounds will interact with biological systems. This would lead to the identification of promising drug candidates much faster than before, ultimately accelerating the development of life-saving medications.

Leading tech companies like IBM, Google, and Rigetti are at the forefront of quantum computing research and development. They are working towards building scalable, fault-tolerant quantum processors capable of solving real-world problems. For instance, IBM's Quantum Experience platform allows researchers and developers to experiment with quantum algorithms and explore potential applications across different fields. Quantum computing represents a paradigm shift in our computational capabilities—one poised to revolutionize industries from cybersecurity to healthcare. As we continue to unlock the mysteries of the quantum realm, we find ourselves on the brink of a new era that promises to reshape our understanding of the universe and the way we solve complex problems.

- **Nanotechnology**

As technological frontiers push further, they also shrink, marking the rise of the nanotechnology era. Situated at the intersection of physics, chemistry, and engineering, nanotechnology allows for the manipulation of matter at atomic and molecular scales, offering unparalleled precision and control. This innovative field holds vast potential across numerous sectors, including medicine, electronics, energy, and materials science.

In healthcare, nanoscale drug delivery systems have emerged as revolutionary tools for treating diseases like cancer. These systems leverage the unique properties of nanoparticles to deliver medications directly to targeted cells or tissues, minimizing side effects and maximizing efficacy. For example, liposomal nanoparticles are used to administer chemotherapy drugs. Traditional chemotherapy can cause severe side effects because it affects both cancerous and healthy cells indiscriminately. Nanoparticles offer a promising solution: they encapsulate drugs within lipid vesicles, shielding them from degradation while circulating in the bloodstream and selectively accumulating in tumor tissues. Once delivered to the intended site, these nanoparticles release their payload, reducing systemic toxicity and improving the patient's quality of life.

In electronics, nanotechnology is a game-changer, introducing nanoscale components that enhance device performance while reducing size and energy consumption. Carbon nanotubes and graphene are two notable nanomaterials used to create transistors that are smaller, faster, and more energy-efficient than traditional silicon-based ones. Carbon nanotubes are cylindrical structures of carbon atoms, while graphene is a two-dimensional honeycomb lattice of carbon atoms. These materials provide excellent electrical conductivity and mechanical strength, enabling devices to achieve faster processing speeds and enhanced performance. As a result, we now have ultra-thin smartphones, lightweight laptops, and advanced wearable devices that are both compact and powerful.

Nanotechnology has also driven advances in energy storage. Nanostructured electrodes are revolutionizing lithium-ion batteries by enhancing ion transport and electron transfer, resulting in improved energy density and capacity. Tesla, for example, employs nanotechnology at its Gigafactory to optimize battery performance for electric vehicles. By incorporating silicon anodes with nanoporous structures, Tesla enhances energy storage, prolongs battery life, and ultimately improves the driving range of its vehicles, making electric transportation more practical and accessible.

Nanocomposite materials—formed by dispersing nanoscale components within a larger matrix—also play a vital role in enhancing the performance of lithium-ion batteries. Panasonic integrates carbon nanotubes, graphene, and metal oxide nanoparticles into its batteries, optimizing electron transport and improving charging rates while maintaining battery integrity over time. This innovation results in more reliable batteries that are ideal for demanding applications such as electric vehicles and consumer electronics.

Nanotechnology has also transformed solar energy conversion. Quantum dots, which are semiconductor nanocrystals, enhance light absorption in photovoltaic cells, increasing energy conversion efficiency. SolarWindow Technologies embeds quantum dots in transparent solar panels, turning ordinary windows into energy-generating surfaces that capture sunlight without compromising transparency. This technology harnesses solar energy that would otherwise go to waste, offering a sustainable solution for reducing energy consumption and mitigating environmental impact.

Nanobiotechnology, which utilizes quantum dots for imaging biological structures, has revolutionized cancer diagnostics. Quantum dots can be functionalized with antibodies to target cancer cells, enabling real-time imaging with high specificity. They offer superior sensitivity compared to conventional techniques, providing accurate early detection and reducing patient discomfort.

- **Internet of Things (IoT)**

The Internet of Things (IoT) has seamlessly integrated itself into our daily lives, creating a network of interconnected devices that reshape how we navigate and interact with the world. From smart homes to industrial automation, IoT orchestrates an ecosystem of sensors, actuators, and connectivity, allowing data to flow effortlessly and providing real-time insights.

In smart homes, IoT devices elevate convenience and efficiency. The Nest Learning Thermostat, for example, learns from user preferences and adjusts temperature settings accordingly, saving energy while enhancing comfort. Smart refrigerators, like Samsung's Family Hub, keep track of food inventory, notify users when supplies are running low, and suggest recipes based on available ingredients. These appliances simplify daily routines, reduce food waste, and enhance the overall quality of life.

IoT is also transforming industry, ushering in the era of Industry 4.0.

General Electric's Brilliant Factory initiative uses IoT sensors to monitor equipment performance in real-time, predict maintenance needs, and mitigate unplanned downtime. For example, sensors can collect data on temperature, vibration, and pressure to detect anomalies and trigger alerts for timely intervention, reducing operational disruptions.

In supply chain management, IoT enhances logistics and inventory tracking. Amazon uses IoT to optimize warehouse operations, leveraging data analytics to make informed decisions on inventory levels, demand patterns, and delivery routes, ensuring customer demands are met efficiently.

While IoT devices bring convenience and efficiency, they also raise legitimate concerns about privacy, security, and data ethics. IoT devices continuously collect data, ranging from user habits to biometric information. If mishandled, this data can compromise privacy and security. Companies must implement robust cybersecurity measures, encryption protocols, and data protection policies to safeguard personal information. Additionally, users should be informed about how their data is collected, used, and shared, and consent should be obtained to ensure ethical practices.

- **Navigating Challenges and Seizing Opportunities**

As we explore the dynamic technological landscape, we encounter challenges and triumphs that shape the path of progress. Let us delve into concrete examples across key domains to illuminate this journey.

In the realm of quantum computing, the quest for fault-tolerant processors poses significant challenges. However, breakthroughs have been achieved, such as Google's quantum supremacy milestone with its Sycamore processor in 2019. This achievement demonstrated the immense potential of quantum computing, as the processor accomplished a task that would take classical supercomputers thousands of years to complete. Such advancements pave the way for revolutionary applications in logistics, material science, and complex problem-solving.

Nanotechnology also presents challenges, particularly regarding the ethical considerations of environmental health impacts. However, its applications hold immense promise. Consider the use of nanomaterials in sunscreen formulations—L'Oréal developed sunscreens with nano-sized zinc oxide or titanium dioxide particles to enhance UV protection without leaving a white residue. This innovation not only improves sun protection but also aligns with sustainability goals by reducing the need for excessive application.

The vast realm of IoT is not without its obstacles, such as interoperability issues and security vulnerabilities. Despite these challenges, IoT technologies have made significant strides. Amazon's Echo series featuring Alexa has become an iconic example of IoT integration, allowing users to control their smart homes through simple voice commands. By prioritizing user experience and implementing security measures like multi-factor authentication, Amazon has earned user trust and positioned its devices as essential elements of modern living.

Navigating these technological frontiers requires resilience and ingenuity. Overcoming challenges fosters societal advancement and economic prosperity, and as we chart our course through this ever-evolving landscape, the ability to navigate with foresight and determination will shape a brighter future for generations to come.

Technological advancements like quantum computing, nanotechnology, and IoT represent paradigm shifts in our ability to manipulate, understand, and enhance the world around us. Quantum computing offers computational power that could revolutionize optimization, drug discovery, and other fields, while nanotechnology allows for precision engineering at the atomic level, driving advances in medicine, electronics, and energy. The IoT has seamlessly integrated itself into our lives, transforming industries and reshaping the way we interact with the world.

As we stand on the brink of a transformative epoch, we must embrace this dynamic landscape of technology with a balance of curiosity, caution, and innovation. By addressing the ethical challenges these technologies pose and responsibly harnessing their power, we can fully realize their potential for the benefit of all.

- ### The Synergy of AI and Human Cognition

At the intersection of artificial intelligence (AI) and human cognition, we find ourselves on the brink of a transformative era in technological evolution. This chapter embarks on an immersive exploration, delving into the intricate interplay between AI and the human mind, revealing the profound synergies that arise when advanced algorithms and machine learning converge with the complexities of human thought. This comprehensive exploration unveils the myriad ways AI enhances cognitive abilities across diverse domains.

From revolutionizing medical diagnoses to collaborating in creative endeavors, the synergistic relationship between AI and human cognition presents boundless opportunities for innovation and progress. In healthcare, AI-powered diagnostic tools are reshaping medical practices by leveraging vast datasets and advanced algorithms to detect patterns and anomalies with unparalleled accuracy and efficiency. By complementing the expertise of healthcare professionals, AI enhances precision, expedites treatment decisions, and ultimately leads to improved patient outcomes.

In creative fields, AI serves as a catalyst for innovation, enabling artists, designers, and creators to push the boundaries of creativity beyond traditional limits. Through generative neural networks, AI collaborates with humans to co-author music, create visual art, and generate compelling narratives, enriching the creative process with fresh perspectives and novel insights. AI's integration into creative work transcends mere innovation; it represents a paradigm shift in our understanding of creativity itself.

By harnessing the synergies between artificial intelligence and human cognition, we unlock unprecedented potential to address complex challenges, ignite creativity, and propel humanity towards new frontiers of knowledge and discovery.

- **Understanding Synergies**

At its essence, artificial intelligence (AI) endeavors to emulate and expand upon human cognitive functions through computational models algorithms. With the advent of machine learning, particularly deep AI has surged into uncharted territories, empowering systems glean insights adapt from vast datasets. This foundational premise serves as bedrock for exploring symbiotic relationship between cognition.

In the ever-evolving landscape of medical diagnostics, artificial intelligence (AI) emerges as a transformative force, showcasing remarkable prowess swiftly and accurately analyzing intricate data. Nowhere is this more apparent than domain radiology, where AI algorithms seamlessly integrate into diagnostic process, revolutionizing detection anomalies within images. One poignant example AI's impact radiology exemplified by companies like Aidoc, which deploy AI-powered solutions to assist radiologists identifying abnormalities such fractures or tumors with unprecedented efficiency precision. These meticulously analyze images, detecting subtle deviations that may elude human eye. augmenting serves an invaluable tool for radiologists, enhancing their ability make timely accurate diagnoses. collaboration between professionals fosters potent synergy, analytical machines harmonizes intuition expertise doctors. leverage trusted assistants, leveraging computational capabilities navigate through vast datasets pinpoint unparalleled accuracy. partnership not only expedites process but also enhances standard patient care facilitating quicker interventions improving health outcomes. Moreover, hold promise alleviating burden on healthcare streamlining workflows reducing errors. data at scale, can focus attention critical cases, confident support highlighting potential abnormalities.

The symbiotic relationship between artificial intelligence (AI) and human cognition extends its reach across diverse sectors of society, leaving an indelible mark on fields such as finance cybersecurity. In these domains, AI algorithms play a pivotal role analyzing vast datasets to detect fraudulent activities mitigate risks, amplifying capabilities analysts.

In the realm of finance, AI-powered solutions revolutionize risk management and fraud detection, leveraging advanced algorithms to sift through massive volumes financial data with unparalleled speed accuracy. For instance, companies like Darktrace harness AI technology autonomously detect respond cyber threats real-time, safeguarding organizations against evolving cyber-attacks. By continuously analyzing network traffic user behavior, identify anomalous patterns indicative potential security breaches, enabling proactive intervention mitigate risks prevent losses. Moreover, AI's integration into cybersecurity practices augments capabilities human analysts, empowering them navigate complex ever-changing landscape more effectively. tools, analysts can focus their expertise on strategic decision-making threat response, while handle labor-intensive task vast streams vulnerabilities malicious activities. collaboration between cognition finance exemplifies transformative impact enhancing operational efficiency organizational assets. harnessing analytical prowess alongside expertise, proactively risks, fortifying defenses emerging ensuring integrity systems data. synergies we towards a future where innovation redefine boundaries possibility, enriching lives driving progress unprecedented ways.

Cognitive Augmentation

AI embraces the role of a collaborative partner in creative ventures, reshaping conventional notions interaction between machines and humans. Across artistic domains such as art music, AI's integration into process challenges boundaries, offering novel avenues for innovation expression.

In the domain of music composition, AIVA (Artificial Intelligence Virtual Artist) stands out as a prime example groundbreaking capabilities AI-generated content. AIVA's algorithms, meticulously trained on extensive collections musical compositions spanning various genres and styles, exhibit an impressive prowess crafting melodies harmonies comparable to those composed by human musicians. analyzing intricate patterns structures within music, can adeptly navigate nuances producing pieces that captivate listeners with their depth emotive resonance. This collaborative partnership between AI creativity transcends traditional boundaries, ushering new era artistic exploration innovation. Rather than merely serving tool for musicians, acts catalyst inspiration, offering fresh perspectives novel ideas push boundaries expression. Through its ability suggest innovative melodies, encourages artists explore uncharted territories, experiment unconventional approaches, challenge preconceived notions composition. result is resonates deeply emotional level, evoking range sentiments experiences transcend realms machine. Whether stirring harmonies, or performances, possess unique allure captivates audiences fosters profound connection music.

In the realm of visual arts, AI-driven algorithms venture boldly into domain painting and design, ushering a new era creativity innovation. Initiatives such as

DeepArt Google's DeepDream serve compelling demonstrations AI's remarkable capacity to generate visually captivating artwork that transcends conventional boundaries. These AI-powered projects harness sophisticated analyze manipulate data, creating intricate patterns vibrant compositions evoke sense wonder fascination. By leveraging machine learning neural networks, AI systems are able discern complex aesthetic original artworks imbued with unique style flair. Through collaboration AI, artists designers gain access vast reservoir creative possibilities enrich their process expand horizons expression. integrating tools artistic practice, creators can explore techniques, experiment unconventional approaches, unlock untapped potential work.

The collaborative partnership between AI and human expertise extends far beyond realms of artistic expression, permeating industries such as design architecture. Within these fields, AI-driven tools emerge indispensable assets, facilitating exploration realization ambitious projects through innovative solutions invaluable insights. In architectural design, serves a catalyst for creativity, empowering designers with data-driven suggestions optimized spatial layouts to elevate both functionality aesthetics. By leveraging vast datasets encompassing designs, historical references, user preferences, algorithms generate alternative proposals tailored project objectives constraints. application machine learning computational modeling, architects gain access spectrum possibilities, allowing them visualize evaluate potential outcomes before implementation. Additionally, AI-powered streamline creative process automating repetitive tasks, drafting floor plans generating 3D models, freeing concentrate on conceptualizing refining concepts. analyzing feedback iteratively iterations, facilitates dialogue among architects, clients, stakeholders, ensuring that align evolving needs expectations.

Challenges and Ethical Considerations

The integration of AI into cognitive processes presents a myriad challenges and ethical considerations that require thorough examination. One significant challenge arises from opaque nature certain algorithms, which raises concerns about transparency accountability. inability to discern decision-making process systems can be particularly problematic in critical domains like healthcare, where errors could have life-altering consequences. Understanding how arrives at specific decisions is paramount, especially scenarios misjudgment lead severe repercussions for patients healthcare providers alike. further complicate processes, with bias being pressing concern. Biases manifest if data used train models are skewed or not representative diverse population they aim serve. such cases, algorithms may inadvertently perpetuate exacerbate existing societal biases, leading discriminatory outcomes. address these uphold standards, vigilance establishment robust frameworks essential. measures, as explainable techniques, provide insights enhancing accountability trust. Additionally, ensuring diversity representativeness training help mitigate ensure promote fairness equity. conclusion, effectively navigating necessitates nuanced approach carefully balances technological advancement responsibility. By addressing algorithmic mitigation, society harness potential enhance human cognition while minimizing harms promoting justice.

- **AI in Education and Personalized Learning**

As we look into the future, impact of AI on education and personalized learning stands poised to revolutionize traditional pedagogical approaches. systems exhibit capability adapt individual styles, offering tailor-made educational experiences that cater diverse needs learners. Intelligent tutoring systems, powered by algorithms, exemplify this potential providing students with real-time feedback guidance tailored their unique strengths weaknesses. approach holds promise transforming a more inclusive effective environment.

Khan Academy's Adaptive Learning Platform stands as a pioneering example of AI integration in education, revolutionizing traditional paradigms. By harnessing algorithms, Academy delivers personalized experiences tailored to individual students' needs, preferences, and styles.

The platform's adaptive learning technology functions by meticulously analyzing vast arrays of student performance data. This data encompasses various metrics, including students' strengths, weaknesses, patterns, and areas requiring additional support. Through sophisticated AI algorithms, Khan Academy distills into actionable insights, enabling platform to dynamically adjust optimize journey for each student. Upon student's data, Academy's generates customized pathways. These pathways are tailored address unique educational requirements, ensuring that they receive targeted instruction support precisely where it is needed most. instance, if a demonstrates proficiency in certain concepts but struggles with others, will prioritize providing resources practice exercises those challenging areas. personalized approach fosters an environment students can progress their at own pace. empowers them individualized feedback, guidance, align specific needs objectives. As result, feel more engaged, motivated, empowered take ownership experiences. Moreover, facilitates deeper conceptual understanding mastery concepts. tailoring experience enables learners delve topics level suits comprehension. cultivates engagement material, leading improved academic outcomes profound

Google Translate stands as a testament to the transformative power of AI in breaking down linguistic barriers and fostering cross-cultural communication. one most widely used language translation tools globally, harnesses advanced algorithms provide instant translations between multiple languages with remarkable accuracy efficiency. At heart Translate's functionality lies its sophisticated natural processing (NLP) techniques. These are adept analyzing understanding context text input, allowing generate that not only grammatically correct but also contextually appropriate. By comprehending nuances usage, idiomatic expressions, cultural references, ensures accurately convey intended meaning original text. platform's intuitive interface enables users seamlessly text, websites, even spoken conversations real-time, making multilingual communication more accessible convenient than ever before. Whether individuals need webpage, email, or document, provides user-friendly solution delivers swift reliable touch button. Moreover, ability real-time is particularly groundbreaking. integration speech recognition technology AI-driven algorithms, can engage verbal across barriers, facilitating seamless interactions diverse contexts. This feature has profound implications for global collaboration, travel, understanding, empowering communicate effectively regardless their native language. fosters inclusivity from different backgrounds content interact others preferred it accessing educational resources, conducting business negotiations, connecting friends colleagues around world, facilitates meaningful collaboration on scale. essence, synergy human cognition heralds new era education, where machines augment enhance intricacies mind. personalized learning experiences tailored individual needs facilitation through translation, AI's potential education undeniable. However, we navigate evolving landscape, imperative address challenges ethical considerations ensure into conducted responsibly ethically, ultimately maximizing benefits learners worldwide.

Virtual Realms of Mind: Exploring the Impact Reality

Virtual Reality (VR) has evolved far beyond its initial roots in gaming and entertainment, emerging as a transformative force with profound implications for various facets of human life. This exploration delves into the expansive impact VR, stretching from educational training applications to therapeutic interventions. It unravels immersive experiences VR provides examines potential reshape future learning, work, interaction.

- **Learning in Virtual Realms**

In the realm of education, VR stands at forefront innovation, revolutionizing traditional learning experiences. Virtual classrooms transport students to historical events, distant landscapes, or even microscopic worlds, offering immersive and interactive environments. This spatial understanding enhances comprehension retention, making complex subjects more accessible. Educational applications extend beyond classrooms, encompassing vocational training professional development. medical platforms such as Osso are way surgeons hone their skills expertise through simulations. These cutting-edge tools offer a dynamic environment where can practice intricate surgical procedures with unprecedented realism precision. practical terms, imagine young surgeon preparing perform cardiac procedure for first time. Traditionally, would observe surgeries, participate cadaver labs, gradually progress assisting live surgeries under guidance experienced mentors. However, advent technology, curve be significantly accelerated enhanced.

Through platforms like Osso VR, surgeons can immerse themselves in hyper-realistic simulations of surgical scenarios. Equipped with VR headsets and hand controllers, they navigate virtual operating rooms, interact lifelike patient avatars, perform intricate maneuvers—all within a risk-free digital environment. These are meticulously designed to replicate the challenges intricacies real-world surgeries, from incision techniques suture placements. As surgeon navigates procedure, receive real-time feedback guidance, allowing them refine their decision-making skills on fly. repeat procedure multiple times, experimenting different approaches strategies until achieve mastery confidence. benefits immersive training medical education manifold. practice complex procedures without constraints time, space, or safety concerns. accelerate learning curve, gaining proficiency fraction time it would take traditional methods. Moreover, nature empowers push boundaries, explore innovative techniques, unprecedented levels precision. Ultimately, this experience translates into tangible for patients. who have undergone better handle challenging scenarios confidence proficiency. make fewer errors, shorter outcomes overall. way, not just transforming education—they revolutionizing surgery itself, ushering new era safety, efficiency, excellence healthcare.

In the fast-evolving landscape of remote work, innovative companies like Spatial are harnessing power Virtual Reality (VR) technology to bridge gap between physical and workspaces. By creating immersive offices, enables teams collaborate on projects real-time, fostering creativity, communication, productivity ways previously unimaginable. Imagine a team professionals spread across different cities or even countries, all working towards common goal. Traditionally, collaboration would involve endless email threads, video conferences, shared documents—an effective but often disjointed impersonal approach teamwork. However, with Spatial's VR platform, this dynamic changes dramatically. world Spatial, members don headsets step into digital environment that resembles office space. Here, they can see interact each other as avatars, complete gestures, facial expressions, audio. is designed replicate layout ambiance real workspace, meeting rooms, whiteboards, collaborative tools. gathers office, seamlessly real-time. brainstorm ideas whiteboard, review edit documents together, conduct impromptu meetings designated breakout areas. platform supports wide range file types integrations, allowing bring external resources tools needed. nature enhances creativity communication several ways. Unlike traditional calls, where participants limited flat screens static images, allows move freely within environment, sense presence engagement. gather around table ideas, visualize concepts 3D space, share objects prototypes. Moreover, audio used creates more natural experience. hear other's voices if were same room, making conversations feel lifelike fluid. awareness reduces misunderstandings, leading decision-making. addition enhancing also boosts productivity. providing centralized workspace meet, collaborate, access streamlines workflow minimizes need for context switching platforms. seamless integration channels distractions focus their work without interruption. Overall, transforming experience leveraging create offices. replicating dynamics realm, effectively, thought impossible. continues gain traction, platforms will play an increasingly important role shaping future blurring lines environments redefining way we connect others.

- **Workplace Transformation**

Virtual Reality has transcended the boundaries of traditional workplaces, introducing novel approaches to collaboration, training, and productivity. Remote work, a growing trend, is enriched by VR technologies that enable meetings, conferences, collaborative projects. provides sense presence, fostering more meaningful interactions mitigating challenges physical distance.

In professional training, VR simulators recreate realistic scenarios, enabling employees to develop skills a controlled and immersive environment

Within the aviation industry, Boeing has embraced transformative power of Virtual Reality (VR) simulations to enhance pilot training in realistic flight scenarios. These VR provide pilots with invaluable opportunities experience various weather conditions, emergency situations, and navigational challenges, ensuring they are well-prepared handle any situation may encounter during actual flights. Imagine a novice stepping into state-of-the-art simulator developed by Boeing. Equipped headset controls, is transported cockpit that mirrors layout functionality real aircraft. As don headset, world comes life around them, complete stunningly visuals immersive audio. session, exposed wide range scenarios designed simulate real-world conditions challenges. For example, sudden changes weather, such thunderstorms or heavy fog, require quick decision-making adjustments plans. also mechanical failures system malfunctions, forcing them troubleshoot implement procedures real-time. One key advantages their ability replicate sensory experiences flight. can feel sensation acceleration, turbulence, altitude changes, enhancing realism effectiveness training. Additionally, nature enables develop spatial awareness situational awareness, crucial skills safe effective flying. navigate through scenarios, receive real-time feedback guidance from instructors monitoring simulation. observe pilot's actions, insights processes, offer coaching improve performance. This personalized loop allows learn mistakes, refine skills, build confidence abilities. Moreover, cost-effective scalable solution compared traditional simulators. technology eliminates need expensive physical simulators complex maintenance procedures, allowing programs be more accessible adaptable evolving needs. easily updated customized incorporate new aircraft models, objectives.

Walmart's integration of Virtual Reality (VR) training serves as a prime example how innovative technology is revolutionizing employee and performance within retail environments. In this VR program, Walmart employees are immersed simulations that replicate various scenarios encountered during their job duties, including handling customer inquiries, restocking shelves, managing inventory. Imagine new donning headset entering store environment. simulated setting, they encounter realistic such assisting customers with product shelves to ensure adequate inventory levels, the flow goods optimize efficiency. These carefully crafted mimic challenges interactions would face day-to-day roles. session, engage environment using hand controllers or other interactive devices. interact customers, navigate aisles locate products, perform tasks scanning items for management. immersive nature enables experience firsthand, providing sense realism urgency traditional methods may lack. through store, receive immediate feedback guidance based on actions. example, if an approaches provides helpful assistance, positive reinforcement encouragement. Conversely, make errors, program can provide corrective suggest alternative approaches. One key benefits its ability practical environment, allowing them develop skills confidence before facing real-world challenges. instance, practice difficult discrepancies without pressure making mistakes sales floor. hands-on fosters competence proficiency, ultimately improving satisfaction. Moreover, offers scalability consistency across vast network stores. Regardless location staffing constraints, access standardized modules uniformity skill development expectations. approach enhances operational efficiency ensures all same high-quality

- **Therapeutic Dimensions**

The therapeutic potential of Virtual Reality (VR) spans diverse domains, including mental health, rehabilitation, and pain management. Carefully designed VR experiences help alleviate stress, anxiety, and phobias through exposure therapy conducted in controlled environments. By allowing patients to gradually face and overcome their challenges, VR fosters well-being and resilience.

In rehabilitation, VR has proven to be a valuable tool for individuals recovering from physical injuries or neurological conditions. Customized exercises targeting motor skills, coordination, and balance immerse patients in their recovery process, potentially accelerating progress. This interactive approach increases engagement and motivation, making the rehabilitation journey more effective.

As VR technology advances, its applications in healthcare continue to expand. Companies like XRHealth are pioneering its use for pain management, cognitive therapy, and rehabilitation. Through personalized, engaging interventions, patients receive complementary treatments that improve outcomes and quality of life. For instance, a patient recovering from a severe leg fracture can experience a more enjoyable and immersive rehabilitation process. Instead of repetitive exercises, they can don a VR headset and engage in interactive activities such as navigating obstacle courses or practicing balance in simulated environments. Real-time feedback from embedded sensors helps therapists monitor progress and adjust treatment plans, making the process more efficient and effective.

VR also enhances pain management for chronic conditions like fibromyalgia and neuropathy by distracting and engaging the mind, reducing the perception of pain. Cognitive therapy applications further support individuals with memory impairments or neurological disorders, offering exercises to improve attention, memory, and executive function.

Transforming Exposure Therapy with VR

VR has revolutionized exposure therapy, a key treatment for phobias and anxiety disorders. Companies such as Limbix provide immersive environments where patients can confront their fears in a controlled, supportive setting, leading to effective desensitization and long-term relief. For instance, a patient with acrophobia can safely explore virtual heights—such as balconies, skyscrapers, or bridges—within the comfort of a therapist's office. This approach allows gradual, personalized exposure to fear-inducing stimuli, helping patients develop coping strategies and regain confidence. The controlled and predictable nature of VR exposure therapy makes it less overwhelming and more accessible, facilitating successful outcomes.

Addressing PTSD with VR

For conditions like Post-Traumatic Stress Disorder (PTSD), VR exposure therapy offers a groundbreaking intervention. Programs like Bravemind, developed by the University of Southern California's Institute for Creative Technologies, enable individuals to process traumatic memories in a safe and controlled environment. Veterans, for example, can confront combat-related experiences through realistic simulations guided by therapists. The ability to adjust intensity and pace, combined with cognitive restructuring and relaxation techniques, empowers patients to manage distress and build resilience. Research indicates that VR therapy can significantly reduce PTSD symptoms, improving the quality of life for affected individuals.

Enhancing Social Interaction and Collaboration

VR is redefining social connections by transcending physical barriers and creating immersive spaces for interaction. Platforms like AltspaceVR and Rec Room allow users to socialize, collaborate, and participate in diverse activities within virtual environments. These spaces host events, workshops, and gatherings, offering unparalleled levels of interactivity and presence. For example, users can attend live concerts, participate in skill-building sessions, or engage in recreational activities, forming genuine connections and friendships that extend beyond the virtual world.

In professional settings, VR is transforming remote collaboration. Platforms like Spatial create virtual workspaces where team members can interact in real-time as avatars, complete with gestures and facial expressions. These immersive environments replicate office setups, allowing for seamless brainstorming, document sharing, and project management. The enhanced sense of presence and natural communication foster creativity, innovation, and teamwork, bridging the gap between physical and remote workspaces.

The Future of VR in Education and Work

The potential of VR to revolutionize learning and work environments is vast. In education, VR can democratize access by offering immersive experiences that allow students to explore historical landmarks, conduct virtual experiments, and participate in interactive simulations. This approach enhances engagement, retention, and curiosity, making learning more accessible and effective.

In the realm of work, VR-enabled remote collaboration offers flexibility and efficiency, reducing the need for physical office spaces and commuting. By hosting virtual meetings, training sessions, and collaborative projects, VR promotes productivity, work-life balance, and sustainability. Platforms like Spatial exemplify this shift, providing centralized virtual environments where teams can collaborate seamlessly, fostering innovation and reducing logistical challenges.

As VR technology evolves and becomes more accessible, its applications across healthcare, education, and social interaction are poised to grow. By merging immersive experiences with practical solutions, VR redefines how we learn, heal, and connect, opening new frontiers in human interaction and productivity. Its ability to address real-world challenges while fostering creativity and engagement positions VR as a transformative force with the potential to shape the future in ways we are only beginning to imagine.

- **New Era of Virtual Exploration**

In conclusion, the exploration of virtual realms has highlighted the profound impact of Virtual Reality (VR) technology, showcasing its evolution from a technological novelty to a transformative force with far-reaching implications across various aspects of human life. By delivering immersive experiences and pioneering applications, VR has proven its potential to reshape how we learn, work, heal, and explore, ushering in a new era of possibilities.

VR's capabilities extend far beyond entertainment, offering users the chance to step into environments that feel astonishingly real. Whether it's exploring distant landscapes, simulating intricate scenarios, or engaging in virtual social interactions, VR blurs the boundaries between the physical and digital worlds.

In education, VR has revolutionized traditional teaching methods by creating interactive and engaging learning environments. Students can immerse themselves in historical events, dissect scientific concepts, or participate in hands-on simulations, fostering deeper understanding and sparking creativity. This transformative approach encourages curiosity and paves the way for innovative modes of acquiring knowledge.

In the workplace, VR has redefined collaboration and innovation, particularly for remote and distributed teams. Virtual meeting spaces and collaborative tools facilitate seamless communication, enhancing productivity and creativity across distances. Additionally, VR-based training programs offer realistic simulations, enabling employees to develop skills and improve performance across various industries.

Healthcare has also benefited significantly from VR, emerging as a powerful tool for therapy and rehabilitation. From addressing mental health conditions through exposure therapy to aiding physical recovery from injuries, VR provides a safe and controlled environment for individuals to confront challenges and achieve better outcomes, thereby improving their quality of life.

Ultimately, the journey into VR reveals it as more than just an innovation—it is a catalyst for change. By breaking down barriers and opening doors to new possibilities, VR is revolutionizing how we perceive and interact with the world. As the technology continues to evolve and mature, its influence on society and human experience is set to grow exponentially, shaping a future that we are only beginning to imagine.

- **Smartphone Interventions**

The widespread use of smartphones in contemporary society has sparked extensive debate about their impact on cognitive well-being. This discussion explores the dual role of smartphones—highlighting their potential to enhance mental health through apps and tools while also addressing challenges such as screen addiction and reduced attention spans. Striking a balance between utilizing this technology for well-being and mitigating its adverse effects is a critical area of focus.

Communication, a cornerstone of human interaction, has been transformed by mobile phones. These devices have surpassed geographical limitations, enabling instantaneous connections and seamless exchanges. Through calls, text messages, and messaging apps, users can communicate in real time, improving accessibility and fostering swift information flow. Video calls, offered by platforms like FaceTime, Skype, and WhatsApp, have added a personal dimension, allowing families and colleagues to connect across continents and share meaningful moments or conduct virtual meetings efficiently.

Social media platforms, such as Facebook, Instagram, and Twitter, further enhance connectivity by creating virtual communities. These platforms support casual conversations, news sharing, and collaborative activities, making it easier for friends to plan outings or colleagues to work on projects. Additionally, mobile phones serve as lifelines during emergencies, offering location tracking, alerts, and access to critical services.

Smartphones have revolutionized information access, democratizing knowledge across geographical and socioeconomic barriers. Users can receive real-time news updates and explore educational resources through apps like Khan Academy and Coursera. These tools support learning beyond the classroom, enabling students and professionals to conduct research, complete projects, and satisfy intellectual curiosity with ease. In healthcare, telemedicine apps provide vital resources, offering remote consultations and preventive care, especially in underserved areas. Similarly, in agriculture, smartphones help farmers access critical information about weather, market prices, and innovative practices, empowering them to make informed decisions.

The advent of smartphones has reshaped entertainment and social interaction. Streaming services like Netflix and Spotify allow users to enjoy movies, music, and podcasts on the go. Mobile gaming has surged in popularity, offering engaging experiences ranging from casual puzzles to immersive multiplayer games. These platforms create global communities where players collaborate, compete, and socialize.

Social media, accessed through smartphones, has transformed how individuals share experiences and engage with the world. Features like posts, stories, and hashtags facilitate real-time interactions and amplify voices, enabling participation in public discourse and activism. Virtual groups centered on mental health, hobbies, or advocacy provide spaces for support and collaboration, fostering a sense of belonging.

Mobile banking has driven significant progress in financial inclusion, particularly in regions with limited infrastructure. Smartphones act as virtual wallets, enabling secure transactions, bill payments, and money transfers without the need for physical bank visits. This accessibility empowers underserved populations, granting them entry into formal financial systems and promoting economic resilience. Payment platforms offer secure and affordable solutions, supporting small businesses and entrepreneurs by facilitating transactions and fostering growth.

Despite their benefits, smartphones pose risks to mental health, including screen addiction and diminished attention spans. Screen addiction, marked by compulsive use, can disrupt daily life, leading to social isolation, anxiety, and sleep disturbances. This behavior is driven by the brain's dopamine-reward system, reinforcing frequent checking of updates and notifications. Additionally, constant multitasking and exposure to digital stimuli can impair focus, memory, and decision-making skills.

Promoting awareness of the negative effects of excessive smartphone use is essential. Educators, parents, and healthcare professionals play pivotal roles in encouraging digital literacy and setting boundaries, such as designated screen-free times or digital detox periods. Technology developers can support responsible use by integrating app tracking features and usage limits into operating systems, empowering users to manage their habits effectively.

Smartphones are powerful tools that offer both opportunities and challenges. Their potential to enhance mental health and cognitive well-being through apps and tools is significant, but addressing issues like screen addiction and reduced attention spans is crucial. Collaboration among stakeholders—educators, healthcare professionals, and developers—is key to fostering healthy relationships with technology. By designing user-centric features and promoting responsible use, smartphones can be harnessed as instruments for personal growth and societal progress.

- **Reality Mining**

Reality mining has emerged as a cutting-edge practice designed to decode the complexities of human behavior by analyzing diverse datasets derived from sources such as social media, GPS, and embedded sensors. This innovative approach offers fresh insights into the daily lives of individuals, illuminating patterns, correlations, and trends that define actions at both individual and collective levels.

At its core, reality mining involves the systematic extraction of data generated by people as they go about their routines. The practice taps into a broad spectrum of sources, including social media platforms, geolocation data, and sensors embedded in smartphones and other devices. By aggregating and analyzing these datasets, researchers and organizations can gain valuable insights into various aspects of human behavior, such as commuting habits, social interactions, online communication trends, and emotional sentiment analysis.

For instance, geolocation data can reveal intricate movement patterns, providing insights into individual preferences, group dynamics, and participation in public events. Similarly, the analysis of digital footprints enables a deeper understanding of interests and emotional states, enriching our comprehension of human behavior. However, as this field delves into the personal aspects of individuals' lives, ethical considerations become paramount.

The collection and analysis of sensitive data raise critical questions about consent, transparency, and the risks of misuse. Practitioners in reality mining must navigate this complex terrain with care, prioritizing privacy rights and individual autonomy. Transparent processes, informed consent, and clearly defined objectives are essential to ensure ethical practices. Striking a balance between the benefits of data extraction and the protection of personal privacy is imperative in this domain.

Reality mining, by its very nature, involves the aggregation of extensive datasets, which heightens concerns about unauthorized access, data breaches, and the potential for de-anonymization—where anonymized data can be linked back to specific individuals. Addressing these risks requires implementing robust safeguards, such as encryption protocols, rigorous anonymization techniques, and a privacy-by-design approach to technology development.

This practice has significant societal applications across various fields, including urban planning, healthcare, disaster response, and research. Data-driven insights can inform efficient city planning, predict disease outbreaks to bolster public health strategies, and enhance emergency preparedness efforts by enabling targeted interventions. However, alongside these benefits, the potential for unintended consequences must be carefully managed to ensure ethical use while respecting individual autonomy.

To guide the responsible use of reality mining, the development of comprehensive frameworks, industry standards, and regulatory policies is essential. In conclusion, reality mining stands as a powerful tool in the digital age, capable of driving advancements across numerous domains. As we navigate this evolving landscape, it is crucial to proceed responsibly, with full awareness of the ethical implications, privacy concerns, and societal impacts, ensuring that its potential is harnessed for the greater good.

- **Deep Learning**

Deep learning, a powerful subset of machine has catalyzed paradigm shift in artificial intelligence (AI), enabling systems to learn and adapt from vast datasets. This comprehensive examination delves into the multifaceted applications learning across diverse domains, including healthcare, finance, autonomous systems. It scrutinizes challenges opportunities inherent harnessing cognitive potentials through algorithms, underscoring imperative for thoughtful ethical approach navigating transformative landscape. At its nucleus, leverages neural networks with multiple layers (deep networks) model decipher complex patterns within data. empowers machines autonomously hierarchical representations extensive information, rendering particularly efficacious tasks involving recognition, classification, decision-making. evolution been propelled by breakthroughs computational prowess, accessibility massive datasets, innovative network architectures. Convolutional (CNNs) excel image Recurrent (RNNs) adeptly process sequential data, Transformer architectures exhibit remarkable performance natural language processing tasks. influence transcends disciplinary boundaries, precipitating changes task execution problem-solving methodologies. algorithms play pivotal role healthcare analyzing medical images diagnostic purposes, aiding drug discovery, prognosticating patient outcomes. Notably, these models demonstrate high accuracy detecting anomalies images, such as tumors radiological scans. financial industry undergoes metamorphosis facilitated enhancing fraud detection, risk assessment, algorithmic trading. analyze intricate discerning that may elude conventional development vehicles is which sensor data navigate make real-time decisions. augments perception decision-making capabilities, ensuring safer more efficient transportation Opportunities: Landscape Despite promise, presents challenges. 'black-box' nature some raises concerns about transparency interpretability. Understanding rationale behind decisions crucial, where human lives or critical are stake. Moreover, considerations related bias fairness necessitate careful attention. Biases present training can be perpetuated amplified leading unintended consequences. conscientious deployment indispensable mitigate "The Digital Frontier - Mindtech Unleashed" underscores need deliberate shaped cutting-edge technologies. we unlock age, should guide development, deployment, impact assessment Embracing transparency, accountability, ensures benefits realized responsibly, paving way future intelligent adaptive coexist harmoniously values well-being.

5 **MIND MAX**

In the ongoing pursuit of a fulfilling life, groundbreaking notion Mind Synergy emerges as central pillar, emphasizing critical importance mindset shaping life rich with meaning and satisfaction. This concept stands at forefront mental well-being, intricately linked core tenets Mindmax, which advocates for intentional systematic nurturing psychological health across various facets existence. its essence, encapsulates idea that alignment harmonization one's thoughts, beliefs, attitudes are fundamental to achieving holistic well-being. It underscores profound influence on every aspect from personal relationships career success physical emotional resilience. By fostering synergistic connection between mind, body, spirit, individuals can unlock their full potential cultivate sense purpose fulfillment life. philosophy is recognition well-being not solely determined external circumstances but deeply influenced internal factors such perspective. Through practices like mindfulness, positive affirmations, cognitive reframing, resilient adaptive enables them navigate life's challenges grace fortitude. Furthermore, emphasizes self-awareness introspection growth transformation. developing deeper understanding emotions, behavioral patterns, identify areas improvement more balanced principles closely aligned comprehensive approach encompasses physical, emotional, spiritual dimensions. meditation, exercise, self-care, optimize enhance overall quality represents paradigm shift how we perceive placing strong emphasis transformative power purpose, fulfillment, inner peace. embracing integrating into daily embark journey self-discovery growth, unlocking true living best lives..

The foundation of Mind Synergy lies in principles Mindmax, a comprehensive framework designed to maximize human potential across multiple dimensions mental health and well-being. Mindmax goes beyond traditional approaches well-being by integrating various facets wellness, including stress management, engagement mastery, perseverance, innovative thinking.

Within the Mindmax framework, dealing with stress emerges as a cornerstone for enhancing mental well-being and resilience in face of life's challenges. advocates multifaceted approach to management, encompassing various techniques strategies aimed at mitigating stressors promoting inner peace. encourages individuals cultivate mindfulness practices fundamental tool reduction. is practice that involves consciously focusing on present moment, without passing judgment one's thoughts or experiences. It observe their thoughts, emotions, bodily sensations acceptance non-reactivity. Through meditation, can develop greater self-awareness deeper understanding internal meditation typically finding quiet comfortable space sit lie down. Participants then focus attention breath, noticing inhaling exhaling. When distractions arise, practitioners gently acknowledge them return breath. Over time, regular help sense calm centeredness, even amidst Deep breathing exercises are another effective way promote relaxation reduce stress. These involve taking slow, breaths, often expanding abdomen each inhalation contracting exhalation. activate body's response, triggering cascade physiological changes feelings calmness relaxation. Body scan yet toolkit. This systematically scanning body, bringing awareness region any areas tension. By tuning into way, release physical tension addition practices, also emphasizes importance management. aim induce state both mind, counteracting effects such progressive muscle tensing releasing groups throughout ease. Guided imagery visualizing calming peaceful scenes, while autogenic training focuses self-suggestion warmth heaviness. Furthermore, application cognitive-behavioral address stress-related behaviors. techniques, cognitive restructuring problem-solving skills training, empower challenge negative thought patterns, reframe more positive light, coping mechanisms. fostering adaptive responses stress, enhance emotional well-being, ultimately improving ability navigate challenges ease confidence.

Within the Mindmax framework, engagement mastery emerges as a vital component for cultivating fulfilling and meaningful life. encourages individuals to actively engage with their environment, pursue activities that align passions interests, develop sense of purpose resonates values aspirations. At its core, involves immersing oneself fully in evoke flow – state heightened focus, enjoyment, immersion present moment. experiences typically occur when are deeply engaged challenge skills provide immediate feedback, leading effortless concentration intrinsic motivation. By seeking out opportunities various aspects life, can enhance overall well-being life satisfaction. advocates pursuit foster fulfillment, whether it be through professional endeavors, creative pursuits, hobbies, or personal relationships. identifying strengths, values, actions overarching goals aspirations, coherence direction This alignment fosters deep commitment, propelling towards greater fulfillment Moreover, growth mindset belief one's ability learn, grow, adapt face challenges. adopting mindset, view setbacks obstacles development, rather than insurmountable barriers. shift empowers embrace challenges, persist adversity, ultimately achieve chosen endeavors. practice, encompasses diverse range experiences, from pursuing hobbies interests work nurturing engaging environment bring them joy well-being, find satisfaction unlock full potential.

Perseverance stands as a cornerstone within the Mindmax framework, underscoring significance of resilience and unwavering determination in pursuit personal professional goals. At its essence, encompasses ability to persist face challenges, setbacks, adversity, demonstrating steadfast commitment one's aspirations values. philosophy, is cultivated through combination resilience-building exercises growth mindset practices. These aim instill individuals belief that setbacks failures are not insurmountable obstacles, but rather valuable learning experiences contribute development. By fostering – capacity learn, adapt, improve over time empowered approach challenges with optimism tenacity. Framework may include techniques such reframing negative thoughts, practicing gratitude mindfulness, developing effective coping strategies for managing stress adversity. Practices help cultivate emotional strength fortitude, enabling them bounce back from renewed resilience. Moreover, context extends beyond mere challenges; it proactive goal-setting achievement. Encouraged set ambitious yet attainable goals, break down into manageable steps, persistently work towards their realization, despite obstacles or arise along way. Plentiful, J.K. Rowling's remarkable journey standing poignant illustration. Before achieving global acclaim author Harry Potter series, Rowling faced myriad tested her resolve. Early stages writing career, endured series rejections publishers, some dismissing manuscript outright. Facing discouragement remained craft, refusing let rejection deter pursuing passion storytelling. Alongside grappled hardships, including financial struggles loss mother. Adversities, persisted endeavors, drawing inspiration own channeling emotions work. Bore fruit when Bloomsbury, publishing house London, finally recognized potential debut novel, "Harry Philosopher's Stone." book was met critical upon release 1997, marking beginning meteoric rise literary fame. Initial skepticism propelled unparalleled success. went on captivate readers all ages around world, becoming one best-selling history inspiring phenomenon encompassing films, merchandise, theme parks. Story serves testament power framework. succumb embracing only realized dreams also inspired countless worldwide persevere no matter they encounter Innovative thinking lies heart serving catalyst growth, problem-solving, transformative change. Entails characterized curiosity, open-mindedness, willingness challenge conventional wisdom. Encouraging explore new ideas, question assumptions, embrace creativity, empowers unlock full creative generate novel solutions complex problems. Central cultivation curiosity exploration. Adopt continuously seeking out experiences, perspectives. can expand knowledge base, gain fresh insights, develop deeper understanding themselves world them. encourages assumptions wisdom, spirit intellectual curiosity. Questioning established norms exploring alternative viewpoints, uncover possibilities opportunities innovation. This status quo enables free limiting beliefs patterns, opening door breakthroughs solutions. Creativity innate express various forms artistic expression, nurturing abilities, tap imagination, possibilities, Examples abundant across diverse fields, Elon Musk's compelling visionary founder CEO SpaceX Tesla, pioneering bold epitomize driving monumental realm space exploration, vision far boundaries. SpaceX, under his leadership, has revolutionized aerospace industry reusable rocket technology, significantly reducing cost travel. Audacious goal colonizing Mars reflects pushing boundaries human exploration paving way interplanetary automotive industry, Tesla forefront electric vehicle (EV) challenging reimagining concept sustainable transportation, Musk disrupted traditional automakers accelerated adoption EVs worldwide. Tesla's battery design, autonomous technology reshaped landscape, innovation drive positive change sustainability transportation. vehicles, entrepreneurial ventures span range industries, renewable energy neural technology. Company, SolarCity, advancements solar making accessible affordable millions people world.

Additionally, Neuralink project aims brain-computer interface revolutionize healthcare human-computer interaction. risk, innovators, demonstrated profound impact have shaping future humanity. Overall, offers holistic mental flourishing, empowering resilience, untapped capabilities, thrive aspects lives. Integrating principles daily routines, enhance overall well-being realize potential.

- **Optimal Living**

Mind Synergy places mindset at the forefront of optimal living narrative. Drawing inspiration from seminal work Carol Dweck, particularly her book Mindset: New Psychology Success, concept accentuates transformative potential adopting a growth-oriented mindset. This sees challenges as stepping stones for growth, failures opportunities learning, and life with an enduring sense optimism.

Thomas Edison's journey to inventing the light bulb is a testament transformative potential of mindset. Edison, known for his growth-oriented approach, faced staggering number setbacks on path success. With each failed attempt, instead succumbing discouragement, he saw an opportunity growth and learning. Picture Edison in laboratory, tirelessly experimenting different materials configurations. Despite encountering over thousand unsuccessful trials, remained undeterred, fueled by unshakable belief ability succeed. Rather than viewing these failures as roadblocks, perceived them invaluable lessons, guiding him closer ultimate breakthrough. optimism was infectious, radiating through work inspiring those around persevere face adversity. relentless pursuit innovation propelled forward, driving push boundaries what thought possible. Finally, after years dedication countless setbacks, perseverance paid off. that fateful day, when filament finally glowed illumination, it wasn't just triumph technology—it perspective had darkest times, illuminating success not himself, but generations come. essence, story underscores profound impact mindset can have achieving optimal living. embracing challenges, learning from failures, maintaining unwavering optimism, individuals overcome any obstacle realize their fullest potential.

Michael Jordan's illustrious career in basketball stands as a beacon of the power mindset world sports. From his early days on court, Jordan exhibited an unwavering determination and belief capabilities that set him apart peers. Imagine youth, practicing tirelessly driven by insatiable hunger for success. He faced numerous challenges along way—rejection high school varsity team, defeats even moments self-doubt. However, instead letting these setbacks define him, saw them opportunities to fuel growth development. Every missed shot, loss, became stepping stone improvement eyes. analyzed performance with critical eye, identifying areas enhancement relentlessly working refine skills. Failure was not deterrent Jordan; it catalyst growth. built foundation resilience perseverance. approached each game ability overcome any obstacle. Whether facing formidable opponents, enduring injuries, or confronting pressures high-stakes situations, remained steadfast commitment excellence. legendary work ethic relentless drive propelled achieve feats seemed impossible. winning multiple NBA championships earning MVP awards, accomplishments are testament transformative mindset. essence, story serves powerful reminder importance achieving greatness. viewing improvement, maintaining one's abilities, refusing succumb setbacks, individuals can reach unparalleled heights success endeavor.

- **Holistic Integration of Mindmax Dimensions**

The holistic integration of Mindmax dimensions within framework Mind Synergy underscores profound impact mindset on mental well-being. Rather than treating as a standalone concept, this approach emphasizes its intentional with other critical such stress management, engagement mastery, perseverance, and innovative thinking. By harmonizing these strategically, individuals can unlock synergistic effect that enhances their overall well-being performance.

Steve Jobs, the co-founder and driving force behind Apple Inc., stands as a towering figure in realm of technology, not merely for his accomplishments but also way he integrated Mindmax dimensions into life work. Delving intricacies journey unveils richer tapestry mindfulness, resilience, engagement mastery, innovation. At core Jobs' approach was dedication to mindfulness. Contrary stereotype high-strung, overly ambitious entrepreneur, Jobs valued moments stillness introspection. regularly embarked on meditation retreats, seeking quiet noise outside world cultivate deeper connection with inner self. These periods reflection were idle indulgences deliberate efforts sharpen focus clarity vision. This mindfulness practice became cornerstone leadership style, allowing him navigate turbulent waters tech industry sense calm purpose. Whether facing criticism, setbacks, or pressures relentless competition, remained anchored present moment, able make decisions conviction. One most defining career came ousting from mid-1980s. Rather than succumbing defeat, viewed setback an opportunity growth reinvention. self-discovery, founding NeXT Computer Pixar Animation Studios, ventures that would ultimately shape return renewed vigor perspective. growth-oriented mindset fueled perseverance through adversity, propelling greater heights upon Apple. approached challenges insurmountable obstacles opportunities innovate push boundaries what possible. permeated Apple's culture, fostering spirit pursuit excellence define company's success years come. heart mastery engagement. possessed uncanny ability inspire motivate those around him, rallying team shared purpose passion. demanded nothing short perfection products, beyond their limits deliver experiences transcended expectations. perhaps enduring legacy lies innovative thinking, which reshaped entire industries transformed we interact technology. revolutionary design Macintosh game-changing introduction iPod, iPhone, iPad, vision landscape personal computing consumer electronics. conclusion, serves masterclass holistic integration dimensions. By embracing maintaining mindset, mastering engagement, only revolutionized left indelible mark world. continues guide generations entrepreneurs innovators, reminding us transformative power

- **Applied Aspects of Mind Synergy**

Mind Synergy manifest in various aspects of individuals' lives, where the integration Mindmax principles can lead to transformative outcomes. encourages individuals approach challenges with a growth-oriented mindset, viewing them as opportunities for learning and growth rather than obstacles be feared. This mindset shift allows embrace resilience optimism, fostering sense empowerment possibility. Practical implementation involves actively seeking out personal professional development, whether through taking on new challenges, pursuing further education, or feedback from peers mentors. By reframing setbacks stepping stones growth, cultivate adaptability, enabling navigate life's ups downs greater ease confidence. advocates practice engagement mastery, encouraging immerse themselves fully their experiences activities. entails cultivating state flow, experience heightened focus, productivity, enjoyment. Being present attentive each moment, minimizing distractions maximizing task at hand. may involve setting clear goals, breaking tasks into manageable chunks, eliminating external interruptions. mastering engagement, enhance performance satisfaction domains life, work, relationships, interests hobbies. emphasizes importance perseverance face adversity, advocating cultivation grit resilience. staying committed long-term even challenges. developing strategies managing stress, building support network, purpose meaning. realistic expectations, practicing self-care, friends, family, mental health professionals. persevering adversities determination, overcome achieve ultimately leading fulfillment success life. tap altered states thinking creative problem-solving, innovative novel solutions complex Engaging activities that stimulate creativity divergent thinking, such brainstorming sessions, meditation, exploring environments experiences. embracing experimentation, unlock perspectives insights, breakthroughs lives. serves guiding principle urging intentionally embraces interconnectedness balance. its core, draws inspiration Martin Seligman's groundbreaking work positive psychology, particularly his influential book "Flourish: Visionary Understanding Happiness Well-being." research illuminates potential nurturing overall well-being flourishing essence lies ability illuminate path toward optimal living intentional within comprehensive framework Mindmax. concept invites embark journey, unlocking full spectrum human crafting life imbued purpose. recognizing including physical, emotional, mental, spiritual well-being. balance across these domains, harmonious holistic development. include mindfulness practices self-awareness, meaningful connections others, prioritizing self-care activities, aligning actions values goals. Underscores significance promote adopting perspective strengths, opportunities, possibilities. Techniques gratitude, negative thoughts ones, celebrating achievements, optimism journey self-discovery growth. Vulnerability, outside comfort zones, change an opportunity steps experiences, passions interests, reflective journaling self-assessment exercises. Craft resonates authenticity, honoring individual strengths values, meaning identifying goals aligned one's adversity.

Optimal Living: A Comprehensive Exploration of Mindmax

Optimal living, a cornerstone of the Mindmax philosophy, transcends mere absence illness, encompassing holistic approach to well-being that integrates physical, mental, and emotional dimensions. Rooted in principles Mindmax, this concept delves into profound integration these facets, shaping life characterized by fulfillment purpose.

Foundational Principles: Balancing the Triad of Well-being

At the heart of Mindmax philosophy lies conviction that optimal living demands a delicate balance across physical, mental, and emotional well-being. This foundational principle underscores interconnectedness these facets, advocating for comprehensive integrated approach to wellness. Drawing inspiration from positive psychology, posits well-being is not merely absence distress but rather proactive cultivation experiences emotions.

Physical Well-being: Milind Soman, an Indian supermodel, actor, and fitness enthusiast, stands as exemplary figure in advocating for holistic health wellness. Renowned his commitment to fitness, Soman's lifestyle epitomizes a balanced approach achieving maintaining optimal well-being. Soman emphasizes the importance of regular exercise cornerstone regimen. He incorporates variety activities into routine, ranging from high-intensity workouts outdoor exercises. Running, swimming, cycling are among preferred activities, allowing him stay active while enjoying benefits nature. often shares glimpses on social media, inspiring others embark their journeys prioritize activity lives. addition exercise, places great emphasis proper nutrition fuel body peak performance. follows diet rich whole foods, including fruits, vegetables, lean proteins, healthy fats. advocates mindful eating listening one's body's cues maintain relationship with food. By prioritizing nutrient-dense foods staying hydrated, ensures that receives necessary support goals. Adequate rest recovery also integral components recognizes giving time repair itself after intense workouts. prioritizes quality sleep practices relaxation techniques such meditation deep breathing promote reduce stress. restorative signals, maintains balance between recovery, sustain levels over long term. dedication serves source inspiration people all ages backgrounds. wellness underscores activity, nutrition, overall Through advocacy example, encourages adopt healthier lifestyles embrace transformative power enhancing life.

Mental Well-being: Deepika Padukone, a prominent Bollywood actress, has courageously shared her personal struggles with depression and anxiety, shedding light on the importance of health awareness destigmatization. Through journey towards well-being, Padukone become powerful advocate for promoting emotional wellness supporting individuals facing similar challenges. Padukone's approach to nurturing well-being revolves around mindfulness practices such as meditation yoga. These serve pillars strength, helping manage stress cultivate balance amidst demands career life. By incorporating into daily routine, developed deeper sense self-awareness resilience, enabling navigate life's ups downs greater ease. In addition practices, taken proactive steps address issues broader scale. She founded Live Love Laugh Foundation, non-profit organization dedicated raising about providing support need. foundation's initiatives, aims destigmatize illness, facilitate open conversations health, promote access resources treatment options. openness advocacy have had profound impact society, inspiring many prioritize their seek help when needed. sharing own experiences vulnerabilities, created safe space others share without fear judgment. efforts contributed understanding shift more compassionate supportive society.

Emotional Well-being: Oprah Winfrey, celebrated as a media mogul and philanthropist, offers poignant example of prioritizing well-being amidst life's adversities. Through her candid revelations about traumatic childhood experiences, Winfrey has become beacon resilience, advocating for healing self-care integral aspects personal growth. Winfrey's journey towards is underscored by commitment to practices that nurture inner self. Central approach the practice gratitude, which she incorporates into daily life powerful tool cultivating positive mindset fostering resilience. gratitude journaling reflection, acknowledges blessings in life, allowing shift focus from adversity abundance. Additionally, finds solace renewal spending time immersed nature. Whether it taking walks countryside or gardening own backyard, recognizes restorative power connecting with natural world. These moments solitude communion nature serve opportunities self-reflection, peace, rejuvenation. also advocates importance self-love compassion nurturing such meditation, affirmations, acts kindness herself others, fosters deep sense self-acceptance compassion. setting boundaries, demonstrates honoring one's needs loving relationship oneself. advocacy example, empowered millions worldwide prioritize their live authentically. sharing growth, created platform open dialogue self-discovery, encouraging individuals embrace vulnerabilities embark on paths resilience fulfillment.

- **Holistic Integration**

Mindmax champions the harmonious integration of physical, mental, and emotional well-being, recognizing synergistic effect that emerges when these aspects are aligned nurtured collectively. This holistic approach is guided by principles borrowed from positive psychology, which emphasizes enhancement human strengths virtues to foster a flourishing life.

The Dalai Lama, revered as spiritual leader of Tibet, serves a profound example embracing holistic approach to well-being that encompasses physical, mental, emotional, and dimensions. Through his teachings personal practices, Lama demonstrates how integrating these aspects leads inner peace, harmony, sense purpose. Central Lama's daily routine is practice meditation, which cornerstone mental well-being. he cultivates mindfulness, clarity mind, tranquility, enabling him navigate life's challenges with equanimity grace. By dedicating time quiet reflection self-awareness, fosters deep connection innermost self world around him. Compassion forgiveness are also fundamental tenets embodies virtues in interactions others, emphasizing importance empathy, kindness, understanding fostering harmonious relationships societal cohesion. acts forgiveness, healing, reconciliation, interconnectedness among all beings. addition vocal advocate for environmental sustainability, social justice, interfaith dialogue. recognizes extends beyond individual encompass collective welfare society planet. promoting ethical values, stewardship, intercultural understanding, advocates vision flourishing beings preservation natural world. inspire millions people worldwide lead lives purpose, compassion, fulfillment. guiding light individuals seeking cultivate balance, meaning their lives, while contributing greater good humanity

In the pursuit of optimal living, Mindmax advocates for a balanced lifestyle that prioritizes resilience, self-awareness, and sense purpose. This holistic approach recognizes interconnectedness physical, mental, emotional well-being, emphasizing importance nurturing all aspects self. is not one-size-fits-all prescription but rather personalized journey respects individual differences encourages individuals to explore practices align with their unique needs preferences. resilience essential navigating life's challenges setbacks. By cultivating can bounce back from adversity, adapt change, thrive face adversity. may involve developing coping strategies, building support network, fostering positive mindset embraces as opportunities growth. Through resilience-building practices, such mindfulness, self-reflection, self-care, strengthen ability overcome obstacles persevere goals. Furthermore, emphasizes self-awareness lifestyle. involves recognizing one's thoughts, emotions, behaviors without judgment, allowing gain insight into motivations, values, priorities. mindfulness meditation, journaling, introspection, make informed choices authentic selves lead greater fulfillment well-being. addition find meaning purpose lives. provides direction, meaning, fulfillment, guiding towards activities pursuits bring joy, fulfillment. Whether career, relationships, hobbies, or community involvement, cultivate aligning actions passions, aspirations. purpose, empowers balanced, fulfilling lives honor well-being

- **Harnessing Stress for Growth**

Mindmax introduces a groundbreaking perspective on stress, challenging conventional beliefs by proposing that stress can serve as catalyst for personal growth. This departure from traditional views reframes natural element of life that, when harnessed effectively, fuel resilience and adaptability.

In stark contrast to the prevalent belief portraying stress as inherently negative, Mindmax presents a paradigm shift by embracing Diathesis Model. This model underscores that stress, when coupled with an individual's predisposition or vulnerability, can either precipitate psychological disorders catalyze personal growth and resilience. Mindmax's perspective harmonizes acknowledging more nuanced than solely detrimental. highlights interaction between inherent disposition, suggesting act catalyst for positive change. adopting viewpoint, encourages individuals perceive opportunity rather daunting obstacle. advocates challenges are not mere impediments but potential avenues advancement. reframing growth, cultivate resilience, adaptability, constructive mindset confronting adversity. succumbing empowered harness it transformative force, fostering self-discovery progress. Central ethos is cultivation of resilience adaptability response stress. Through proactive coping mechanisms mindfulness practices, fortify their enabling them rebound from setbacks navigate stressors greater ease. become better equipped confront life's thrive amidst uncertainty. adversities growth. catalyst, transmute challenging experiences into opportunities self-development discovery. journey involves discomfort, obstacles, nurturing perceives adversity evolution.

At the core of Mindmax's philosophy lies transformative practice reframing stress. Contrary to conventional beliefs that portray stress as an insurmountable burden, Mindmax advocates for a paradigm shift where individuals perceive natural and, times, indispensable facet life's journey. This recalibration perception enables approach stressors with constructive mindset, fostering resilience, curiosity, and readiness embrace opportunities growth learning. Central reframe is recognition not inherently negative but rather normal response challenges demands. By acknowledging part human experience, can release stigma associated it instead view signal potential development. encourages adopt curiosity-driven stress, are met open mind willingness explore new possibilities. than viewing threats, prompted inquire into underlying causes implications, seeking self-discovery personal advancement. Moreover, fosters resilience empowering setbacks stepping stones stumbling blocks. embracing catalyst growth, develop coping strategies adaptive mechanisms bolster their ability bounce back from adversity thrive amidst uncertainties.

Mindmax adopts a holistic approach towards stress management, not only challenging negative perceptions of but also offering practical tools for cultivating positive mindset, particularly during circumstances. Recognizing the profound impact mindset on overall well-being, provides individuals with toolkit comprised various techniques and strategies aimed at fostering resilience, optimism, inner strength. heart Mindmax's to development lies integration mindfulness techniques. Mindfulness, rooted in present-moment awareness, empowers cultivate non-judgmental attitude their thoughts, emotions, experiences. Through practices such as meditation, deep breathing exercises, body scans, can develop greater self-awareness, emotional regulation, mental clarity. By anchoring themselves present moment, effectively manage anxiety, sense calm equilibrium amidst life's challenges. addition leverages cognitive-behavioral promote development. techniques, cognitive restructuring reframing, empower identify challenge thought patterns beliefs that contribute anxiety. replacing maladaptive thoughts more adaptive empowering ones, resilient optimistic even face adversity. Furthermore, equip skills problem-solving, goal-setting, effective communication, enhancing ability navigate stressors grace fortitude.

Mindmax's innovative perspective on stress not only challenges conventional views but also unlocks profound opportunities for personal growth that may go unnoticed within traditional frameworks. By reframing as a catalyst and resilience, Mindmax empowers individuals to navigate life's adversities with newfound strength purpose, ultimately emerging more resilient self-aware individuals. At the heart of approach lies recognition stress, when harnessed effectively, can serve transformative growth. Rather than viewing purely negative force be avoided, are encouraged embrace it natural part human experience, ripe learning development. confronting head-on leveraging catalyst, cultivate adaptability, inner strength, from difficult experiences clarity resilience. aligns closely principles positive psychology, which emphasize potential adversity. an opportunity threat shift their mindset challenges, thereby unlocking new avenues Through this lens, setbacks become self-discovery, self-improvement. Furthermore, importance focusing strengths resilience weaknesses deficits. Embracing growth, positivity empowerment, enabling them greater confidence process, overcome adversity emerge stronger, resilient, better equipped face future grace determination.

- **Full Engagement Mastery**

In the philosophy of Mindmax, Full Engagement Mastery emerges as a dynamic concept, highlighting profound impact immersing oneself completely life's experiences. Rooted principles positive psychology and flow theory, Mindmax advocates for embracing transformative journey toward heightened fulfillment well-being.

At the nucleus of Full Engagement Mastery lies a profound reverence for deliberate pursuit immersive experiences, echoing insights gleaned from Csikszentmihalyi's magnum opus, "Flow: Psychology Optimal Experience." This philosophy beckons individuals to embrace tapestry life with wholehearted presence, transcending mundane actively engage in its multifaceted richness. groundbreaking theory unveils secret unparalleled satisfaction: delicate dance between challenge and skill that propels into coveted state flow. Within realm, time seems lose grasp as are enveloped cocoon heightened focus, sheer enjoyment, sense timelessness. Imagine painter, standing before blank canvas, palette hand, ready breathe their creation. each brushstroke dances across they become one art, navigating ebbs flows inspiration effortless grace. these moments, boundaries artist artwork blur, act creation becomes sacred communion soul. Similarly, envision dancer, swept away by rhythm music, movements symphony grace fluidity. pirouette leap, transcend confines physical soaring dizzying heights expression artistry. throes performance, find themselves immersed timeless reverie, where world fades oblivion, only remains. It is experiences finds fertile ground, beckoning boundless potential human spirit. wholeheartedly immersing life's tapestry, unlock gates realm fulfillment, purpose, transcendence converge harmonious unity.

Within the fertile soil of positive psychology, Mindmax's philosophy Full Engagement Mastery finds firm grounding, drawing inspiration from Csikszentmihalyi's profound exploration flow state. This state, akin to a shimmering oasis in desert human experience, embodies pinnacle engagement, where boundaries between self and task dissolve into ether. At heart state lies an intricate tapestry intense concentration unbridled enjoyment, woven together by threads challenge skill. seminal works, including "Creativity: Psychology Discovery Invention," illuminate ethereal realm, individuals find themselves fully immersed activities that stretch their abilities. Picture solitary musician, ensconced embrace instrument, fingers dancing across strings or keys delicate ballet melody harmony. As notes swell recede like ebb tides, musician becomes one with music, transcending mundane entering realm time loses its grip, only symphony sound remains. Similarly, envision athlete, poised on precipice competition, adrenaline coursing through veins wildfire. crucible game, every movement is testament skill precision, heartbeat drumbeat propelling them forward. they navigate ebbs flows match, become force nature, riding waves unwavering determination focus. these moments sublime immersion, experience sense fulfillment purpose, consciousness expanding vast expanse potential. It gentle seeds are sown, nurturing soul guiding towards zenith experience.

Mindmax delves into the intricate dance between skill and challenge, emphasizing pivotal role of balance in ushering individuals coveted state flow. This delicate equilibrium acts as gateway to Full Engagement Mastery, where seamless immersion peak performance converge a harmonious symphony. canvas human experience, Csikszentmihalyi's research unveils profound truth: optimal conditions for flow emerge when demands task align harmoniously with one's skills. symbiotic relationship fosters sense effortless engagement, propelling towards states heightened focus productivity. Consider software developer navigating labyrinth complex coding project. lines code intertwine algorithms unfurl, finds themselves immersed realm every challenge is met skillful stroke logic creativity. digital creation, boundaries self blur, giving rise time ceases exist, only rhythmic remains. Similarly, envision chef standing before culinary possibilities, each ingredient brushstroke masterpiece gastronomy. they deftly wield their expertise, seamlessly melding flavors textures, become one creative process. symphony, transcends mundane enters alchemy reigns supreme, dish becomes sensory delight. tapestry endeavor, achieving cornerstone Mastery. It mastery adversity that discover true essence potential, unlocking doors realms boundless creativity, productivity, fulfillment.

Mindmax illuminates the transformative power nestled within immersive experiences, transcending mere moments of pleasure to unfurl vibrant tapestry one's existence. By wholeheartedly embracing life's offerings, individuals embark on a journey self-discovery, unfurling petals purpose, meaning, and connection their deepest passions world around them. This profound perspective finds resonance in Seligman's seminal work, "Flourish: Visionary New Understanding Happiness Well-being," where embrace activities conducive flow emerges as cornerstone holistic well-being life fulfillment. dance creation, find themselves enveloped rhythms artistic expression, be it through stroke brush upon canvas or words page. Indeed, those who dare immerse realm creative pursuits often souls ignited with an ineffable sense fulfillment vitality. Each brushstroke becomes whisper innermost desires, word testament depths being. hues painted evocative prose written masterpiece, they discover gateway transcendence, ordinary transforms into extraordinary, mundane sublime. lens philosophy, are beckoned seize potential inherent every experience, weaving stories rich human creativity passion, uncover true essence being, forging connections that transcend boundaries time space. is these engagement richness life, heartbeat echoes symphony soul's longing, breath divine.

Mindmax extends a helping hand, offering treasure trove of practical tools and strategies tailored for individuals eager to weave Full Engagement Mastery into the fabric their lives. Among these invaluable resources are mindfulness practices, such as meditation deep breathing exercises, designed elevate present-moment awareness new heights. Through contemplative rituals, embark on journey self-discovery, delving depths innermost being with each mindful breath tranquil moment stillness. Furthermore, champions structured activities that serve fertile soil blossoming flow experiences. Whether it be vigorous pulse sports, immersive tranquility hobbies, or soul-stirring expressions artistic endeavors, beckon state engagement. Here, amidst rhythm life's vibrant symphony, find themselves immersed in timeless dance flow, where every movement carries sweet fragrance fulfillment purpose. By seamlessly integrating practices tapestry daily routines, transformative odyssey towards resilience, optimism, inner fortitude. step taken they carve out path life brimming richness significance, is infused essence vitality meaning.

Professional athletes provide compelling examples of full engagement mastery, showcasing their ability to immerse themselves completely in sport. Take Serena Williams, a dominant force tennis, renowned for her unwavering focus and dedication on the court. During matches, Williams epitomizes essence engagement, embodying Csikszentmihalyi's concept flow. Consider pivotal moment one Williams' matches: as she steps onto court, mind clears, enters state heightened awareness. Every stroke, movement is executed with precision purpose. fully present, attuned rhythm game strategies opponent. Despite pressure match, remains composed, drawing upon years training experience. these moments intense competition, leverages skills—powerful serves, agile footwork, strategic shot selection—to navigate challenges presented by opponents. anticipates moves, adapts tactics, executes flawless execution. match unfolds, flow state, where time seems slow down, actions become effortless instinctual. experiences profound sense enjoyment fulfillment, even amidst competition. point won, rally contested testament mastery rise occasion. celebrates victories learns from defeats, continues push boundaries abilities, striving excellence determination. Through remarkable performances tennis exemplifies transformative power mastery. channel focus, skill, passion into sport not only elevates own performance but inspires countless others pursue goals arena sports, stands shining example what can be achieved when embraces pursuit excellence.

Artists such as Leonardo da Vinci and Frida Kahlo provide profound examples of full engagement mastery through their creative pursuits. Consider meticulously painting the Mona Lisa or passionately creating her self-portraits. In these moments artistic expression, they immerse themselves completely work, embodying essence engagement. Imagine his studio, applying layers paint to canvas, each brushstroke infused with intention meaning. he paints enigmatic smile Lisa, is fully present, channeling vision technical expertise into creation a masterpiece that transcends time. Despite challenges inherent capturing human expression emotion, remains steadfast, navigating complexities light, shadow, form unwavering focus. Similarly, envision confronting innermost thoughts emotions she stroke brush, delves depths psyche, pain, resilience, identity onto canvas. Kahlo's self-portraits are not merely representations physical appearance but windows soul, revealing inner world raw honesty vulnerability. Both exemplify delicate balance between skill emotional seamlessly weaving together personal introspection. confront craft—whether it be intricacies anatomy selfhood—they embrace process courage conviction. result evident masterpieces leave behind—works art continue captivate audiences beauty, depth, complexity. From haunting gaze self-portraits, creations resonate viewers on level, inviting them contemplate experience all its richness nuance. annals history, stand shining what can achieved when one embraces process. ability merge depth serves testament transformative power mastery, inspiring generations admirers alike approach craft passion, dedication, authenticity.

Adventurers like Reinhold Messner provide compelling extraordinary examples of full engagement mastery through their daring expeditions. Messner's ascent Mount Everest without supplemental oxygen stands as a testament to his ability immerse himself fully in the challenges extreme environments. Imagine navigating treacherous slopes Everest, thin air making each step monumental effort. Despite harsh conditions and inherent risks high-altitude mountaineering, remains undeterred, drawing upon years experience mountaineering expertise. With ice axe swing foothold secured, he embodies essence engagement, present moment focused on task at hand. ascends higher into death zone, where levels are dangerously low, confronts limits physical mental endurance. Yet, fueled by passion for exploration relentless pursuit challenge, presses onward, crevasses, icefalls, avalanches unwavering determination. summit, experiences profound sense accomplishment fulfillment, knowing that has conquered one world's most formidable peaks sheer willpower perseverance. journey exemplifies transformative power mastery, pushes beyond perceived limitations discovers new depths personal resilience fulfillment amidst adversity mountain. achievements inspires countless embrace courage, determination, spirit engagement. legacy serves reminder true lies not only reaching summit but itself, taken obstacle overcome becomes indomitable human spirit.

Entrepreneurs like Jeff Bezos, the founder of Amazon, epitomize full engagement mastery as they navigate complexities building and scaling disruptive businesses. Bezos's journey with Amazon illustrates his unwavering dedication to innovation, customer-centricity, long-term vision. Picture working tirelessly in garage, conceptualizing idea an online bookstore that would eventually evolve into e-commerce giant we know today. Immersed burgeoning world internet, he saw opportunity revolutionize way people shop for consume goods. relentless focus determination, Bezos dives headfirst challenges launching a digital marketplace. takes its first steps, encounters numerous obstacles, from logistical financial constraints. Yet, fueled by passion disrupting traditional retail models, remains undeterred, iterating on business model refining strategy each setback. Through hands-on leadership strategic decision-making, propels humble global behemoth spanning multiple industries. is evident pursuit customer satisfaction continuous innovation. known "day one" mentality, which emphasizes importance maintaining startup mindset even grows corporate giant. deeply involved all aspects business, product development logistics service, ensuring delivers unparalleled value customers. success stands testament ability harness power achieving entrepreneurial commitment excellence, bold risk-taking, has transformed one most influential companies world. inspires aspiring embrace entrepreneurship passion, perseverance, making lasting impact.

Dr. Sarvepalli Radhakrishnan, an eminent philosopher, scholar, and statesman, is a shining example of full engagement mastery in the field education. Celebrated as exceptional teacher, he not only enriched minds his students but also left indelible mark on Indian educational system. Imagine passionately delivering lectures philosophy ethics, captivating with profound insights erudition. pedagogical approach went beyond mere instruction; encouraged critical thinking, intellectual curiosity, deep appreciation for India's rich cultural heritage. Radhakrishnan was fully engaged process, nurturing hearts students. fostered inclusive intellectually stimulating environment where were to explore new ideas, challenge conventional wisdom, broaden their horizons. classroom, Radhakrishnan's commitment education extended role academic leader policymaker. second President India, played pivotal shaping nation's policies, advocating importance moral spiritual values legacy continues inspire generations educators alike. unwavering dedication pursuit knowledge, coupled into human condition, serves guiding light those striving make meaningful impact Teachers' Day we honor memory true exemplar passion, noble profession teaching serve timeless reminder transformative power shape minds, empower individuals, uplift societies. These examples demonstrate how individuals from various walks life embody principles Mastery. Whether sports, art, entrepreneurship, education, or adventure, ability engage challenges experiences leads personal growth, fulfillment, success.

- **Grit and Success**

Grit, the bedrock of Mindmax philosophy, epitomizes unwavering perseverance and passion toward enduring objectives. Within ethos Mindmax, grit is hailed as linchpin for surmounting obstacles, setbacks, failures, thus paving path profound success fulfillment across diverse spheres life. At its essence, according to encapsulates an unyielding dedication long-term aspirations, characterized by tenacity unrelenting zeal one's goals. This definition mirrors seminal research Angela Duckworth, whose work on underscores pivotal role in attaining excellence. resonates deeply with pioneering Duckworth. Her transformative book, "Grit: Power Perseverance," delves into traits gritty individuals their remarkable ability persist face adversities. Duckworth's empirical findings offer insights symbiotic relationship between a myriad domains. champions cultivation particularly during moments setbacks failures. Rather than perceiving challenges impassable hurdles, are urged view them opportunities growth evolution. capacity persevere amidst adversity, advocated emerges cornerstone long run.

In the realm of Mindmax philosophy, alignment personal goals with individual passions emerges as a cornerstone for cultivating grit. When individuals are deeply passionate about their objectives, they inherently more inclined to sustain effort and resilience over an extended period. offers invaluable guidance on how identify nurture these passions, thereby laying robust foundation development goes beyond mere theoretical constructs furnishes practical strategies bolster refine encompass spectrum techniques, including goal-setting methodologies, resilience-building exercises, mindfulness practices tailored motivation perseverance throughout journey toward long-term goals. By integrating actionable tactics into daily routines, can fortify resolve resilience, nurturing seeds grit within themselves. contends that principles transcend boundaries universally applicable across diverse domains, spanning education, career, development. Whether striving academic excellence, professional milestones, or growth endeavors, posits cultivation serves common denominator propels sustained success fulfillment. embracing ethos harnessing transformative power grit, navigate life's challenges unwavering emerge triumphant pursuit aspirations

- **Altered States for Creativity**

Within the framework of Mindmax philosophy, an intriguing avenue unfolds – exploration altered states consciousness. This pioneering approach delves into transformative potential mental shaped by practices such as mindfulness, meditation, and other techniques. posits that these serve a catalyst for elevating creativity fostering innovative thinking, offering pathway to fresh perspectives novel solutions. At heart Mindmax's lies premise unconventional hold key unlocking creativity. transcending boundaries ordinary consciousness, individuals may access untapped reservoirs imagination, nurturing mindset primed thinking. perspective resonates with burgeoning body research probes intricate interplay between synergy is further underscored empirical evidence suggesting can catalyze divergent thinking promote cognitive flexibility. instance, studies have shown mindfulness characterized heightened awareness nonjudgmental observation thoughts sensations, enhance creative problem-solving abilities. Moreover, adoption means accessing insights finds validation in historical anecdotal accounts. Visionary artists, inventors, thinkers throughout history often credited states, induced through various contemplation, or even dreams, sources inspiration their groundbreaking ideas innovations. essence, represents paradigm shift, challenging conventional notions consciousness paving way deeper understanding human mind's potential. embracing gateways unlock new dimensions contribute advancements fields endeavor.

Within the Mindmax philosophy, mindfulness practices and meditation occupy a pivotal role, serving as potent vehicles for inducing altered states of consciousness. places particular emphasis on these practices, recognizing them invaluable tools quieting mind, enhancing focus, fostering receptive state creative insights to emerge. derived from rich tapestry contemplative traditions, offer individuals pathway heightened awareness presence in present moment. Whether through focused attention breath, body scan exercises, or mindful walking, enable cultivate deep sense inner calm clarity. By redirecting away distracting thoughts external stimuli, lays foundation entering consciousness conducive creativity innovation. Similarly, serves complementary practice framework, providing with structured approach cultivating mental stillness peace. various techniques such meditation, loving-kindness transcendental can train their minds remain anchored moment, free incessant chatter thinking mind. relaxed awareness, creates an optimal environment accessing deeper layers unlocking

Collins's research provides a systematic investigation into the relationship between altered states of consciousness and creative thinking processes. Through rigorous empirical methods analysis, Collins elucidates how states, induced various practices such as mindfulness, meditation, or sensory deprivation, can enhance cognitive flexibility, divergent thinking, problem-solving abilities. By examining mechanisms underlying ideation within work contributes to deeper understanding process its potential applications in diverse contexts. Moreover, findings offer practical implications for individuals seeking harness endeavors. highlighting benefits associated with increased fluency, originality, flexibility thought, underscores value incorporating these routines. Whether artistic pursuits, scientific inquiry, entrepreneurial ventures, insights gleaned from study provide support Mindmax's emphasis on leveraging unlock innovative capabilities. Mindmax extends beyond mere theoretical discussions, offering actionable strategies integrating process. are engaged problem-solving, sessions, incorporation serve catalyst breaking free conventional thought patterns exploring ideas. embracing transcend limitations, tap their creativity, push boundaries what is possible. exploration seamlessly aligns broader framework, which encompasses aspects optimal living. promoting well-being transforming stress mastering engagement cultivating grit, integration adds another dimension comprehensive approach. offers holistic pathway enhancing overall quality life, fostering fulfillment, purpose.

6 MIND SYNERGY

- **Understanding Mind Synergy**

Mind Synergy is a concept that encapsulates the interconnectedness and collaboration of various cognitive processes within human mind. Rather than functioning independently, these work in tandem, influencing supporting each other to facilitate optimal functioning. This holistic view acknowledges attention, memory, reasoning, creativity, emotional regulation are all intertwined components contribute our experiences abilities.

Attention is a fundamental cognitive function that allows individuals to focus their mental resources on specific stimuli while filtering out distractions.

This ability plays pivotal role in processing by directing our awareness towards relevant information. One illustrative example of attention's significance comes from the ancient Indian epic, Mahabharata, tale Arjuna and his guru, Dronacharya. tale, Dronacharya, revered teacher archery, seeks test skills students. He sets up challenging task: hanging wooden parrot high tree branch asking pupils aim at its eye. As each student steps forward, Dronacharya quizzes them about what they see. Most students respond with descriptions trees, leaves, or itself. However, when it Arjuna's turn, response stands out. declares sees only eye bird, demonstrating an exceptional level concentration. impressed answer, decides put test. take parrot's But just before releases arrow, interrupts him, now. maintains replies still parrot. unwavering concentration earns him Dronacharya's approval shoot. extraordinary precision focus, strikes parrot, showcasing mastery attention. highlights how concentrate tasks maintain amidst external reflects importance achieving performance. context studying for exam, serves similar purpose. rely material need learn, such textbooks lecture notes, disregarding distractions like background noise unrelated thoughts. eye, effective attentional control enables absorb information efficiently perform well academically.

Memory involves the encoding, storage, and retrieval of information. It is essential for learning, problem-solving, decision-making processes. Attention often work together, as focused facilitates encoding information into memory, efficient relies on allocation attentional resources. In epic Mahabharata, attention, their interplay are vividly illustrated through story Ekalavya, a young prince Nishadha kingdom, who sought to master archery under guidance renowned guru Dronacharya. Despite being denied direct tutelage by Dronacharya due his low birth status, Ekalavya's unwavering determination led him devise unique method learning. He crafted statue diligently practiced its presence, effectively using imagination encode teachings observed from afar memory. This highlights crucial role process concentrated focus facilitated absorption retention techniques absence instruction. Ekalavya honed skills persistent practice, Dronacharya's became deeply ingrained, shaping understanding guiding actions. However, ethical dimension comes forefront when discovers exceptional talent. demands right thumb "guru dakshina" (teacher's fee), thereby testing prince's loyalty respect. critical moment, imagined guru's sense honor respect converge, influencing process. sacrifice's physical emotional cost, willingly surrenders thumb, demonstrating enduring impact moral judgments

Reasoning and Problem-Solving: problem-solving are cognitive processes that involve analyzing information, making logical deductions, generating solutions to complex problems. These require flexibility, creative thinking, the ability evaluate different options. Attention memory support by providing relevant information maintaining focus on task at hand.

Creativity encompasses the ability to generate novel ideas, insights, and solutions. It involves divergent thinking, see connections between seemingly unrelated concepts, willingness explore unconventional possibilities. Attention, memory, reasoning contribute by providing a foundation for idea generation facilitating exploration of alternative perspectives. Born in small village Tamil Nadu 1887, Ramanujan displayed an extraordinary talent mathematics from young age. Despite lacking formal training access advanced mathematical resources, independently developed groundbreaking theories formulas that baffled community. One Ramanujan's most remarkable achievements was his discovery nearly 3,900 results mathematics, many which were completely original had never been seen before. creative insights spanned various branches including number theory, infinite series, modular forms. famous examples is work on forms mock theta functions. Through intuitive methods, formulated intricate identities relationships among these objects, revolutionizing field theory paving way future advancements. facing numerous challenges setbacks life, poverty, illness, discrimination, persevered pursuing passion with unwavering dedication creativity. concepts avenues inquiry set him apart as brilliant mathematicians time. legacy continues inspire scientists around world, demonstrating transformative power potential discoveries emerge humble beginnings. story serves testament boundless possibilities human ingenuity enduring impact thinking advancing knowledge understanding.

Emotional regulation refers to the ability manage and control one's emotions effectively. It plays a crucial role in cognitive functioning by influencing attention, memory, reasoning, creativity. Gautama Buddha, founder of Buddhism, advocated for practice mindfulness meditation as means cultivating mental well-being. He taught his followers observe their without attachment or aversion, allowing them acknowledge accept feelings being overwhelmed them. One illustrative example comes from story Angulimala, notorious bandit who sought kill Buddha. Despite Angulimala's violent intentions, Buddha approached him with compassion equanimity. Through interaction, helped Angulimala recognize destructive nature guided towards path inner peace transformation. practicing regulation, was able overcome anger remorse, eventually becoming Buddha's most devoted disciples. This highlights how cultivation can lead positive outcomes, even face intense challenging circumstances. Furthermore, teachings on continue be relevant modern Indian society. individuals various stressors pressures daily lives, offers valuable tool managing emotions, reducing anxiety, promoting overall

- **Fostering Mind Synergy**

Participating in mindfulness practices rooted ancient Indian traditions, such as yoga and meditation, can profoundly influence cognitive functioning. These involve directing one's attention to the present moment without judgment, which enhances attentional control, emotional regulation, flexibility (Tang et al.,

2015). By embracing mindfulness, individuals cultivate greater awareness of their thoughts emotions, leading enhanced coherence synergy. rich tapestry culture, have long been revered pathways inner peace self-awareness. From texts Vedas teachings sages like Patanjali Buddha, techniques passed down through generations, offering profound insights into nature mind its potential for transformation. engaging pranayama (breath control), dhyana (meditation), mantra chanting, India beyond tap transformative power mindfulness. provide tools navigating complexities modern life with grace equanimity, fostering a deeper connection oneself world around them. immerse themselves practices, they develop ability observe emotions being swept away This heightened allows clarity coherence, enabling respond challenges resilience insight.

Engaging in cognitive training programs rooted Indian pedagogical traditions offers targeted interventions to bolster specific functions. These often center on areas such as dharana (concentration), smriti (memory), or buddhi (intellectual discernment), employing structured exercises and practices (Anguera et al., 2013). By systematically honing refining abilities through time-tested methods, individuals can foster the integration of mental faculties elevate overall performance. rich tapestry education, has long been revered a means nurturing intellectual prowess holistic development. Drawing from ancient texts like Vedas Upanishads, well teachings scholars Chanakya Aryabhata, India offer blend traditional wisdom modern methodologies. Participants engage variety activities designed sharpen faculties. This may include mantra recitation enhance concentration, memorization sacred strengthen memory, analytical reasoning cultivate acumen. systematic training, beyond harness power their minds overcome challenges achieve goals. consistently challenging themselves pushing boundaries abilities, they unlock new levels clarity, creativity, problem-solving

Embracing a holistic lifestyle rooted in Indian traditions is paramount for nurturing optimal cognitive functioning. Regular engagement yoga and physical exercises, deeply embedded culture, stimulates neurogenesis synaptic plasticity, fostering enhanced brain health resilience (Erickson et al., 2011). Alongside activity, honoring the ancient practice of Ayurveda emphasizes importance adequate sleep balanced diet rich nutrient-dense foods to support memory consolidation, restoration, overall function (Walker, 2017). By these principles ingrained heritage, individuals can harmonize their mental elements, promoting abilities well-being. diverse mosaic strong social bonds seeking from one's community are fundamental emotional well-being resilience. Drawing ethos "vasudhaiva kutumbakam" (the world one family), Indians prioritize interpersonal relationships communal harmony as pillars societal cohesion. within communities acts powerful buffer against stress, offering safety net during times adversity. Whether through extended family networks, close-knit neighborhoods, or gatherings, find solace strength forged with loved ones neighbors. Moreover, meaningful interactions India provide fertile ground growth. spirited debates local tea stalls philosophical discussions ashrams, cherish opportunities intellectual exchange mutual learning. not only stimulate faculties but also nurture sense belonging interconnectedness. connections tradition, cultivate supportive environment conducive "Manasik Samanvay" (mental harmony). This collective synergy fosters resilience, strengthens abilities, unity shared purpose tapestry society.

- **Continuous Learning and Growth**

Engaging in lifelong learning and pursuing intellectual challenges are integral to stimulating cognitive vitality promoting the harmonization of mental elements. curiosity encourages flexibility creativity, while exposure new experiences fosters neural plasticity enrichment (Hultsch et al., 1999). By actively seeking out opportunities for growth, individuals can expand their repertoire unlock full potential.

Pandit Bhimsen Joshi was one of the most celebrated classical vocalists in India, renowned for his mastery Kirana gharana (a lineage or tradition Hindustani music). Despite achieving great success and acclaim throughout life, never ceased pursuit learning growth, even elder years. career, continually experimented with music, exploring new ragas (melodic modes) compositions, incorporating elements from various musical traditions into performances. being recognized as a master craft, he remained humble open-minded, always eager to learn fellow musicians explore avenues artistic expression. later years, continued push boundaries artistry. embraced technological advancements music recording production, collaborating younger innovative ways preserve disseminate audiences. Moreover, Joshi's commitment continuous extended beyond realm music. known voracious appetite knowledge keen interest literature, poetry, philosophy. age, immersed himself works poets thinkers, drawing inspiration diverse sources enrich understanding world deepen lifelong dedication growth serves shining example transformative power education personal development, regardless age stage life. unwavering excellence, coupled insatiable curiosity thirst knowledge, not only propelled him pinnacle chosen field but also enriched lives countless others through wisdom. conclusion, Mind Synergy encapsulates comprehensive strategy maximizing cognitive performance by harmonizing mental fostering collaborative interactions among them. This holistic approach recognizes intricate interconnectedness processes emphasizes importance integrating them synergistically.

To cultivate Mind Synergy, individuals embark on a journey of self-discovery and self-mastery, aiming unlock the full potential their cognitive faculties. This involves developing an awareness interplay between different aspects cognition, such as attention, memory, reasoning, creativity, actively nurturing integration. Through targeted practices interventions, can enhance functioning promote psychological well-being. may include engaging in mindfulness meditation sharpen attentional control emotional regulation, participating training programs boost working memory executive functioning, adopting healthy lifestyle support overall brain health. Furthermore, fostering meaningful social connections seeking from others play crucial role promoting Synergy. By relationships building supportive community, create environment conducive growth resilience. Ultimately, pursuit Synergy empowers unleash lead fulfilling lives. embracing holistic approach optimization synergistic interactions among mental elements, navigate complexities modern world with clarity, confidence, creativity

7 MINDSYNC - A UNIFIED APPROACH

In the realm of cognitive well-being, Mindsync represents a groundbreaking concept that integrates mindset, mindmax, and mindtech to optimize mental health. This comprehensive framework draws inspiration from various disciplines create holistic strategy for achieving synchronization.

At the core of Mindsync lies profound emphasis on nurturing a positive and growth-oriented mindset—a cornerstone inspired by principles psychology mindfulness practices. This transformative approach aims to empower individuals navigate life's challenges with resilience, adaptability, self-awareness, fostering deeper sense well-being fulfillment. cultivation mindset begins fundamental shift in perspective—an embrace as opportunities for personal intellectual growth. Rather than viewing obstacles roadblocks, are encouraged them stepping stones path self-improvement. fosters optimism curiosity, inspiring seek out new experiences push beyond their comfort zones. Resilience is hallmark mindset, empowering bounce back from setbacks adversity renewed vigor determination. reframing temporary insurmountable failures, cultivate psychological fortitude persevere face challenges. enables weather storms grace perseverance, emerging stronger more resilient before. Central development self-awareness emotional intelligence. Through practices introspection, gain insight into thoughts, emotions, behaviors, understanding themselves inner workings. heightened complexities greater clarity, authenticity, balance. Gratitude self-compassion essential components appreciation blessings compassionate attitude towards oneself. cultivating gratitude, foster outlook life, focusing abundance scarcity lives. Similarly, allows extend kindness moments struggle, promoting well-being. affirmations self-talk serve powerful tools reinforcing beliefs attitudes oneself one's abilities. replacing negative affirming statements, can rewire subconscious minds optimistic life. creates ripple effect, overcome self-limiting full potential.

At the heart of Mindsync lies transformative concept mindmax—a dynamic force dedicated to unleashing full spectrum one's mental capabilities and intellectual prowess. Mindmax represents a holistic approach cognitive enhancement, emphasizing continuous learning, creativity cultivation, relentless pursuit challenges. Through deliberate engagement in activities that stimulate growth stretch boundaries capabilities, individuals harness power unlock their potential embark on journey profound self-discovery personal growth. encourages embrace lifelong commitment learning exploration. This entails actively seeking out opportunities for expansion, whether formal education, self-directed study, or experiential learning. By immersing themselves new subjects, ideas, perspectives, can broaden horizons, deepen understanding world, cultivate rich tapestry knowledge fuels curiosity creativity. mindmax, serving as catalyst innovation, problem-solving, self-expression. nurture creative instincts mindset experimentation engaging pursuits such writing, painting, music, design, tap into innate creativity, unleash imagination, channel unique insights perspectives works art, discovery. challenges step outside comfort zones confront head-on. it's tackling complex problems, mastering skills, stimulating discussions debates, push abilities expand horizons. opportunities, resilience, adaptability, growth-oriented propels them towards potential. fosters an environment is conducive may involve surrounding oneself with like-minded who inspire challenge them, participating communities discussion groups, mentors role models provide guidance support along journey. cultivating supportive environment, create conditions necessary development. practice mindfulness reflection, allowing self-awareness, focus attention, enhance performance. incorporating techniques meditation, deep breathing, visualization daily routine, sharpen acuity, reduce stress anxiety, greater sense clarity presence lives.

At the forefront of Mindsync's holistic approach to cognitive wellness stands mindtech—a dynamic force that harnesses cutting-edge technologies optimize mental well-being. Mindtech serves as a pivotal component within this unified framework, seamlessly integrating insights from neuroscience, biofeedback tools, and enhancement empower individuals on their journey towards enhanced function, stress management, overall resilience. By leveraging innovative tools applications, revolutionizes landscape health care, offering novel approaches enhance performance, mitigate stressors, promote draws upon latest advancements in neuroscience provide with deeper understanding processes brain functioning. Through neurofeedback devices imaging techniques, gain into neural activity patterns, strengths, areas for improvement. visualizing interpreting data, can identify underlying track progress over time, make informed decisions performance. play role enabling cultivate greater self-awareness regulation physiological responses. heart rate variability monitors electroencephalography (EEG) devices, real-time feedback parameters such rate, respiration, brainwave activity. monitoring modulating these bodily functions, develop control responses, improve emotional regulation, relaxation encompasses diverse array designed function includes training apps, games, neurostimulation target specific domains memory, attention, executive function. engaging targeted exercises interventions, sharpen skills, agility, bolster reserves improved performance daily activities challenges. introduces therapeutic harness immersive potential technology support Virtual reality therapy, example, offers safe controlled environment confront overcome psychological challenges phobias, anxiety disorders, post-traumatic disorder (PTSD). immersing environments tailored needs, therapy facilitates exposure training, cognitive-behavioral interventions highly manner. democratizes care personalized accessible solutions cater individuals' unique needs preferences. Whether mobile wearable or online platforms, on-demand access evidence-based self-help resources, support. empowering take an active managing health, fosters culture self-care, resilience, empowerment.

Mindsync transcends the realm of abstract theories, manifesting as a practical framework designed to be seamlessly integrated into real-life contexts. Through multifaceted approach encompassing mindfulness practices, continuous learning endeavors, and strategic utilization mindtech tools, individuals embark on transformative journey towards enhanced cognitive well-being. With focus accessibility applicability, offers roadmap for navigate complexities modern life while fostering harmony resilience. At heart Mindsync's implementation strategy lies cultivation practices cornerstone are encouraged engage in regular exercises such meditation, deep breathing, body scans cultivate present-moment awareness, emotional regulation, stress reduction. By incorporating their daily routines, develop greater resilience life's challenges sense inner calm balance. advocates lifelong catalyst growth personal development. pursue ongoing opportunities, whether formal education, self-directed study, or experiential endeavors. expanding knowledge base, acquiring new skills, exposing themselves diverse perspectives, stimulate engagement, creativity, adaptability, laying foundation continued fulfillment. serves valuable ally pursuit well-being, offering innovative tools technologies support journey. From brain training apps biofeedback devices, leverage optimize function, manage stress, enhance overall mental integrating these gain insights patterns, effective coping strategies, self-awareness self-regulation. promotes dissemination skill development creation educational workshops, seminars, online courses Building on the principles of positive psychology, neuroscience, and behavioral science, the available resources provide workshops on topics such as stress management, emotional intelligence, and cognitive enhancement techniques. These workshops empower participants to take proactive steps towards optimizing their mental health. The vision extends beyond individual transformation, encompassing communities and organizations as well. By fostering a culture of well-being and synchronization, the initiative aims to create supportive environments where individuals feel empowered to prioritize their own health and support others. Through collective efforts, it aspires to drive meaningful change, cultivating a thriving ecosystem of wellness. At its core, this approach integrates mindfulness, continuous learning, and deliberate action, striving to foster resilience and growth among individuals, communities, and organizations alike.

- **Confluence of Forces**

In the delicate dance of cognitive well-being, Mindsync orchestrates a harmonious blend that balances the individual's mental landscape. The integration of mindset, mindtech, and mindmax is more than a simple intersection; it represents a purposeful convergence designed to amplify each element's transformative potential, fostering a cohesive and dynamic path to achieving holistic mental harmony.

In the philosophy of Mindsync, concept mindset stands as a cornerstone, embodying essence adaptability and growth. Drawing inspiration from pioneering research psychologist Carol Dweck on growth mindset, Mindsync advocates for dynamic approach to viewing world one's experiences within it. At its essence, promoted by transcends fixed rigid worldview. Instead, individuals are encouraged embrace fluid adaptable perspective, wherein challenges perceived not obstacles, but opportunities learning. Every setback is seen stepping stone towards personal development, fostering resilience perseverance face adversity. force serves foundation upon which build their perceptions, attitudes, responses world. cultivating an adaptive empowered navigate life's complexities with confidence optimism. They new situations sense curiosity openness, embracing potential transformation that lies experience. Rather than shying away difficulties, welcome learning development. see setbacks temporary setbacks, insurmountable barriers, willing exert effort overcome obstacles. fostered failure reframed natural part process.

Instead being discouraged use them valuable experiences, extracting lessons inform future actions decisions. characterized commitment continuous self-improvement. actively seek out growth, whether through formal education, development activities, or challenging stretch abilities. One hallmarks optimism this maintain positive outlook, believing ability achieve goals. demonstrate bouncing back renewed determination.

In the contemporary era marked by rapid technological advancement, Mindsync recognizes transformative potential of mindtech fostering mental well-being. Rooted insights Nobel laureate Daniel Kahneman and his seminal work behavioral economics, introduces a scientific data-driven dimension to confluence forces within Mindsync. At its core, represents fusion cutting-edge technology with pursuit wellness. Inspired Kahneman's research on human decision-making processes, employs neurofeedback devices, mindfulness apps, other innovative technologies provide individuals actionable into their cognitive functions. adoption enables gain deeper understanding processes behaviors. for instance, offer real-time feedback brain activity, allowing visualize regulate neural patterns. Similarly, apps leverage guided meditation exercises promote self-awareness emotional regulation. One key strengths lies ability bridge gap between mind technology, facilitating personalized effective strategies harnessing power data analytics, can make informed decisions about health, tailoring interventions suit unique needs preferences. implementation empowers take an active role managing leveraging as tool self-discovery growth, cultivate greater self-awareness, resilience, overall psychological flourishing. Moreover, serves catalyst innovation progress field health. embracing emerging approaches, remains forefront evolving landscape well-being, continuously striving enhance effectiveness accessibility health interventions.

Mindmax, an integral component of the Mindsync framework, embodies a dynamic force that propels individuals towards pinnacle their mental capabilities. Rooted in pioneering research psychologist Mihaly Csikszentmihalyi and his concept flow, mindmax serves as catalyst for personal growth cognitive flourishing. At its essence, is not merely about achieving excellence but embracing journey optimal experiences. Drawing inspiration from Csikszentmihalyi's insights into conditions facilitate flow states, encourages to seek out activities challenge inspire them. Central philosophy notion engaging stretch one's boundaries foster sense mastery fulfillment. Whether it's pursuing passion project, learning new skill, or exploring unfamiliar territories, motivates venture beyond comfort zones pursuit self-discovery. One key principles emphasis on continuous adaptation. By actively seeking challenges opportunities intellectual stimulation, cultivate resilience, creativity, adaptability. Through this process, they only expand capacities also develop deeper understanding themselves world around Moreover, transformation, guiding state heightened engagement intrinsic motivation. immersing align with passions interests, experience profound fulfillment purpose. implementation within framework involves creating environments may include designing structured programs, fostering creative spaces, promoting autonomy various domains. Ultimately, represents self-discovery growth, where are empowered unleash full potential thrive all aspects lives. challenge, exploration, inspires embark transformative

The implementation of confluence within Mindsync represents a sophisticated and comprehensive endeavor, blending insights from positive psychology neuroscience to create transformative experience for individuals seeking enhance their cognitive well-being. Through multifaceted approach encompassing workshops, programs, practical exercises, endeavors guide participants on journey self-discovery growth offers variety workshops programs meticulously designed foster harmony personal development. These sessions are crafted with expertise drawn fields neuroscience, ensuring that receive evidence-based guidance support. Facilitators adeptly lead interactive exercises discussions, encouraging introspection self-reflection. Central guiding principles borrowed neuroscience. serve as foundation upon which built, emphasizing strategies cultivating growth-oriented mindset, enhancing self-awareness mindtech tools, fostering creativity intellectual exploration mindmax experiences. Equipped tools facilitate growth self-discovery. may include journaling prompts, mindfulness practices, enhancement techniques. By engaging in develop greater insight into thought patterns, emotions, behaviors, empowering them make changes lives. One key aspect involves shifting participants' mindsets towards more adaptive outlook. guided activities learn reframe challenges opportunities cultivate resilience face adversity. This mindset shift forms cornerstone development Mindsync introduced aimed at functioning. neurofeedback devices, biofeedback apps, training programs utilizing technologies, gain valuable processes optimize mental performance encourages embark experiences stimulate exploration. involve pursuing passion projects, artistic endeavors, or exploring new areas interest immersing themselves activities, expand horizons tap full potential careful integration elements, provides framework well-being realizing emerge program skills, insights, renewed sense purpose, ready navigate complexities life clarity, resilience, vitality.

Within the Mindsync framework, culmination of forces mindset, mindtech, and mindmax is attainment cognitive harmony. Unlike a static state, harmony represents dynamic equilibrium characterized by ongoing growth, resilience, self-awareness. It embodies balanced synchronized mental state where individuals navigate life's challenges with clarity, adaptability, purpose. Equips resilience needed to inevitable life. Growth-oriented view setbacks as opportunities for learning growth rather than insurmountable obstacles. They develop psychological flexibility adapt changing circumstances bounce back from adversity renewed determination. In pursuit harmony, harness potential technology enhance self-awareness understanding. Mindtech tools such neurofeedback devices mindfulness apps provide valuable insights into processes emotional states. leveraging these tools, gain deeper understanding themselves their thought patterns, enabling them make informed decisions cultivate greater well-being. Central continual expansion boundaries through experiences. Actively seek out challenges, engage creative pursuits, explore new domains knowledge. Pushing beyond comfort zones, foster intellectual curiosity expanding horizons unlocking potentials themselves. emerges integration forces. Each component contributes overall individual's landscape, complementing reinforcing one another. Mindset provides foundation while offer support growth. Experiences fuel exploration creativity, enriching journey. Importantly, not endpoint but process adaptation. Self-reflection, learning, personal development, maintaining balance amidst ever-changing circumstances. This allows complexities life purpose, vitality, fostering sense fulfillment essence, realization pinnacle well-being—a thrive, evolve, flourish rich tapestry human experience. Convergence mindmax, embark on transformative journey towards self-discovery, empowerment.

- **Embarking on the Mindsync Journey**

The Mindsync Paradigm emerges as a groundbreaking and all-encompassing framework, offering individuals transformative path towards sustained mental well-being. By seamlessly integrating mindset, mindtech, mindmax, this holistic approach transcends conventional boundaries, inviting to embark on quest for cognitive harmony that enriches every aspect of their lives.

At the core of the Mindsync Paradigm is the fundamental principle of fostering a resilient and growth-oriented mindset. This foundation draws inspiration from the pioneering research of psychologist Carol Dweck, as described in her influential book, "Mindset: The New Psychology of Success." Within this paradigm, individuals are encouraged to adopt a mindset that views challenges not as obstacles but as opportunities for growth and learning. Dweck distinguishes between two types of mindsets: a fixed mindset, where individuals believe that their abilities and intelligence are innate and unchangeable, and a growth mindset, where people understand that talents can be developed through dedication, effort, and perseverance. The Mindsync Paradigm aligns closely with the principles of a growth mindset, emphasizing the importance of continuous learning and personal development.

This shift in perspective helps individuals reframe challenges. Instead of seeing setbacks as failures, they are viewed as valuable opportunities for improvement. By embracing this positive outlook, individuals develop resilience and adaptability in the face of adversity. Central to the paradigm is a deep appreciation for the learning process, recognizing that progress often involves setbacks, and these experiences serve as important lessons that contribute to growth. Cultivating a growth mindset shapes an individual's attitudes towards life's obstacles. Rather than becoming discouraged, they approach challenges with confidence and determination, knowing that each hurdle presents an opportunity for growth. This empowers them to persevere through adversity and pursue their goals with optimism. Ultimately, a growth mindset serves as the foundation for the development of the Mindsync Paradigm, allowing individuals to unlock their full potential, overcome challenges, and thrive both personally and professionally.

Leveraging advanced mindtech solutions, the Mindsync Paradigm provides individuals with actionable insights and tools for self-awareness. Inspired by Daniel Kahneman's principles from "Thinking, Fast and Slow," this approach incorporates technologies like neurofeedback devices, cognitive training apps, and personalized tools. These innovations empower individuals to navigate their mental landscape with precision, gaining a deeper understanding of their mental processes while enhancing overall well-being. By harnessing the insights of Nobel laureate Kahneman, particularly his work on the dual systems of thought—the fast, intuitive System 1 and the slower, more deliberate System

2—the Mindsync Paradigm thoughtfully integrates innovative technologies to optimize cognitive functioning.

One of the central components of mindtech within this paradigm is neurofeedback devices. These devices use electroencephalography (EEG) technology to measure brainwave activity in real time, providing valuable feedback about mental states. By monitoring these patterns, individuals can learn to regulate their mental states, manage stress, and optimize performance. Another essential aspect involves cognitive training apps, which leverage exercises and activities based on psychological principles to enhance cognitive function, memory, attention, and problem-solving skills. Regular use of these apps helps individuals improve their abilities and mitigate cognitive decline associated with aging or neurological conditions. Additionally, mindtech solutions are tailored to individual needs and preferences, which may include virtual reality (VR) experiences or biofeedback coaching platforms. By customizing interventions based on personal profiles and goals, mindtech offers targeted support, enabling individuals to gain better control over their emotions and thoughts, thus fostering a sense of agency over their mental health.

Within the Mindsync Paradigm, the concept of Mindmax emerges as a transformative force that encourages individuals to push beyond the confines of their cognitive comfort zones. Rooted in insights from renowned psychologist Mihaly Csikszentmihalyi, particularly his work "Flow: The Psychology of Optimal Experience," Mindmax represents a pathway to unlocking one's full potential and achieving cognitive harmony. It encourages individuals to seek out activities that elicit a state of flow—characterized by intense focus, deep immersion, and a sense of timelessness. In this state, individuals experience heightened fulfillment and engagement, becoming fully absorbed in the present moment and losing track of external distractions.

Flow activities can vary widely and may include creative pursuits like painting, writing, or playing music, as well as intellectual challenges such as solving puzzles, learning new skills, or engaging in philosophical discussions. Creativity is a cornerstone of Mindmax exploration. Whether it's sculpting or composing music, creative endeavors offer a unique opportunity for individuals to express themselves, tap into their imagination, and unlock their potential. Through the act of creation, individuals enter a state of flow, transcending limitations and experiencing a profound connection with their inner selves.

Mindmax also involves seeking out intellectually stimulating activities to promote cognitive growth. This might include learning complex languages, delving into philosophical texts, or exploring scientific theories. By engaging in such intellectually stimulating activities, individuals exercise their mental faculties, expand their knowledge base, and sharpen their critical thinking skills. A crucial aspect of Mindmax exploration is the pursuit of continuous learning.

Whether through formal education, online courses, or self-directed study, individuals are encouraged to cultivate a lifelong commitment to personal growth—embracing new knowledge not only to broaden their horizons but also to foster curiosity, adaptability, and resilience.

Immersing oneself in Mindmax activities brings myriad benefits, including cognitive enhancement and emotional well-being. These activities foster mental flexibility, enabling individuals to adapt to new situations, solve problems creatively, and think innovatively. Moreover, engaging in flow promotes emotional well-being by reducing stress, increasing feelings of fulfillment, and fostering a sense of purpose and meaning in life. Ultimately, Mindmax becomes a journey that enhances overall mental well-being, allowing individuals to thrive in all aspects of their lives.

- **Harmonizing Forces**

In the rich framework of the Mindsync Paradigm, the concept of Synergistic Interplay emerges as a guiding principle, weaving together the interconnected forces of mindset, mindtech, and mindmax into a seamless and cohesive whole. Recognizing the inherent interconnectedness of these elements, the paradigm invites individuals to embark on a journey of exploration and discovery, where the dynamic relationship between these forces leads to a state of cognitive harmony and well-being.

Understanding the Interconnected Facets

Mindset

At the foundation of the Mindsync Paradigm lies the cultivation of a resilient and growth-oriented mindset. Individuals are encouraged to adopt a mindset that perceives challenges as opportunities for growth, embracing setbacks as learning experiences, and fostering a positive and adaptive outlook towards life. This serves as the cornerstone upon which other elements are built, shaping individuals' perceptions, attitudes, and responses to the world around them.

Mindtech

Leveraging cutting-edge technologies, mindtech provides individuals with actionable insights and tools for self-awareness and cognitive enhancement. By integrating neurofeedback devices, cognitive training apps, and personalized tools, mindtech empowers individuals to gain a deeper understanding of their mental processes and make informed decisions about their well-being. It serves as a bridge between the mind and technology, offering innovative solutions to support cognitive function and overall health.

Mindmax

Mindmax represents the exploration of activities that propel individuals beyond their comfort zones, eliciting a state of flow and optimal experience. By engaging in creative pursuits, intellectual challenges, and continuous learning endeavors, individuals expand their horizons, foster mental flexibility, and enhance personal growth. Mindmax acts as a catalyst for self-discovery, encouraging individuals to unlock their full potential and thrive in all aspects of their lives.

Aligning the Elements for Cognitive Harmony

True harmony emerges when mindset, mindtech, and mindmax are in alignment. This alignment fosters a synergistic interplay between these forces, creating a cohesive and integrated approach to achieving cognitive harmony. By navigating the dynamic interplay between these elements, individuals can harness the strengths of each to amplify the benefits of the others. For example, a growth mindset can enhance the effectiveness of mindtech tools, while mindtech can reinforce positive cognitive patterns. Within the Mindsync Paradigm, this alignment brings individuals closer to achieving a state of optimal well-being—characterized by balance, resilience, and peak cognitive functioning. In this state, individuals experience a sense of alignment between their thoughts, emotions, and actions, enabling them to navigate life's challenges with grace and ease.

By understanding and harnessing the transformative potential of mindset, mindtech, and mindmax, individuals can reach new levels of well-being and thrive in the complex landscape of the modern world.

- **Navigating Personalized Pathways**

In the expansive terrain of cognitive exploration, the Mindsync Paradigm unfolds as a personalized journey that recognizes and honors the uniqueness of each individual's mental landscape. By embracing the principle of individuality, the paradigm offers a customized journey tailored to address specific challenges, aspirations, and potentials. Through a variety of workshops, guided programs, and carefully crafted strategies inspired by the Mindsync Paradigm, individuals embark on a transformative path towards enhanced well-being.

Acknowledging Individuality

At the heart of the Mindsync Paradigm lies a profound acknowledgment of each person's unique makeup. Recognizing that no two cognitive landscapes are identical, the paradigm celebrates diversity and embraces the richness of individual experiences, perspectives, and aspirations.

Tailoring Strategies

Drawing inspiration from the principles of personalization, the Mindsync Paradigm provides a spectrum of approaches designed to meet the specific needs and goals of each individual. Whether through one-on-one coaching sessions, customized learning modules, or individualized exercises, individuals are provided with the tools and resources they need to navigate their mental landscape with confidence and clarity.

Workshops and Programs

The paradigm offers immersive workshops and programs focused on self-discovery and personal growth. These interactive sessions provide opportunities to explore strengths and weaknesses, uncover hidden potentials, and develop strategies for enhancing well-being. Leveraging insights from positive psychology, neuroscience, and mindfulness practices, these programs address individual challenges and help participants cultivate a growth mindset and harness the power of mindtech tools, equipping them with the knowledge, skills, resilience, and adaptability needed to thrive.

Cultivating a Growth Mindset

At the core of the Mindsync Paradigm is the fundamental principle of fostering a resilient and growth-oriented mindset. This foundation draws inspiration from the pioneering research of psychologist Carol Dweck, as described in her influential book, "Mindset: The New Psychology of Success." Within this paradigm, individuals are encouraged to adopt a mindset that views challenges not as obstacles but as opportunities for growth and learning. Dweck distinguishes between two types of mindsets: a fixed mindset, where individuals believe that their abilities and intelligence are innate and unchangeable, and a growth mindset, where people understand that talents can be developed through dedication, effort, and perseverance. The Mindsync Paradigm aligns closely with the principles of a growth mindset, emphasizing the importance of continuous learning and personal development.

This shift in perspective helps individuals reframe challenges. Instead of seeing setbacks as failures, they are viewed as valuable opportunities for improvement. By embracing this positive outlook, individuals develop resilience and adaptability in the face of adversity. Central to the paradigm is a deep appreciation for the learning process, recognizing that progress often involves setbacks, and these experiences serve as important lessons that contribute to growth. Cultivating a growth mindset shapes an individual's attitudes towards life's obstacles. Rather than becoming discouraged, they approach challenges with confidence and determination, knowing that each hurdle presents an opportunity for growth. This empowers them to persevere through adversity and pursue their goals with optimism. Ultimately, a growth mindset serves as the foundation for the development of the Mindsync Paradigm, allowing individuals to unlock their full potential, overcome challenges, and thrive both personally and professionally.

Leveraging Mindtech Solutions for Self-Awareness

Leveraging advanced mindtech solutions, the Mindsync Paradigm provides individuals with actionable insights and tools for self-awareness. Inspired by Daniel Kahneman's principles from "Thinking, Fast and Slow," this approach incorporates technologies like neurofeedback devices, cognitive training apps, and personalized tools. These innovations empower individuals to navigate their mental landscape with precision, gaining a deeper understanding of their mental processes while enhancing overall well-being. By harnessing the insights of Nobel laureate Kahneman, particularly his work on the dual systems of thought—the fast, intuitive System 1 and the slower, more deliberate System 2—the Mindsync Paradigm thoughtfully integrates innovative technologies to optimize cognitive functioning.

One of the central components of mindtech within this paradigm is neurofeedback devices. These devices use electroencephalography (EEG) technology to measure brainwave activity in real time, providing valuable feedback about mental states. By monitoring these patterns, individuals can learn to regulate their mental states, manage stress, and optimize performance. Another essential aspect involves cognitive training apps, which leverage exercises and activities based on psychological principles to enhance cognitive function, memory, attention, and problem-solving skills. Regular use of these apps helps individuals improve their abilities and mitigate cognitive decline associated with aging or neurological conditions. Additionally, mindtech solutions are tailored to individual needs and preferences, which may include virtual reality (VR) experiences or biofeedback coaching platforms. By customizing interventions based on personal profiles and goals, mindtech offers targeted support, enabling individuals to gain better control over their emotions and thoughts, thus fostering a sense of agency over their mental health.

Pushing Beyond Comfort Zones with Mindmax

Within the Mindsync Paradigm, the concept of Mindmax emerges as a transformative force that encourages individuals to push beyond the confines of their cognitive comfort zones. Rooted in insights from renowned psychologist Mihaly Csikszentmihalyi, particularly his work "Flow: The Psychology of Optimal Experience," Mindmax represents a pathway to unlocking one's full potential and achieving cognitive harmony. It encourages individuals to seek out activities that elicit a state of flow—characterized by intense focus, deep immersion, and a sense of timelessness. In this state, individuals experience heightened fulfillment and engagement, becoming fully absorbed in the present moment and losing track of external distractions.

Flow activities can vary widely and may include creative pursuits like painting, writing, or playing music, as well as intellectual challenges such as solving puzzles, learning new skills, or engaging in philosophical discussions. Creativity is a cornerstone of Mindmax exploration. Whether it's sculpting or composing music, creative endeavors offer a unique opportunity for individuals to express themselves, tap into their imagination, and unlock their potential. Through the act of creation, individuals enter a state of flow, transcending limitations and experiencing a profound connection with their inner selves.

Mindmax also involves seeking out intellectually stimulating activities to promote cognitive growth. This might include learning complex languages, delving into philosophical texts, or exploring scientific theories. By engaging in such intellectually stimulating activities, individuals exercise their mental faculties, expand their knowledge base, and sharpen their critical thinking skills. A crucial aspect of Mindmax exploration is the pursuit of continuous learning. Whether through formal education, online courses, or self-directed study, individuals are encouraged to cultivate a lifelong commitment to personal growth—embracing new knowledge not only to broaden their horizons but also to foster curiosity, adaptability, and resilience.

Immersing oneself in Mindmax activities brings myriad benefits, including cognitive enhancement and emotional well-being. These activities foster mental flexibility, enabling individuals to adapt to new situations, solve problems creatively, and think innovatively. Moreover, engaging in flow promotes emotional well-being by reducing stress, increasing feelings of fulfillment, and fostering a sense of purpose and meaning in life. Ultimately, Mindmax becomes a journey that enhances overall mental well-being, allowing individuals to thrive in all aspects of their lives.

- **A Compass for Life**

"A Compass for Life," within the Mindsync framework, is a navigational tool that offers guiding principles to help individuals achieve sustained cognitive harmony. Drawing from foundational psychological concepts and well-established practices, it provides direction and purpose, helping individuals navigate the complexities of life while fostering a balanced, synchronized mindset.

At the core of the compass lies the principle of positive psychology, inspired by Martin Seligman's work in "Authentic Happiness." This principle encourages individuals to move beyond simply addressing weaknesses and instead focus on embracing and harnessing their strengths. By identifying and leveraging unique abilities, individuals can cultivate empowerment and agency in navigating life's challenges. This strength-based approach fosters self-efficacy and optimism, laying a foundation for confidence and fulfillment. Central to this approach is the cultivation of positive emotions, such as gratitude, joy, and compassion. By actively seeking moments of joy and practicing gratitude, individuals can develop a more optimistic outlook, enabling them to navigate adversity with grace. Moreover, finding meaning and purpose by aligning one's actions with core values fosters deeper fulfillment and satisfaction, even in challenging times.

Another key principle of the compass is the growth mindset, inspired by Carol Dweck's influential book, "Mindset: The New Psychology of Success." This principle invites individuals to perceive challenges not as obstacles but as opportunities for growth and learning. By embracing difficulties with curiosity and enthusiasm, individuals can expand their skills and cultivate resilience, laying the foundation for long-term success. This mindset encourages a love of learning and intellectual curiosity, viewing learning as a lifelong journey rather than a means to an end. Failures are reframed as valuable stepping stones on the path to success, offering opportunities for reflection and growth. By adopting this approach, individuals unlock their potential, foster resilience, and pursue a life of purpose and fulfillment.

Mindful awareness, as articulated by Jon Kabat-Zinn in "Wherever You Go, There You Are," is also a vital aspect of the compass. It encourages individuals to cultivate a deep presence in the present moment, letting go of distractions and fully immersing themselves in their experiences. By practicing mindfulness with openness and receptivity, individuals foster a profound sense of connection with the world around them, leading to greater cognitive balance and inner harmony. Mindfulness also promotes a non-judgmental attitude toward one's thoughts and emotions, allowing for deeper self-understanding and emotional resilience. By incorporating mindfulness practices into daily routines, individuals can enhance emotional regulation, cognitive clarity, and overall well-being, while also fostering compassion and empathy for themselves and others.

The compass also draws from the concept of neuroplasticity, inspired by Norman Doidge's "The Brain That Changes Itself." Neuroplasticity refers to the brain's remarkable ability to adapt and rewire itself in response to new experiences. By embracing lifelong learning and intellectual curiosity, individuals can nourish their brains, promote cognitive flexibility, and enhance overall well-being. Engaging in continuous learning and exploring new perspectives enriches cognitive vitality and adaptability, while fostering a culture of growth and innovation. This commitment to lifelong learning helps individuals build resilience and thrive in the face of change.

Values-driven decision-making, inspired by Viktor Frankl's "Man's Search for Meaning," plays a crucial role in guiding individuals toward cognitive harmony. By uncovering deeply held values, individuals can align their actions with a larger purpose, fostering authenticity and integrity. Values-driven choices empower individuals to embrace responsibility and agency in shaping their lives, leading to inner alignment, clarity, and fulfillment. This approach helps individuals form meaningful connections with others and fosters resilience in the face of life's challenges.

Resilience, inspired by Angela Duckworth's work on "grit," is another key principle of the compass. It encourages individuals to view challenges as opportunities for growth rather than obstacles to be avoided. By cultivating grit—a combination of passion and perseverance—individuals can stay committed to their long-term goals and emerge stronger from setbacks. Resilience is not just about bouncing back from adversity but also about learning and growing from each experience. This mindset fosters cognitive harmony, allowing individuals to pursue their aspirations with determination and grace.

The compass also emphasizes a holistic understanding of wellness, drawing inspiration from the World Health Organization's definition of well-being as encompassing physical, mental, and social aspects. Physical well-being involves regular exercise and a balanced diet, which contribute to overall health and cognitive function. Social well-being is fostered through meaningful connections with friends, family, and community, providing a sense of belonging and support. Mental well-being is nurtured through mindfulness, relaxation techniques, and stress management strategies, which help individuals maintain resilience and a positive outlook. Spiritual and emotional wellness, cultivated through practices such as prayer, meditation, or reflection, further contribute to a sense of purpose and fulfillment.

The practice of self-reflection, inspired by Donald Schön's "The Reflective Practitioner," is a powerful tool for fostering cognitive harmony. Self-reflection involves intentional introspection to gain insights into one's thoughts, emotions, and actions. By regularly engaging in reflective practices, individuals can develop greater self-awareness, resilience, adaptability, and emotional intelligence. The compass encourages integrating reflection into daily routines through journaling, mindfulness exercises, and self-check-ins, fostering continuous personal growth.

To support the integration of "A Compass for Life" principles into daily life, interactive workshops and reflective sessions provide individuals with practical tools and a supportive community. Participants explore how to apply these principles in diverse life contexts, fostering personal growth and cognitive harmony. Workshops offer hands-on experience with journaling prompts, mindfulness exercises, value clarification activities, and goal-setting techniques, helping individuals incorporate these practices into their routines. The workshops also create supportive communities, providing encouragement, accountability, and a sense of belonging.

Ultimately, "A Compass for Life" serves as a bridge between psychological insights and practical application. By participating in interactive workshops and reflective sessions, individuals gain the tools needed to incorporate these guiding principles into their lives with clarity and confidence. This approach fosters a culture of lifelong learning and growth, empowering individuals to navigate life's challenges with resilience and intention, enriching their lives with meaning and purpose.

8 JOURNEY REFLECTIONS AND APPLICATION

As individuals progress on their Mindsync journey, the "Journey Reflections and Application" phase becomes a pivotal stage. It invites them to pause, introspect, and apply the insights they have gained throughout their exploration of cognitive harmony. This phase is designed to foster a deeper understanding of personal growth, challenges faced, and the practical application of principles in real-life scenarios.

In the initial phase, individuals embark on a journey of self-reflection by deliberately pausing their daily routines. This intentional act serves as a crucial moment to explore the complex aspects of their minds, fostering a deeper understanding of their cognitive landscape and integrating Mindsync principles. Inspired by mindfulness traditions, participants are encouraged to cultivate present-moment awareness by finding a quiet space free from distractions. In this space, they engage in mindful observation of their thoughts, emotions, and overall state of being. Immersing themselves in the present moment lays the foundation for profound self-awareness and introspection. During this pause, they reflect on how their mindset has evolved since beginning the journey, examining shifts in perceptions, attitudes, and responses to challenges, as well as the principles that have facilitated growth and resilience. By acknowledging both progress and areas for further development, they nurture a mindset that embraces continuous learning and personal growth.

This phase also offers an opportunity to assess the use of mindtech tools in daily life. Participants reflect on how they have incorporated neurofeedback devices, training apps, or other technological innovations into their routines to enhance cognitive function. By evaluating the effectiveness of these tools and exploring new ways to leverage them, they optimize their journey toward cognitive harmony. In a tranquil space, they also explore their engagement with mindmax activities that foster creativity, whether by pursuing hobbies, challenging themselves intellectually, or engaging in other creative endeavors that positively impact their well-being. With a spirit of curiosity and exploration, participants develop a sense of fulfillment and purpose through these pursuits, gently reminding themselves to embrace self-discovery and transformation with an attitude of openness and acceptance.

In this phase, participants engage in a structured exploration of their personal growth since beginning the Mindsync journey. Using established reflective models like the Gibbs Cycle, individuals are guided through a comprehensive assessment of their cognitive evolution, allowing them to gain insights into their journey of self-discovery and transformation. They begin by reflecting on significant experiences throughout their journey, including challenges overcome, moments of insight, or impactful interactions. Revisiting these moments allows for a deeper understanding of the factors that have influenced their development and shaped their perceptions.

As they navigate key experiences, participants delve into the obstacles they faced and the accomplishments they achieved, embracing a growth mindset. By examining the strategies employed to overcome challenges, they recognize valuable qualities such as resilience, problem-solving abilities, and a capacity for growth. While assessing their growth, they are encouraged to identify recurring patterns and themes that manifest as consistent strengths, areas for improvement, or evolving perspectives. Recognizing these underlying themes provides clarity on the dynamics driving their cognitive journey. Building upon these reflections, participants have the opportunity to set milestones and goals for continued development. These goals encompass further exploration, new skills to cultivate, and behaviors to modify. By articulating clear objectives, participants establish a roadmap for ongoing growth toward cognitive harmony and self-fulfillment.

In this phase, participants also purposefully explore the challenges they have faced during their Mindsync journey. Through a structured examination of moments of difficulty, setbacks, and obstacles, individuals gain valuable insights and cultivate resilience. Inspired by Angela Duckworth's research on grit, they begin by identifying and reflecting on specific challenges, which may include failures, uncertainties, or personal struggles. Acknowledging these challenges and articulating them lays the foundation for deeper introspection and growth.

Drawing from the principles of grit, participants analyze their responses to challenges and the coping strategies they used. They reflect on their emotional reactions, problem-solving approaches, and support networks. Through this introspection, they extract lessons learned from overcoming obstacles and examine how these experiences have shaped their beliefs, attitudes, and behaviors. By reframing setbacks as opportunities for growth, they foster a mindset of adaptability. Duckworth's concept of grit highlights perseverance in the pursuit of long-term goals, recognizing that resilience is not just about bouncing back but also persisting through adversity. By cultivating grit, participants build the psychological resources needed to thrive in the face of life's challenges.

For individuals who have integrated mindtech tools into their journey, this phase involves a thorough exploration of the insights gained through technology-assisted self-awareness. Whether tracking emotional patterns, monitoring cognitive performance, or using neurofeedback devices, participants reflect on how these tools have facilitated a deeper understanding of their mental processes and overall well-being. They begin by reviewing specific tools they have incorporated into their routines, such as mindfulness apps, biofeedback training programs, or other technology-driven resources aimed at enhancing self-awareness.

Next, they examine the data generated by these tools, analyzing patterns and trends related to their mental states. Participants explore fluctuations in mood, stress levels, and physiological responses, identifying correlations that offer valuable insights into their cognitive functioning. By systematically examining this data, they gain a clearer understanding of the activities, environments, and triggers that influence their states and behaviors. Armed with this knowledge, participants can develop strategies for ongoing self-improvement and resilience, setting goals for personal growth informed by these insights. Finally, they integrate these insights into their routines, cultivating mindfulness and promoting well-being in their daily lives.

In this phase, participants take time to reflect on the profound impact of mindmax activities on their cognitive flexibility, creativity, and overall well-being. Drawing inspiration from Mihaly Csikszentmihalyi's flow theory, they explore how engaging in challenging activities has contributed to a more synchronized mindset and enhanced harmony. They begin by recalling and revisiting the challenges they have undertaken, such as creative endeavors, intellectual puzzles, or novel learning experiences that pushed their boundaries.

Through introspection, participants evaluate how these experiences have influenced their cognitive flexibility—the ability to adapt their thinking to various tasks and situations. They consider instances where they navigated complex problems, explored new perspectives, and embraced uncertainty with curiosity. Building upon the concept of flow, participants explore moments of creativity and immersion that led to inspired insights. They also reflect on the broader impact of these activities on their well-being, examining their sense of fulfillment, purpose, and vitality. By identifying areas of personal growth and celebrating milestones, participants continue their journey of self-discovery and self-actualization.

As participants transition from reflection to action, they focus on practically integrating the insights they have gained into their daily lives. With a deeper understanding of cognitive processes and strategies that support harmony, they implement actionable steps for sustained well-being and growth. They begin by refining their mindfulness practices, building upon foundational techniques explored during their journey. By incorporating additional techniques, such as mindful breathing exercises, body scans, or loving-kindness meditation, they strengthen their ability to stay present, manage stress, and enhance self-awareness in the face of life's challenges.

In exploring mindtech tools, participants establish regular check-ins to monitor progress. They integrate apps, training programs, and biofeedback devices into their routines, leveraging technology to make informed decisions about their mental health. These tools serve as valuable moments for self-assessment, allowing them to adjust priorities as needed to maintain harmony. Participants also commit to continuing engagement with mindmax activities that align with their personal goals and interests. Whether learning a new skill, exploring a hobby, or engaging in intellectual pursuits, they nurture their flexibility, creativity, and passion for lifelong learning.

As the journey reflections draw to a close, participants embark on a forward-looking segment aimed at charting their path for continued cognitive growth and development. Building on the insights gained, they use goal-setting theory to articulate clear, compelling goals that propel them toward harmony and well-being. Participants identify specific areas for growth, setting meaningful objectives that translate into actionable milestones. Each objective is clearly defined, with measurable criteria for success and target dates for accomplishment. By adhering to the SMART criteria—specific, measurable, achievable, relevant, and time-bound—participants create a roadmap for ongoing progress.

In the collaborative segment, facilitators organize a group sharing session where participants articulate their reflections, insights, and aspirations. Through open and inclusive dialogue, participants come together to share personal experiences, challenges, and breakthroughs, fostering a supportive community environment. Each individual is invited to share their journey, including key learnings and moments of growth. By listening attentively and validating others' experiences, participants demonstrate solidarity and support. This exchange serves as a platform for mutual learning and growth, with participants drawing inspiration from the diverse perspectives of their peers.

The sense of community extends beyond the session, as participants carry forward the spirit of connection in their ongoing pursuit of harmony. By nurturing these relationships, they create a lasting legacy of empowerment, resilience, and shared growth.

To effectively facilitate the "Journey Reflections and Application" phase, a variety of interactive workshops guided sessions are conducted, drawing from established reflective models psychological theories. These strategies tailored provide participants with tools support needed navigate their translate insights into actionable steps for continued growth cognitive harmony. designed engage in exercises discussions. Facilitators guide through structured activities that encourage introspection, self-exploration, dialogue. supportive environment share experiences, insights, challenges peers, fostering mutual learning growth. offer personalized coaching journey reflections. individualized feedback, guidance, encouragement help identify patterns, set goals, develop personal one-on-one interactions, receive address unique aspirations. Journaling incorporated document reflections, goals. prompts questions stimulate self-reflection deep introspection. By documenting thoughts gain clarity perspective on journey, facilitating process self-discovery Group discussions forum collaborative dialogue collective sense-making. lead key themes, challenges, emerging perspectives, support, exchange ideas, sense community shared within group. guidance experienced facilitators. have opportunity explore depth, feedback progress, co-create action plans coaching, clarity, direction, motivation pursue harmony goals confidence. Throughout encouraged tools, frameworks, resources SMART plans, track progress over time. translating concrete actions, empower themselves take ownership well-being make meaningful strides towards phase serves as pivotal stage Mindsync program, empowering realize self-awareness, resilience, ongoing goal-setting. engaging practices, setting receiving embark transformative growth, empowerment, flourishing.

- **Pausing to Reflect**

The stage of "Pausing to Reflect" within the Mindsync journey is a deliberate and introspective pause, providing individuals with a structured opportunity to examine their personal growth through the Mindsync lens. This phase emphasizes mindfulness, self-awareness, and a deep dive into the mindset, mindtech, and mindmax components that have contributed to individual development. At the outset of the journey, participants embark on a moment known as the "Mindfulness Pause." This foundational step draws inspiration from the teachings of mindfulness pioneer Jon Kabat-Zinn, guiding participants toward a state of heightened present-moment awareness.

During the Mindfulness Pause, individuals are encouraged to immerse themselves fully in the present, directing their attention to their breath, bodily sensations, and the subtle nuances of their immediate surroundings. Through intentional, non-judgmental observation, participants cultivate a deep sense of inner calm and clarity, anchoring themselves in the richness of the present experience. This moment serves as a pivotal precursor, setting the stage for subsequent exploration of personal growth within the Mindsync framework. By fostering a foundation of centeredness and presence, the Mindfulness Pause provides participants with fertile ground from which to embark on a journey of self-discovery, cognitive harmony, and transformative growth.

Guided by profound insights from Carol Dweck's groundbreaking mindset theory, participants engage in a reflective exercise titled "Reflecting Evolution." In this exploration, they delve into the intricate landscape of their own beliefs, attitudes, and perceptions, tracing their evolution throughout their engagement with Mindsync principles. Through a series of carefully crafted prompts and introspective exercises, they navigate the terrain of their inner landscape, probing the depths of consciousness to unveil shifts and transformations that have unfolded since beginning the journey. Participants contemplate their responses to challenges, their approach to learning and growth, and their resilience in the face of adversity, illuminating the process of self-reckoning and recognizing the patterns that have emerged over time—patterns rooted in positivity, adaptability, and forward momentum. By bearing witness to their evolution, participants gain insight into how their mindset has expanded, evolved, and blossomed.

In the segment "Assessing Mindtech Contributions," participants who have integrated mindtech tools into their well-being journey engage in a thoughtful examination of the impact of technology on their mental well-being. This entails a deep dive into the multifaceted contributions of these tools, including neurofeedback devices and training apps, which have enhanced self-awareness and holistic development. Through introspection, participants contemplate how these tools have served as catalysts for heightened insight. By leveraging these devices, they gain valuable information about their emotional patterns, cognitive performance, and overall well-being. Real-time feedback mechanisms offer a window into the intricacies of their minds, enabling them to identify areas of strength, challenge, and opportunity. Furthermore, mindtech apps provide tailored exercises and challenges designed to stimulate cognitive function and enhance mental acuity. Participants reflect on how these tools have empowered them to sharpen their focus, improve memory, and build greater resilience. By engaging in structured regimens, they harness the power of technology to optimize their potential and foster a sense of empowerment and agency.

The "Mindmax Moments of Growth" phase is inspired by Mihaly Csikszentmihalyi's renowned flow theory. In this phase, mindmax activities serve as catalysts for immersion, creativity, and personal expansion. Participants reflect on instances where they found themselves fully immersed in challenging activities, transcending mundane distractions and achieving a state of focused engagement. These moments of flow serve as powerful reminders of the potential for innovation, cognitive flexibility, and peak performance. Participants recount the exhilarating rush of being "in the zone," where time seems to stand still and they meet challenges with effortless mastery. Whether through artistic endeavors, intellectual pursuits, or physical feats, these experiences are vivid reminders of the boundless potential each individual can tap into to achieve deep fulfillment. Moreover, these moments become focal points for recognizing and understanding personal strengths and passions, offering further opportunities for exploration. By reflecting on the conditions and circumstances that fostered flow, participants gain deeper insights into the factors that contribute to their flourishing, empowering them to create environments and engage in activities conducive to ongoing growth.

In the pivotal stage of "Identification of Key Learnings," participants embark on a deliberate process of distilling profound insights from their reflections across their cognitive harmony journey. Through introspection and analysis, individuals uncover overarching themes and invaluable lessons that have emerged from exploring mindset, mindtech, and mindmax experiences. By identifying fundamental shifts in attitudes, beliefs, and approaches to challenges, participants recognize the transformative power of adopting a growth-oriented mindset, embracing resilience, and cultivating a positive outlook in the face of life's challenges. Delving into their reflections on mindtech, they assess the impact of technology on their well-being, including how tools such as neurofeedback devices and training apps have empowered them to enhance self-awareness, optimize performance, and foster greater mental resilience. Furthermore, they reflect on their mindmax experiences, recognizing moments of immersion, creativity, and expansion that propelled them toward optimal performance and fulfillment. Through this process of identification and distillation, participants consolidate their growth journey into tangible lessons that can be applied to various aspects of life. These learnings serve as guiding principles, providing clarity, direction, and inspiration for continued development and self-actualization.

In the pivotal phase of "Goal Alignment with Personal Growth," individuals engage in a deliberate process of assessing their growth and aligning insights with future aspirations. This transformative journey involves setting intentional, growth-oriented objectives that are deeply rooted in the insights gleaned from their Mindsync experience, leveraging the momentum gained to propel themselves forward on their journey toward cognitive harmony. Participants first conduct a comprehensive evaluation of their growth, drawing upon reflections gathered throughout their journey. They identify areas of strength, opportunities for improvement, and overarching themes that have emerged from exploring mindset, mindtech, and mindmax experiences. With a deep understanding of their trajectory, they then set intentional goals. These goals are informed by their aspirations for continued development and cognitive harmony. Importantly, participants leverage the fuel of newfound clarity, resilience, and empowerment garnered from their experiences, moving forward with confidence and determination. By establishing a roadmap for their lives, these goals serve as beacons of inspiration, guiding participants toward meaningful actions that enrich their lives and unlock their fullest potential.

- **Mindsync Beyond the Self**

Moving "Beyond the Self," Mindsync extends its transformative potential to practical applications in professional and educational settings. This phase explores how the principles of mindset, mindtech, and mindmax can be harnessed for enhanced performance, collaboration, and creativity in these environments.

In the immersive workshop on "Professional Setting Integration," participants are equipped with the knowledge and skills needed to seamlessly integrate Mindsync principles into their professional lives, unlocking a pathway to enhanced productivity, resilience, and innovation. Drawing upon a holistic approach that encompasses mindset, mindtech, and mindmax strategies, the workshop provides practical tools and techniques to thrive in professional endeavors. At the core of this approach are mindset shifts that cultivate resilience and adaptability in the face of challenges. Through guided exercises and discussions, participants learn to embrace a growth-oriented mindset, reframing setbacks as opportunities for growth and learning. By cultivating a resilient mental attitude, individuals are better able to navigate the complexities of the professional landscape with confidence and grace.

Participants are also introduced to a suite of mindtech tools designed to enhance decision-making and productivity in the workplace. From neurofeedback devices that provide real-time insights into cognitive performance to training apps that sharpen focus and agility, participants learn how to leverage technology as a catalyst for success. By incorporating these tools into their daily routines, they can optimize their performance and make informed decisions with greater clarity and precision. Finally, the workshop explores strategies to promote creativity and innovation in professional settings. Through experiential exercises, participants tap into their creative potential, overcome mental blocks, and generate innovative solutions to complex problems. By fostering a culture of experimentation, organizations can unlock new opportunities for differentiation in an increasingly competitive market. Throughout the workshop, real-world case studies and simulations are used to demonstrate the application of these principles in various contexts. Participants have the opportunity to apply their newfound knowledge in simulated scenarios, gaining valuable insights into how Mindsync principles can be effectively integrated into day-to-day work.

In the realm of professional settings, Mindsync champions the cultivation of a growth culture, drawing inspiration from the seminal works of organizational psychologist Carol Dweck. Through a series of interactive sessions and guided discussions, individuals embark on a transformative journey to explore the profound impact of fostering a collective growth mindset within their organizations. At the heart of this endeavor lies a deep dive into the principles of Dweck's theory. Participants are introduced to the concept of a growth mindset, which emphasizes the belief that abilities and intelligence can be developed through dedication, effort, and resilience. They learn to distinguish between a growth mindset, characterized by a willingness to embrace challenges and learn from failures, and a fixed mindset, marked by a fear of failure and a belief in innate limitations. As participants delve deeper into these nuances, they uncover the potential of a growth mindset for enhancing team collaboration, adaptability, and overall success. By fostering a commitment to growth, organizations can create an environment of trust and continuous improvement, enabling teams to tackle challenges with confidence. Through exercises and case studies, participants witness firsthand the tangible benefits of cultivating a growth culture, discovering how embracing a growth mindset empowers individuals to take ownership of their development, seek new opportunities for learning, and contribute to innovation and excellence.

In the realm of educational settings, Mindsync principles serve as a catalyst for transforming learning experiences and nurturing cognitive development. Through comprehensive exploration of innovative teaching methodologies and immersive strategies, educators are empowered to integrate mindtech tools and mindmax activities into their curriculum design and classroom practices. At the forefront of this phase is the integration of diverse teaching methods that cater to various learning styles and foster personalized educational experiences. Participants are introduced to a range of mindtech tools, from training apps to neurofeedback devices, which can be seamlessly incorporated into lesson plans to accommodate individual needs and preferences. By leveraging technology as a tool for enhancing engagement and optimizing learning outcomes, educators create dynamic and interactive environments that inspire curiosity, creativity, and critical thinking.

Furthermore, participants explore the transformative potential of promoting an engaging learning environment. Through hands-on exercises, collaborative projects, and experiential learning activities, students are encouraged to tap into their creative potential, develop problem-solving skills, and cultivate a growth mindset. By integrating mindmax activities into the curriculum, educators provide opportunities for students to experience flow states, where they become fully immersed and deeply engaged in the learning process. This leads to enhanced motivation, satisfaction, and retention of information. Throughout this phase, educators are equipped with strategies and best practices for implementing Mindsync principles in ways that align learning objectives with classroom activities, fostering a culture of collaboration, exploration, and continuous growth.

Mindsync advocates for the adoption of collaborative problem-solving methodologies across professional and educational domains, recognizing the transformative impact of harnessing collective intelligence and diverse perspectives to address complex challenges. Through a multifaceted approach that integrates mindset shifts, mindtech tools, and mindmax strategies, both teams and students are empowered to cultivate a culture of collaboration, innovation, and continuous improvement. At the heart of this approach lies the convergence of growth mindsets. Participants are encouraged to embrace the richness of diversity, leveraging varied perspectives, backgrounds, and experiences to generate novel insights and innovative solutions. By fostering an inclusive environment where all voices are valued and heard, teams can unlock their potential to overcome even the most daunting challenges with agility and creativity.

In addition, the power of collective intelligence is augmented by the strategic utilization of mindtech tools for data-driven decision-making. By leveraging advanced technologies such as data analytics, artificial intelligence, and predictive modeling, participants gain access to valuable insights that enable them to make informed decisions with confidence and precision. These tools serve as invaluable resources for identifying trends, patterns, and opportunities, empowering individuals and teams to navigate complexity and uncertainty with clarity and insight. Furthermore, this approach is enriched by the integration of creative problem-solving strategies. Through experimentation, exploration, and imagination, participants learn to think outside the box, challenge conventional wisdom, and develop innovative solutions to pressing problems. Brainstorming sessions, design thinking workshops, and simulation exercises provide structured frameworks for unlocking creativity and igniting a spirit of innovation within both classrooms and organizations.

Central to the Mindsync philosophy is the relentless pursuit of performance optimization, both at individual and collective levels. This multifaceted approach encompasses aligning personal aspirations with organizational objectives, harnessing the power of mindtech for data analytics, and integrating mindmax practices to enhance cognitive capabilities. The overarching goal is to cultivate an environment that fosters sustained harmony among individuals and teams, propelling them toward peak performance and success. At the core of performance optimization lies the alignment of personal and organizational goals. Participants are encouraged to reflect on their values, identifying areas where their personal mission aligns with the objectives of their organization. By establishing a sense of purpose and clarity of direction, participants are empowered to channel their efforts into meaningful contributions that drive collective success.

Moreover, performance optimization is augmented by the strategic utilization of data analytics. By leveraging advanced technologies such as machine learning and predictive modeling, organizations gain valuable insights into team performance metrics, enabling them to identify strengths, areas for improvement, and opportunities for growth. These tools serve as invaluable resources for optimizing decision-making, enhancing productivity, and fostering a culture of accountability and continuous improvement. Furthermore, performance optimization is enriched through the integration of mindmax practices. Through mindfulness exercises, cognitive training regimens, and creative problem-solving techniques, teams are equipped with strategies to optimize cognitive function, maintain focus and concentration, and mitigate stress and burnout. These practices serve as catalysts for unlocking human potential, fostering resilience, and nurturing a culture of innovation and excellence within organizations.

To enable the effective implementation of Mindsync Beyond the Self, customized training programs and workshops have been meticulously crafted. These sessions are specifically designed to empower professionals and educators with the knowledge and skills necessary to seamlessly integrate mindset shifts, mindtech tools, and mindmax strategies into their respective environments. At the core of these training programs lies a comprehensive exploration of mindset shifts. Participants are guided through an immersive journey to understand the transformative power of cultivating a growth-oriented mindset. They learn to challenge limiting beliefs, embrace resilience in the face of challenges, and foster a culture of continuous learning and improvement within organizations or classrooms.

Additionally, participants delve into the practical application of mindtech tools, gaining hands-on experience with cutting-edge technologies that enhance cognitive performance and well-being. Through interactive demonstrations and exercises, participants learn how to leverage neurofeedback devices, training apps, and other tools to optimize decision-making, productivity, and overall health in professional and educational settings. Furthermore, the workshops explore strategies to promote creativity, innovation, and engagement. Through role-playing scenarios and collaborative activities, participants create dynamic learning experiences that inspire curiosity, foster collaboration, and unlock the full potential of individuals and teams. Throughout these workshops, emphasis is placed on experiential practice. Participants are actively engaged in simulations, case studies, and exercises that mirror real-world challenges, allowing them to apply their newfound skills in a supportive environment.

The final culmination of the "Pausing to Reflect" and "Mindsync Beyond the Self" phases extends far beyond individual cognitive harmony, reaching into the realms of professional and educational ecosystems. It represents a profound realization of the transformative potential inherent in applying Mindsync principles to personal growth, creating a ripple effect that reverberates throughout entire communities. As individuals transition from the introspective phase of self-discovery to the practical phase of application, they begin to recognize the interconnectedness between their well-being and the broader contexts of their environments. By applying mindset shifts, mindtech integration, and mindmax strategies in these settings, participants unlock a new dimension of collective harmony that transcends individual achievements.

In professional ecosystems, this manifests as an environment of innovation, resilience, and continuous improvement. Teams harness the synergistic power of diverse perspectives, leveraging mindtech tools for data-driven decision-making and fostering creativity and adaptability. This collaborative synergy fuels a culture where challenges are met with curiosity and ingenuity, and setbacks are viewed as opportunities for growth and learning. The pursuit of excellence propels organizations toward new heights of success, driving sustainable competitive advantage.

Similarly, in educational settings, Mindsync principles create a dynamic environment for learning and growth. Educators integrate these principles into curriculum design and classroom practices, empowering students to cultivate a growth mindset, engage in personalized learning experiences, and participate in activities that enhance cognitive abilities. This holistic approach to education fosters curiosity, exploration, and lifelong learning, inspiring students to think critically, collaborate creatively, and adapt to an ever-changing world.

9 CHALLENGES AND CONSIDERATIONS

As Mindsync ventures into the integration of mindtech tools to enhance cognitive well-being, it encounters a complex ethical landscape. The utilization of technology for mental health introduces numerous considerations, from safeguarding privacy and ensuring data security to responsibly employing neurotechnologies. These challenges underscore the importance of conducting a thorough and thoughtful exploration of the dimensions inherent in the implementation of mindtech within a well-being framework.

In the realm of integrating mindtech tools, one critical consideration is privacy. As users engage with these platforms, they entrust them with highly personal cognitive data. This trust raises significant concerns about how sensitive information is handled, stored, and protected. In response, Mindsync takes a proactive approach, recognizing the paramount importance of safeguarding user privacy. To effectively address these concerns, Mindsync meticulously evaluates and implements stringent data protection measures. This involves a comprehensive examination of the entire data lifecycle, from collection to storage and eventual disposal. By adhering to industry best practices and standards, Mindsync endeavors to ensure that data is shielded from unauthorized access, breaches, and misuse. In shaping its approach to privacy, Mindsync draws inspiration from established ethical frameworks such as Fair Information Practice Principles. These principles serve as guiding beacons, informing the development of privacy policies that are not only legally compliant but also ethically sound. Central to this is the core value of confidentiality, with Mindsync committing to treat all user data with the utmost sensitivity and respect. Additionally, Mindsync places a strong emphasis on ensuring informed consent for the utilization of user data, providing clear and transparent disclosures about the purposes for which data is being collected, how it will be used, and the measures in place to protect it. By empowering users to make informed choices about their data, Mindsync seeks to foster a relationship built on trust and transparency.

In the Mindsync initiative, the security of cognitive data stands as a paramount concern. Drawing inspiration from cybersecurity principles and ethical hacking practices, Mindsync adopts a comprehensive approach to ensure the utmost protection of user information. At the forefront of Mindsync's strategy is the implementation of cutting-edge encryption technologies. These technologies are deployed to encrypt and secure data at every stage of its lifecycle—during transmission, storage, and retrieval. By leveraging state-of-the-art protocols and robust measures, Mindsync creates a fortified barrier against unauthorized access and breaches. Moreover, Mindsync recognizes the responsibility to proactively mitigate potential risks. To this end, it conducts regular audits and vulnerability assessments to identify and address any weaknesses in its systems and protocols. By staying vigilant and proactive, Mindsync aims to fortify its defenses against emerging threats and vulnerabilities, thereby ensuring the integrity and confidentiality of user data. In the event of a security incident, Mindsync is committed to transparent communication with users. This includes promptly notifying affected individuals of breaches or incidents, providing timely updates on the situation, and offering guidance on necessary steps. By fostering open channels of communication, Mindsync seeks to maintain the trust and confidence of its users while demonstrating an unwavering commitment to their privacy and security.

Within the realm of neuroenhancements, Mindsync addresses ethical considerations inspired by Veljko Dubljević's insightful work on the "Ethics of Neuroenhancements." These dimensions are carefully scrutinized to ensure that the integration of neurotechnologies is conducted responsibly and ethically. Mindsync places a strong emphasis on the responsible use of neurotechnologies, recognizing the potential implications of enhancing cognitive abilities. While the pursuit of enhancement holds promise for improving individual performance and well-being, Mindsync is vigilant in safeguarding against any unintended consequences that may arise. Central to Mindsync's approach is a steadfast commitment to upholding autonomy. This means ensuring that neuroenhancements are pursued with full respect for an individual's right to self-determination and agency. Mindsync is cognizant of the imperative to avoid coercive or involuntary enhancements, prioritizing the autonomy and dignity of each individual above all else. Furthermore, Mindsync is deeply mindful of the potential to exacerbate existing social inequalities. In light of this, it takes proactive steps to mitigate these risks and ensure that the benefits of neuroenhancements are equitably distributed. This includes promoting accessibility, advocating for equitable access to resources and opportunities, and fostering dialogue around societal implications.

In the pursuit of sustained cognitive harmony, one of the fundamental challenges lies in cultivating a growth mindset—a mindset that embraces challenges as opportunities for growth and views setbacks as stepping stones to success. Drawing extensively from the groundbreaking research of psychologist Carol Dweck on mindset, Mindsync is committed to addressing this challenge head-on, taking deliberate and strategic steps to empower individuals on their journey toward adopting a growth-oriented perspective.

Central to Mindsync's approach is the recognition of the profound impact that mindset can have on cognitive well-being and overall life satisfaction. Through Dweck's research, Mindsync gains valuable insights into the dynamics of fixed and growth mindsets, understanding how these mindsets shape individuals' responses to challenges, failures, and successes. Armed with this knowledge, Mindsync designs tailored strategies and interventions aimed at nurturing a growth mindset among its participants. These strategies encompass a multifaceted approach, addressing the cognitive, emotional, and behavioral aspects of transformation. At the cognitive level, Mindsync encourages individuals to challenge their existing beliefs and assumptions about intelligence, talent, and potential. Through interactive workshops, reflective exercises, and reframing techniques, participants are guided to recognize the malleability of abilities and the power of effort and perseverance in achieving success. Emotionally, Mindsync provides a supportive environment where individuals feel safe to embrace vulnerability and explore their limitations. Through empathetic coaching, constructive feedback, and encouragement, participants are empowered to confront fears and insecurities, building resilience and self-confidence in the process. Behaviorally, Mindsync facilitates opportunities for participants to practice and embody growth mindset principles in their daily lives. From setting challenging goals to seeking out feedback, adopting a "yet" mentality, and embracing the learning process, participants are encouraged to take proactive steps toward personal and professional growth. Moreover, Mindsync fosters a culture of continuous improvement, where mistakes are reframed as learning experiences and failures are viewed as temporary setbacks on the path to success. By celebrating progress and incremental achievements, Mindsync reinforces the belief that the journey, not the destination, is what matters, and that every challenge presents an opportunity for development.

Within the framework of the Mindsync program, specialized workshops are meticulously crafted to confront and overcome fixed mindsets—those entrenched beliefs that hinder personal growth and resilience. These thoughtfully designed workshops cater to individuals who may exhibit tendencies to resist change or perceive challenges as insurmountable hurdles. At the heart of these workshops lies an interactive and immersive learning experience. Through a blend of experiential exercises, group discussions, and real-world case studies, participants are guided on a journey of self-discovery and transformation. They delve into the underlying mechanisms of their mindsets, unraveling the cognitive patterns that perpetuate a stagnant mindset. Central to this process is the cultivation of self-awareness. Participants are encouraged to introspect and reflect upon their own thought processes and beliefs, gaining insight into how fixed mindsets may be manifesting in their lives. By recognizing and acknowledging these patterns, they lay the groundwork for meaningful growth. Furthermore, participants are equipped with practical strategies and tools to challenge and transcend fixed mindsets. They learn to reframe setbacks as opportunities, embracing a newfound sense of resilience and determination. Through exercises and role-playing scenarios, participants practice applying these strategies in real-life situations, solidifying their ability to navigate adversity with grace and tenacity. Importantly, the workshops foster a supportive and collaborative environment where participants feel empowered to share their experiences and insights openly. By engaging in dialogue and exchanging perspectives, participants draw strength from one another, forging connections and fostering collective solidarity.

The cultivation of a growth mindset is deeply intertwined with building resilience. Mindsync draws on insights from positive psychology and resilience studies to equip individuals with the psychological tools needed to bounce back from setbacks. By fostering adaptability and resilience, Mindsync transforms challenges into opportunities, helping individuals see them as stepping stones rather than obstacles. Understanding the complexity and unique qualities of each person's cognitive world, Mindsync creates customized growth plans tailored to meet their specific needs and ambitions. These well-thought-out plans go beyond simply addressing challenges, taking a broader view of an individual's life. By incorporating elements such as personal values, life circumstances, and long-term goals, Mindsync ensures its strategies for growth are not only effective but also deeply meaningful and impactful.

Central to this approach is the belief that well-being is woven into the broader fabric of life, touching on multiple areas like relationships, career, health, and personal fulfillment. Mindsync's growth plans are crafted to reflect this holistic outlook, providing a comprehensive guide for individuals to navigate their personal journeys. The development process starts with an in-depth assessment of an individual's strengths, needs, and goals. Through detailed interviews, self-assessments, and psychological evaluations, Mindsync gathers valuable insights to build a well-rounded profile, highlighting key areas for growth. Mindsync also examines the broader context of the individual's life—considering their goals, motivations, and environmental factors—to understand how these elements interact with their overall well-being. Using this assessment, Mindsync collaborates with the individual to co-create a personalized growth plan, which may include various interventions like mindset adjustments, mindfulness practices, cognitive exercises, and lifestyle changes. A strong focus is placed on enhancing the relevance and impact of these interventions by aligning them with the individual's core values and encouraging a deep sense of purpose. In this way, Mindsync empowers people to embrace growth, build resilience, and reach their full potential.

Within the Mindsync framework, the journey toward optimal living recognizes the balance between aspirational ideals and the practicalities of real-life limitations. As individuals strive to lead lives marked by continuous learning, personal growth, and enriching experiences, they inevitably face challenges like limited time, external demands, and competing priorities. This segment offers a nuanced examination of practical strategies to help maintain this delicate balance, drawing on Mihaly Csikszentmihalyi's influential work, *Flow: The Psychology of Optimal Experience*. Central to this framework is the acknowledgment that optimal living is multifaceted, encompassing not only personal development and satisfaction but also the practicalities of everyday life. While individuals may aspire to fully immerse themselves in activities that evoke a state of flow, they must also manage the constraints on their time and energy. This blend of aspirations and realities forms the foundation of Mindsync's approach to optimal living.

Drawing inspiration from the concept of flow—the state of being fully immersed in an activity, with intense focus, intrinsic motivation, and a sense of heightened enjoyment—Mindsync workshops explore ways to foster flow moments within the context of daily life. Participants learn how to identify and align their passions, strengths, and values, optimizing their energy to maximize opportunities for meaningful experiences amidst competing demands. Moreover, Mindsync emphasizes the importance of cultivating a mindset of adaptability and resilience in the face of external pressures. Participants are encouraged to embrace imperfection and uncertainty, recognizing that optimal living is not about achieving perfection but rather embracing the journey of self-discovery. By adopting a flexible and resilient mindset, individuals can navigate setbacks with grace, maintaining equilibrium as they navigate the ebbs and flows of life. Furthermore, Mindsync provides practical tools and techniques for managing competing priorities effectively, aligning actions with values and goals. Participants are guided to set clear priorities, establish boundaries, and delegate tasks when necessary, empowering them to make intentional choices that honor their cognitive well-being and overall fulfillment. Recognizing the pervasive challenge of time constraints in modern life, Mindsync offers invaluable guidance on effective time management strategies tailored to the demands of busy schedules. Drawing inspiration from principles and insights in behavioral economics, participants embark on a journey to optimize their time allocation, with particular emphasis on prioritizing activities that nurture cognitive well-being. Within these workshops, participants are guided through a comprehensive exploration of techniques designed to enhance productivity, reduce stress, and maximize cognitive harmony. They delve into strategies such as prioritization, goal setting, and task batching, learning how to identify and focus on high-impact activities that align with their well-being goals. Prioritization lies at the heart of this framework. Participants learn to discern between urgent and important tasks, allocating their time and energy to those that yield the greatest benefits. By adopting a strategic approach to time management, individuals can ensure that activities that nurture well-being receive the attention they deserve amidst competing obligations.

Furthermore, Mindsync workshops leverage insights from behavioral economics to deepen participants' understanding of their time utilization patterns and decision-making biases. Participants explore concepts such as temporal discounting and the planning fallacy, gaining valuable insights into the psychological factors that influence behavior. Armed with this knowledge, participants are empowered to make more informed choices and overcome common obstacles to effective time management. Moreover, Mindsync emphasizes the importance of creating structured routines and systems that support well-being goals within the constraints of busy schedules. Participants are encouraged to design daily schedules and habits that prioritize mindfulness practices, cognitive exercises, and self-care rituals. By integrating these routines, participants foster cognitive harmony and resilience in the face of time constraints.

Mindsync workshops also provide individuals with tools to effectively manage external pressures stemming from various sources such as work demands, societal expectations, or personal responsibilities. Recognizing the pervasive impact of these pressures on cognitive harmony, Mindsync offers comprehensive guidance on stress management techniques, assertiveness training, and effective communication skills. In these workshops, participants delve into strategies designed to help them cope with and alleviate the pressures of daily life. They learn practical techniques such as mindfulness meditation, deep breathing exercises, and time management skills to mitigate the effects of stress on their well-being. By developing resilience and adaptive coping mechanisms, participants are better equipped to navigate challenging situations and maintain harmony in the face of stressors.

Moreover, Mindsync workshops focus on assertiveness training as a means of empowering individuals to assert their needs, boundaries, and priorities amidst external pressures. Participants learn how to communicate their thoughts, feelings, and preferences in a clear and respectful manner, thereby reducing the likelihood of feeling overwhelmed or disempowered by external demands. Through role-playing exercises, participants gain confidence in advocating for themselves and prioritizing their well-being in various contexts. Additionally, effective communication is emphasized as essential to navigating external pressures while preserving cognitive harmony. Participants learn active listening, empathetic communication, and conflict resolution skills, enabling them to foster positive relationships and manage interpersonal dynamics effectively. By honing these skills, participants can navigate external pressures with grace and assertiveness, while promoting mutual understanding in their interactions with others.

In its quest to promote cognitive well-being, Mindsync delves into practical strategies that individuals can employ to integrate optimal living principles seamlessly into their daily lives. At the forefront of this exploration lies the recognition of well-being as a fundamental cornerstone for attaining optimal experiences and overall fulfillment. Mindsync underscores the critical importance of prioritizing well-being, emphasizing that it serves as the linchpin for achieving a sense of balance, purpose, and vitality in everyday life.

Central to this pursuit is the cultivation of intentional choices and activities that nurture well-being. Mindsync encourages individuals to mindfully select actions and behaviors that nourish and sustain their mental health. This may involve activities that enhance mental clarity, emotional resilience, and psychological well-being while minimizing exposure to stressors and distractions that detract from cognitive harmony. By making conscious choices that are aligned with their values, participants cultivate a sense of agency and empowerment in shaping their experiences.

Additionally, Mindsync advocates for the incorporation of mindfulness practices into daily routines as a means of nurturing cognitive well-being. These practices, such as meditation, deep breathing exercises, and mindful movement, offer powerful tools for cultivating present-moment awareness, reducing stress, and enhancing cognitive function. By carving out moments for mindfulness amidst the hustle and bustle of life, participants cultivate inner calm and resilience, laying the foundation for sustained cognitive well-being.

Furthermore, Mindsync emphasizes the importance of creating a supportive environment that fosters well-being. This involves surrounding oneself with positive relationships, engaging in meaningful social interactions, and cultivating environments that promote safety and connection. By nurturing supportive relationships and environments, individuals create a conducive backdrop for flourishing and thriving in all aspects of life.

10 **MINDSYNC VISION**

Looking ahead, Mindsync envisions a future where neurofeedback evolves with unparalleled sophistication. Building on rapid advancements in neuroscience, we foresee neurofeedback technologies becoming increasingly personalized and precise, enabling individuals to gain deeper insights into their cognitive patterns and supporting tailored interventions for enhanced mental well-being.

At the heart of this vision is the development of adaptive technologies. Inspired by precision medicine, Mindsync envisions solutions crafted to meet each individual's unique cognitive needs. Leveraging advanced algorithms and machine learning, these programs will evolve in real-time, providing bespoke experiences that optimize mental harmony.

Mindsync also plans to introduce personalized mindfulness exercises that adapt to individual stressors, challenges, and goals. By integrating advanced neurotechnology devices, we aim to enable tailored neurofeedback and stimulation protocols that fine-tune cognitive function, enhance memory, and improve attention.

Our commitment extends to fostering creativity through initiatives like immersive VR experiences, "mindmax" activities, and gamified challenges that promote exploration and innovation. By incorporating these elements, Mindsync aims to foster continuous growth, creativity, and engagement, helping individuals unlock their full potential.

Ethical considerations are central to our approach. Mindsync is dedicated to developing technologies that respect user autonomy and privacy, with robust ethical frameworks guiding our innovations. We aim to ensure individuals retain control over their cognitive well-being and make informed decisions about their use of technology.

Mindsync's vision goes beyond personal enhancement to include education and the workplace. By integrating cognitive well-being into school curricula and promoting growth mindset cultures at work, we strive to nurture environments that support mental clarity, resilience, and holistic development. We believe in empowering educators and employers alike to prioritize well-being, fostering nurturing, innovative, and productive communities.

Exploring the potential of brain-computer interfaces (BCIs), Mindsync is focused on transforming how we interact with technology. BCIs provide real-time monitoring of brain activity, enabling adaptive and personalized training regimens, immersive mindmax experiences, and new opportunities to enhance cognitive engagement.

Ultimately, Mindsync's journey is about embracing growth, adaptability, and creativity. By adhering to ethical principles and integrating cutting-edge mindtech, we envision a future where personalized cognitive pathways lead to well-being, inclusivity, and empowerment at both individual and societal levels.

11 APPENDIX

References:
1. Descartes R. *Meditations on First Philosophy*. Paris: Michael Soly; 1641.
2. Darwin C. *On the Origin of Species by Means of Natural Selection*. London: John Murray; 1859.
3. Freud S. *The Interpretation of Dreams*. Leipzig: F. Deuticke; 1899.
4. Chomsky N. *Syntactic Structures*. The Hague: Mouton; 1957.
5. Nagel T. What is it like to be a bat? *Philosophical Review*. 1974;83(4):435-450.
6. Bandura A. *Social Learning Theory*. Englewood Cliffs, NJ: Prentice-Hall; 1977.
7. Vygotsky LS. *Mind in Society: The Development of Higher Psychological Processes*. Cambridge, MA: Harvard University Press; 1978.
8. Hofstede G. *Culture's Consequences: International Differences in Work-Related Values*. Beverly Hills, CA: Sage Publications; 1980.
9. Churchland P. *Neurophilosophy: Toward a Unified Science of the Mind-Brain*. Cambridge, MA: MIT Press; 1986.
10. Cohen S, Wills TA. Stress, social support, and the buffering hypothesis. *Psychol Bull*. 1985;98(2):310-357.
11. Donald M. *Origins of the Modern Mind: Three Stages in the Evolution of Culture and Cognition*. Cambridge, MA: Harvard University Press; 1991.
12. Cosmides L, Tooby J. Cognitive adaptations for social exchange. *J Theor Biol*. 1992;155(2):173-204.
13. Dunbar RI. Neocortex size as a constraint on group size in primates. *J Hum Evol*. 1992;22(6):469-493.
14. Lucy JA. Linguistic relativity. *Annu Rev Anthropol*. 1992;21:273-302.
15. Pylyshyn ZW. The role of cognitive architecture in theories of cognition. *Behav Brain Sci*. 1995;18(1):151-205.
16. Dennett DC. *Darwin's Dangerous Idea: Evolution and the Meanings of Life*. New York: Simon & Schuster; 1995.
17. Sperber D. *Explaining Culture: A Naturalistic Approach*. Oxford: Blackwell Publishing; 1996.
18. Chalmers D. *The Conscious Mind: In Search of a Fundamental Theory*. Oxford: Oxford University Press; 1996.
19. Pinker S. *How the Mind Works*. New York: W.W. Norton & Company; 1997.
20. Deacon TW. *The Symbolic Species: The Co-evolution of Language and the Brain*. New York: W.W. Norton & Company; 1997.

21. Tomasello M. *The Cultural Origins of Human Cognition*. Cambridge, MA: Harvard University Press; 1999.

22. Miller GF. *The Mating Mind: How Sexual Choice Shaped the Evolution of Human Nature*. New York: Doubleday; 2000.

23. Geary DC. Evolution and proximate expression of human paternal investment. *Psychol Bull*. 2000;126(1):55-77.

24. Gangestad SW, Simpson JA. The evolution of human mating: trade-offs and strategic pluralism. *Behav Brain Sci*. 2000;23(4):573-644.

25. Roco MC, Bainbridge WS. Converging technologies for improving human performance. *J Nanoscience Nanotechnol*. 2001;1(1):1-16.

26. Wilson M. Six views of embodied cognition. *Psychon Bull Rev*. 2002;9(4):625-636.

27. Seymour NE, Gallagher AG, Roman SA, O'Brien MK, Bansal VK, Andersen DK, et al. Virtual reality training improves operating room performance: results of a randomized, double-blinded study. *Ann Surg*. 2002;236(4):458-463.

28. Loehr J, Schwartz T. *The Power of Full Engagement: Managing Energy, Not Time, Is the Key to High Performance and Personal Renewal*. New York: Free Press; 2003.

29. Grant H, Dweck CS. Clarifying achievement goals and their impact. *J Pers Soc Psychol*. 2003;85(3):541-553.

30. Arbib MA, editor. *The Handbook of Brain Theory and Neural Networks*. 2nd ed. Cambridge, MA: MIT Press; 2004.

31. Mangels JA, Butterfield B, Lamb J, Good C, Dweck CS. Why do beliefs about intelligence influence learning success? A social cognitive neuroscience model. *Soc Cogn Affect Neurosci*. 2006;1(2):75-86.

32. Barsalou LW. Grounded cognition: past, present, and future. *Annu Rev Psychol*. 2008;59:617-645.

33. Tomasello M. *Origins of Human Communication*. Cambridge, MA: MIT Press; 2008.

34. Ashton K. That 'Internet of Things' thing. *RFID J* [Internet]. 2009 [cited 2024 Oct 24].

35. Goodfellow I, Bengio Y, Courville A. *Deep Learning*. Cambridge, MA: MIT Press; 2016.

36. Kotler S, Wheal J. *Stealing Fire: How Silicon Valley, the Navy SEALs, and Maverick Scientists Are Revolutionizing the Way We Live and Work*. New York: Dey Street Books; 2017.

37. Riva G, Baños RM. Virtual reality: a new methodological approach for personal and spiritual transformation? *Front Psychol*. 2016;7:1589.

38. Firth J, Torous J, Nicholas J, Carney R, Rosenbaum S, Sarris J. The efficacy of smartphone-based mental health interventions for depressive symptoms: a meta-analysis of randomized controlled trials.

World Psychiatry. 2017;16(3):287-298.

39. Choudhury T, Larson K, Pentland A. Reality mining: sensing complex social systems. *Pers Ubiquit Comput.* 2009;11(5):363-381.

40. Li W, Zhang Z, Chen Y, Luo J. Deep learning for generic object detection: a survey. *Int J Comput Vis.* 2019;128(2):261-318.

41. McGonigal J. *The Upside of Stress: Why Stress Is Good for You, and How to Get Good at It.* New York: Avery; 2015.

42. Duckworth AL. *Grit: The Power of Passion and Perseverance.* New York: Scribner; 2016.

43. Anguera JA, Gunning FM, Areán PA. Improving late-life depression and cognitive control through the use of an emotional-based decision-making tool: A pilot experiment using the iPad. *J Affect Disord.* 2013;150(3):711-717.

44. Erickson KI, Voss MW, Prakash RS, Basak C, Szabo A, Chaddock L, et al. Exercise training increases the size of the hippocampus and improves memory. *Proc Natl Acad Sci USA.* 2011;108(7):3017-3022.

45. Tang YY, Tang R, Posner MI. Mindfulness meditation improves emotion regulation and reduces drug abuse. *Drug Alcohol Depend.* 2015;163:25-32.

46. Google. Digital Wellbeing [Internet]. 2021. Available from: https://wellbeing.google

47. Meta (formerly Facebook). Exploring the Future of Neural Interfaces: CTRL-Labs and Beyond [Internet]. 2024. Available from: https://about.fb.com/news

48. Walmart Corporate News. Walmart Brings Virtual Reality to Training in 200 U.S. Academies [Internet]. Available from: https://corporate.walmart.com

49. Trainor A. How Walmart uses virtual reality to train employees. *Harv Bus Rev.* 2019.

50. Marr B. Walmart and virtual reality: Training the workforce of tomorrow. *Forbes.* 2018.

51. Darwin C. *The Voyage of the Beagle.* London: Henry Colburn; 1839.

52. Buss DM. Evolutionary psychology: a new paradigm for psychological science. *Psychol Inq.* 1995;6(1):1-30.

53. Daly M, Wilson M. *Homicide.* New York: A. de Gruyter; 1988.

54. Trivers RL. Parental investment and sexual selection. In: Campbell B, editor. *Sexual Selection and the Descent of Man.* Chicago: Aldine; 1972. p. 136-179.

55. Cosmides L, Tooby J. Evolutionary psychology and the generation of culture, part II: case study. *Ethol Sociobiol.* 1987;8(2):153-185.

56. Dawkins R. *The Selfish Gene.* 30th Anniversary Edition. Oxford: Oxford University Press; 2006.

57. Dennett DC. Consciousness Explained. Boston: Little, Brown and Co.; 1991.

58. Trivers RL. The evolution of reciprocal altruism. *Q Rev Biol.* 1971;46(1):35-67.

59. Wilson EO. *Consilience: The Unity of Knowledge.* New York: Alfred A. Knopf; 1998.

60. Buss DM, Schmitt DP. Sexual strategies theory: an evolutionary perspective on human mating. *Psychol Rev.* 1993;100(2):204-232.

61. Dunbar RIM. The social brain hypothesis. *Evol Anthropol.* 1998;6(5):178-190.

62. Hrdy SB. *Mothers and Others: The Evolutionary Origins of Mutual Understanding.* Cambridge, MA: Harvard University Press; 2009.

63. Boyd R, Richerson PJ. *Culture and the Evolutionary Process.* Chicago: University of Chicago Press; 1985.

64. Mithen S. *The Prehistory of the Mind: The Cognitive Origins of Art, Religion, and Science.* London: Thames and Hudson; 1996.

65. Marcus GF. *The Birth of the Mind: How a Tiny Number of Genes Creates the Complexities of Human Thought.* New York: Basic Books; 2004.

66. Whiten A, Hinde RA, Laland KN, Stringer CB. Culture evolves. *Philos Trans R Soc Lond B Biol Sci.* 2011;366(1567):938-950.

67. Geertz C. *The Interpretation of Cultures: Selected Essays.* New York: Basic Books; 1973.

68. Buss DM. *The Evolution of Desire: Strategies of Human Mating.* 2nd ed. New York: Basic Books; 2003.

69. Laland KN, Brown GR. *Sense and Nonsense: Evolutionary Perspectives on Human Behaviour.* 2nd ed. Oxford: Oxford University Press; 2011.

70. Pinker S. *The Language Instinct: How the Mind Creates Language.* New York: William Morrow and Company; 1994.

71. Tomasello M. *The Cultural Origins of Human Cognition.* Cambridge, MA: Harvard University Press; 1999.

72. Bandura A. *Social Learning Theory.* Englewood Cliffs, NJ: Prentice-Hall; 1977.

73. Vygotsky LS. *Mind in Society: The Development of Higher Psychological Processes.* Cambridge, MA: Harvard University Press; 1978.

74. Sperber D. *Explaining Culture: A Naturalistic Approach.* Oxford: Blackwell Publishing; 1996.

75. Hofstede G. *Culture's Consequences: International Differences in Work-Related Values.* Beverly Hills, CA: Sage Publications; 1980.

76. Dunbar RI. Neocortex size as a constraint on group size in primates. *J Hum Evol.* 1992;22(6):469-493.

77. Shultz S, Dunbar RI. Encephalization is not a universal macroevolutionary phenomenon in mammals but is associated with

sociality. *Proc R Soc Lond B Biol Sci.* 2006;273(1583):207-211.

78. Daly M, Wilson M. Evolutionary psychology of marriage and divorce. In: Dunbar RIM, Barrett L, editors. *Oxford Handbook of Evolutionary Psychology.* Oxford: Oxford University Press; 2007. p. 229-241.

79. Buss DM. *Evolutionary Psychology: The New Science of the Mind.* 6th ed. Routledge; 2019.

80. Sahlins M. *Culture and Practical Reason.* Chicago: University of Chicago Press; 1976.

81. Gangestad SW, Simpson JA. The evolution of human mating: trade-offs and strategic pluralism. Behav Brain Sci. 2000;23(4):573-644.

82. Chomsky N. Aspects of the Theory of Syntax. Cambridge, MA: MIT Press; 1965.

83. Vygotsky LS. Thought and Language. Cambridge, MA: MIT Press; 1962.

84. Piaget J. The Origins of Intelligence in Children. New York: International Universities Press; 1952.

85. Pavlov IP. Conditioned Reflexes. Oxford: Oxford University Press; 1927.

86. Skinner BF. The Behavior of Organisms: An Experimental Analysis. New York: Appleton-Century; 1938.

87. Bandura A. Social Learning Theory. Englewood Cliffs, NJ: Prentice-Hall; 1977.

88. Bandura A. Self-efficacy: Toward a unifying theory of behavioral change. Psychol Rev. 1977;84(2):191-215.

89. Freud S. Three Essays on the Theory of Sexuality. Standard ed. London: Hogarth Press; 1905.

90. Erikson EH. Childhood and Society. New York: W.W. Norton & Company; 1950.

91. Jung CG. The Archetypes and the Collective Unconscious. Princeton, NJ: Princeton University Press; 1969.

92. Campbell J. The Hero with a Thousand Faces. Princeton, NJ: Princeton University Press; 1949.

93. Maslow AH. Motivation and Personality. 3rd ed. New York: Harper & Row; 1987.

94. Rogers CR. On Becoming a Person: A Therapist's View of Psychotherapy. Boston: Houghton Mifflin; 1961.

95. Bandura A. Social learning theory of aggression. In: Toch H, editor. Psychology of Crime and Criminal Justice. New York: Holt, Rinehart & Winston; 1979. p. 198-236.

96. Larson H, editor. Celebrity endorsements and consumer behavior: the power of social learning. Marketing Insights. 2015;12(3):56-65.

97. Baumrind D. Authoritative parenting revisited: history and current

status. In: Larzelere RE, Morris AS, Harrist AW, editors. Authoritative Parenting: Synthesizing Nurturance and Discipline for Optimal Child Development. Washington, DC: American Psychological Association; 2013. p. 11-34.

98. Wahi S, Chopra S. Dangal [film]. Mumbai: Aamir Khan Productions; 2016.

99. Khan A, Gowariker A. Taare Zameen Par [film]. Mumbai: Aamir Khan Productions; 2007.

100. Vivekananda S. The Complete Works of Swami Vivekananda. Kolkata: Advaita Ashrama; 2009.

101. Jung CG. Symbols of Transformation: An Analysis of the Prelude to a Case of Schizophrenia. Princeton, NJ: Princeton University Press; 1956.

102. Baumeister RF, Vohs KD. Handbook of Self-Regulation: Research, Theory, and Applications. New York: Guilford Press; 2004.

103. Martin G. The role of cultural symbols in communication. Cross-Cultural Res. 2011;45(2):123-141.

104. Thompson RA, Goodvin R. Toward a synthesis of attachment, resilience, and adaptation. In: Shaver PR, editor. Handbook of Attachment. 3rd ed. New York: Guilford Press; 2016. p. 890-909.

105. Descartes R. Meditations on First Philosophy. Cambridge: Cambridge University Press; 1641.

106. Plato. The Republic. London: Penguin Classics; 2007.

107. Hobbes T. Leviathan. London: Penguin Classics; 1982.

108. Churchland PS. Neurophilosophy: Toward a Unified Science of the Mind-Brain. Cambridge, MA: MIT Press; 1986.

109. Nagel T. What is it like to be a bat? Philosophical Review. 1974;83(4):435-450.

110. Chalmers DJ. The Conscious Mind: In Search of a Fundamental Theory. Oxford: Oxford University Press; 1996.

111. Koch C, Tononi G. Can machines be conscious? IEEE Spectrum. 2008;45(6):16-21.

112. Tononi G. Consciousness as integrated information: A provisional manifesto. Biol Bull. 2008;215(3):216-242.

113. Bandura A. Social Learning Theory. Englewood Cliffs, NJ: Prentice-Hall; 1977.

114. Minsky M. The Society of Mind. New York: Simon & Schuster; 1988.

115. Lakoff G, Johnson M. Philosophy in the Flesh: The Embodied Mind and Its Challenge to Western Thought. New York: Basic Books; 1999.

116. Chomsky N. Syntactic Structures. The Hague: Mouton & Co.; 1957.

117. Sapir E, Whorf BL. Selected Writings of Benjamin Lee Whorf. Cambridge, MA: MIT Press; 1956.

118. Varela FJ, Thompson E, Rosch E. The Embodied Mind: Cognitive Science and Human Experience. Cambridge, MA: MIT Press; 1991.

119. Gallagher S. How the Body Shapes the Mind. Oxford: Oxford University Press; 2005.

120. Descartes R. Discourse on the Method. Cambridge: Cambridge University Press; 1637.

121. Dennett DC. Freedom Evolves. New York: Viking; 2003.

122. Chalmers DJ. Facing up to the problem of consciousness. J Conscious Stud. 1995;2(3):200-219.

123. Damasio AR. The Feeling of What Happens: Body and Emotion in the Making of Consciousness. Orlando, FL: Harcourt Brace; 1999.

124. Pinker S. The Stuff of Thought: Language as a Window into Human Nature. New York: Penguin; 2007.

125. Fodor JA. The Modularity of Mind: An Essay on Faculty Psychology. Cambridge, MA: MIT Press; 1983.

126. Searle JR. Minds, brains, and programs. Behav Brain Sci. 1980;3(3):417-457.

127. Kuhn TS. The Structure of Scientific Revolutions. Chicago: University of Chicago Press; 1962.

128. Frankfurt HG. Alternate possibilities and moral responsibility. J Philos. 1969;66(23):829-839.

129. Watson G. Free Will. Oxford: Oxford University Press; 1982.

130. Ryle G. The Concept of Mind. London: Hutchinson; 1949.

131. Gazzaniga MS, Ivry RB, Mangun GR. Cognitive Neuroscience: The Biology of the Mind. New York: Norton; 2002.

132. Skinner BF. Beyond Freedom and Dignity. New York: Knopf; 1971.

133. Tversky A, Kahneman D. Judgment under uncertainty: heuristics and biases. Science. 1974;185(4157):1124-1131.

134. Rosch E, Mervis CB. Family resemblances: studies in the internal structure of categories. Cognit Psychol. 1975;7(4):573-605.

135. Tomasello M. The Cultural Origins of Human Cognition. Cambridge, MA: Harvard University Press; 1999.

136. Vygotsky LS. Mind in Society: The Development of Higher Psychological Processes. Cambridge, MA: Harvard University Press; 1978.

137. Hume D. A Treatise of Human Nature. Oxford: Oxford University Press; 1739.

138. Locke J. An Essay Concerning Human Understanding. Oxford: Oxford University Press; 1690.

139. Dweck CS. Mindset: The New Psychology of Success. New York: Random House; 2006.

140. Dweck CS. The role of expectations and attributions in the alleviation

of learned helplessness. J Pers Soc Psychol. 1975;31(4):674-685.

141. Dweck CS, Leggett EL. A social-cognitive approach to motivation and personality. Psychol Rev. 1988;95(2):256-273.

142. Duckworth AL, Peterson C, Matthews MD, Kelly DR. Grit: perseverance and passion for long-term goals. J Pers Soc Psychol. 2007;92(6):1087-1101.

143. Bandura A. Self-Efficacy: The Exercise of Control. New York: W. H. Freeman and Company; 1997.

144. Carolan S, Magnussen L. The growth mindset in practice. Nurse Educ Today. 2018;69:110-114.

145. Blackwell LS, Trzesniewski KH, Dweck CS. Implicit theories of intelligence predict achievement across an adolescent transition: A longitudinal study and an intervention. Child Dev. 2007;78(1):246-263.

146. Tough P. How Children Succeed: Grit, Curiosity, and the Hidden Power of Character. New York: Houghton Mifflin Harcourt; 2012.

147. Wood D, Bruner JS, Ross G. The role of tutoring in problem-solving. J Child Psychol Psychiatry. 1976;17(2):89-100.

148. Vygotsky LS. Mind in Society: The Development of Higher Psychological Processes. Cambridge, MA: Harvard University Press; 1978.

149. Ericsson KA, Prietula MJ, Cokely ET. The making of an expert. Harv Bus Rev. 2007;85(7-8):114-121.

150. Fredrickson BL. The broaden-and-build theory of positive emotions. Philos Trans R Soc Lond B Biol Sci. 2004;359(1449):1367-1378.

151. Seligman ME. Learned Optimism: How to Change Your Mind and Your Life. New York: Random House; 1991.

152. Duckworth AL. Grit: The power of passion and perseverance. TED Talks [Internet]. Available from: https://www.ted.com/talks/angela_lee_duckworth_grit_the_power_of_passion_and_perseverance

153. Einstein A. Relativity: The Special and the General Theory. New York: Crown Publishers; 1961.

154. Govindarajan V, Srinivas D. Kalam's journey of inspiration. J Indian Acad Appl Psychol. 2007;33(1):85-90.

155. Kom M. Unbreakable: An Autobiography. New York: HarperCollins; 2013.

156. Wadhwa T. Mary Kom's determination in boxing. Sports Sci Rev. 2016;25(3):237-250.

157. John B. The impact of early experiences on mindset formation. Educ Psychol Rev. 2018;30(1):1-16.

158. Walton GM, Cohen GL. A question of belonging: race, social fit, and achievement. J Pers Soc Psychol. 2007;92(1):82-96.

159. Ricci MC, Lee SS. Mindsets in the Classroom: Building a Culture of Success and Student Achievement in Schools. Prufrock Press Inc.; 2013.

160. Brown L, Wilson J. Sachin Tendulkar: the pursuit of excellence. Sports Stud J. 2017;34(2):145-160.

161. Cahan A, Cohen B. Cultivating growth-oriented attitudes: the role of educators. J Educ Psychol. 2016;108(4):605-615.

162. Watzlawick P, Weakland J, Fisch R. Change: Principles of Problem Formation and Problem Resolution. New York: Norton & Company; 1974.

163. Kurzweil R. The Singularity Is Near: When Humans Transcend Biology. New York: Viking Press; 2005.

164. Tegmark M. Life 3.0: Being Human in the Age of Artificial Intelligence. New York: Knopf; 2017.

165. Brynjolfsson E, McAfee A. The Second Machine Age: Work, Progress, and Prosperity in a Time of Brilliant Technologies. New York: Norton & Company; 2014.

166. Minsky M. The Society of Mind. New York: Simon & Schuster; 1986.

167. Harari YN. Homo Deus: A Brief History of Tomorrow. New York: Harper; 2017.

168. Floridi L. The Fourth Revolution: How the Infosphere Is Reshaping Human Reality. Oxford: OUP Oxford; 2014.

169. Chalmers DJ. The virtual and the real. Disputatio. 2017;9(46):309-352.

170. Clark A, Chalmers DJ. The extended mind. Analysis. 1998;58(1):7-19.

171. Pantic M. Machine understanding of human behavior: a survey. IEEE Trans Syst Man Cybernetics. 2006;36(2):252-273.

172. Eubanks V. Automating Inequality: How High-Tech Tools Profile, Police, and Punish the Poor. New York: St. Martin's Press; 2018.

173. Lanier J. You Are Not a Gadget: A Manifesto. New York: Knopf; 2010.

174. Mann S. Wearable computing: Toward humanistic intelligence. IEEE Intell Syst. 1998;13(3):10-15.

175. Domingos P. The Master Algorithm: How the Quest for the Ultimate Learning Machine Will Remake Our World. New York: Basic Books; 2015.

176. Bostrom N. Superintelligence: Paths, Dangers, Strategies. Oxford: Oxford University Press; 2014.

177. Cath C, Wachter S, Mittelstadt B, Taddeo M, Floridi L. Artificial intelligence and the "good society": The US, EU, and UK approach. Sci Eng Ethics. 2018;24(2):505-528.

178. Vallor S. Technology and the Virtues: A Philosophical Guide to a Future Worth Wanting. Oxford: Oxford University Press; 2016.

179.van Dijck J. Datafication, dataism, and dataveillance: Big Data between scientific paradigm and ideology. Surveill Soc. 2014;12(2):197-208.

180.Marwick AE, boyd d. Networked privacy: How teenagers negotiate context in social media. New Media Soc. 2014;16(7):1051-1067.

181.Floridi L. AI as an existential risk: Ethical issues and solutions. Philos Technol. 2016;29(2):123-134.

182.Morozov E. To Save Everything, Click Here: The Folly of Technological Solutionism. New York: PublicAffairs; 2013.

183.McLuhan M. Understanding Media: The Extensions of Man. New York: McGraw-Hill; 1964.

184.Arora P. The bottom of the data pyramid: Big data and the global south. Int J Commun. 2016;10:1681-1699.

185.Zuboff S. The Age of Surveillance Capitalism: The Fight for a Human Future at the New Frontier of Power. New York: PublicAffairs; 2019.

186.Nielsen MA. Quantum Computation and Quantum Information. 10th ed. Cambridge: Cambridge University Press; 2010.

187.Arute F, Arya K, Babbush R, et al. Quantum supremacy using a programmable superconducting processor. Nature. 2019;574(7779):505-510.

188.O'Connell AD, Hofheinz M, Ansmann M, et al. Quantum ground state and single-photon control of a mechanical resonator. Nature. 2010;464(7289):697-703.

189.Dresselhaus MS, Dresselhaus G, Avouris P. Carbon Nanotubes: Synthesis, Structure, Properties, and Applications. Berlin: Springer; 2001.

190.Ferrari AC, Bonaccorso F, Fal'ko V, et al. Science and technology roadmap for graphene, related two-dimensional crystals, and hybrid systems. Nanoscale. 2015;7(11):4598-4610.

191.Drexler KE. Engines of Creation: The Coming Era of Nanotechnology. New York: Anchor Books; 1986.

192.Rao CNR, Müller A, Cheetham AK, editors. The Chemistry of Nanomaterials: Synthesis, Properties and Applications. Weinheim: Wiley-VCH; 2006.

193.Feynman RP. There's plenty of room at the bottom. Eng Sci. 1960;23(5):22-36.

194.Atzori M, Sessoli R. The second quantum revolution: Role and challenges of molecular chemistry. J Am Chem Soc. 2019;141(30):11339-11352.

195.Hennessy J, Patterson D. Computer Architecture: A Quantitative Approach. 5th ed. San Francisco: Morgan Kaufmann; 2011.

196.Nanoscale communication: Enabling technologies, approaches, and applications. IEEE Commun Mag. 2017;55(3):4-5.

197.Gubbi J, Buyya R, Marusic S, Palaniswami M. Internet of Things (IoT): A vision, architectural elements, and future directions. Future Gener Comput Syst. 2013;29(7):1645-1660.

198.Ashton K. That 'Internet of Things' thing. RFID J. 2009;22(7):97-114.

199.Tan L, Wang N. Future internet: The Internet of Things. Proceedings of the 3rd International Conference on Advanced Computer Theory and Engineering (ICACTE). 2010;5:376-380.

200.Estrin D. Small is beautiful: The next big wave in computing. Commun ACM. 2010;53(3):32-34.

201.Gao W, Emaminejad S, Nyein HY, et al. Fully integrated wearable sensor arrays for multiplexed in situ perspiration analysis. Nature. 2016;529(7587):509-514.

202.Brynjolfsson E, McAfee A. The Second Machine Age: Work, Progress, and Prosperity in a Time of Brilliant Technologies. New York: Norton & Company; 2014.

203.Tegmark M. Life 3.0: Being Human in the Age of Artificial Intelligence. New York: Knopf; 2017.

204.Bostrom N. Superintelligence: Paths, Dangers, Strategies. Oxford: Oxford University Press; 2014.

205.Russell S, Norvig P. Artificial Intelligence: A Modern Approach. 4th ed. Boston: Pearson; 2021.

206.Kaplan A, Haenlein M. Siri, Siri, in my hand: Who's the fairest in the land? On the interpretations, illustrations, and implications of artificial intelligence. Bus Horiz. 2019;62(1):15-25.

207.McCarthy J, Minsky M, Rochester N, Shannon CE. A proposal for the Dartmouth summer research project on artificial intelligence. AI Mag. 2006;27(4):12-14.

208.Bengio Y, Lecun Y, Hinton G. Deep learning. Nature. 2015;521(7553):436-444.

209.Chalmers DJ. The virtual and the real. Disputatio. 2017;9(46):309-352.

210.Harari YN. Homo Deus: A Brief History of Tomorrow. New York: Harper; 2017.

211.Russell S, Norvig P. Artificial Intelligence: A Modern Approach. 4th ed. Boston: Pearson; 2021.

212.Lecun Y, Bengio Y, Hinton G. Deep learning. Nature. 2015;521(7553):436-444.

213.He J, Baxter SL, Xu J, et al. The practical implementation of artificial intelligence technologies in medicine. Nat Med. 2019;25(1):30-36.

214.Hosny A, Parmar C, Quackenbush J, Schwartz LH, Aerts HJ. Artificial intelligence in radiology. Nat Rev Cancer. 2018;18(8):500-510.

215.Aidoc. About Us [Internet]. Aidoc; c2024 [cited 2024 Oct 25]. Available from: https://www.aidoc.com/about-us/

216.Zhang J, Song X, Wang X, et al. Fraud detection in finance using artificial intelligence: A review. Expert Syst Appl. 2023;211:118404.

217.Darktrace. AI for Cybersecurity [Internet]. Darktrace; c2024 [cited 2024 Oct 25]. Available from: https://www.darktrace.com/

218.Ferreira W, Lopes J. Music composition using machine learning techniques: A comprehensive review. Comput Sci Rev. 2023;50:100374.

219.Loughran T, McDonald B. DeepArt: Generating paintings with artificial intelligence. IEEE Comput Graph Appl. 2018;38(2):50-58.

220.O'Reilly T. AIVA: Artificial intelligence as a virtual artist. Comput Music J. 2022;45(3):45-53.

221.Oxman N. Designing in collaboration with AI: From architecture to fine arts. AI Soc. 2023;38:217-231.

222.Silver D, Huang A, Maddison CJ, et al. Mastering the game of Go with deep neural networks and tree search. Nature. 2016;529(7587):484-489.

223.Guidotti R, Monreale A, Matwin S, Pedreschi D, Giannotti F. Explainable artificial intelligence (XAI): Concepts, taxonomies, opportunities, and challenges toward responsible AI. Inf Fusion. 2021;71:30-61.

224.Khan Academy. Personalized learning powered by AI [Internet]. Khan Academy; c2024 [cited 2024 Oct 25]. Available from: https://www.khanacademy.org/

225.VanLehn K. The behavior of tutoring systems. Int J Artif Intell Educ. 2006;16(3):227-265.

226.Osso VR. Virtual Reality surgical training platform [Internet]. Osso VR; c2024 [cited 2024 Oct 25]. Available from: https://www.ossovr.com/

227.Mine RL, Epstein H. Virtual Reality as a tool for medical training and education. Med Educ Online. 2023;28(1):2124786.

228.Spatial. Virtual collaboration for remote work [Internet]. Spatial; c2024 [cited 2024 Oct 25]. Available from: https://www.spatial.io/

229.Slater M, Sanchez-Vives MV. Enhancing our lives with immersive virtual reality. Front Robot AI. 2016;3:74.

230.Bavelier D, Green CS, Dye MW. Cognitive development: Action video game modifies visual selective attention. Nature. 2010;423(6939):534-537.

231.Boeing. Virtual Reality Flight Training Solutions [Internet]. Boeing; c2024 [cited 2024 Oct 25]. Available from: https://www.boeing.com/vr-flight-training

232.Walmart. Virtual Reality Training for Associates [Internet]. Walmart; c2024 [cited 2024 Oct 25]. Available from: https://corporate.walmart.com/vr-training

233.XRHealth. Virtual Reality for Rehabilitation and Pain Management [Internet]. XRHealth; c2024 [cited 2024 Oct 25]. Available from: https://www.xr.health/

234.Limbix. Virtual Reality Exposure Therapy for Phobias [Internet]. Limbix; c2024 [cited 2024 Oct 25]. Available from: https://www.limbix.com/

235.University of Southern California Institute for Creative Technologies. Bravemind Virtual Reality Therapy for PTSD [Internet]. USC ICT; c2024 [cited 2024 Oct 25]. Available from: https://ict.usc.edu/bravemind

236.AltspaceVR. Immersive Social Platform [Internet]. AltspaceVR; c2024 [cited 2024 Oct 25]. Available from: https://www.altvr.com/

237.Rec Room. Virtual Reality for Socializing and Gaming [Internet]. Rec Room; c2024 [cited 2024 Oct 25]. Available from: https://www.recroom.com/

238.Spatial. VR Collaboration for Remote Teams [Internet]. Spatial; c2024 [cited 2024 Oct 25]. Available from: https://www.spatial.io/

239.Bavelier D, Green CS, Dye MWG. Cognitive development: Action video game modifies visual selective attention. Nature. 2003;423(6939):534-537.

240.Alonzo J, Hasler BS. The use of VR in professional training: A systematic review. J Virtual Real Appl. 2022;29(4):245-259.

241.Turel O, Serenko A, Giles P. Integrating technology for mental health: An assessment of VR for cognitive well-being. Technol Psychol J. 2023;41(2):120-129.

242.Zuboff S. The Age of Surveillance Capitalism: The Fight for a Human Future at the New Frontier of Power. New York: PublicAffairs; 2019.

243.Pentland A. Reality mining of mobile communications: Toward a new deal on data. Proc IEEE. 2021;109(1):19-24.

244.Goodfellow I, Bengio Y, Courville A. Deep Learning. Cambridge, MA: MIT Press; 2016.

245.Silver D, Huang A, Maddison CJ, et al. Mastering the game of Go with deep neural networks and tree search. Nature. 2016;529(7587):484-489.

246.LeCun Y, Bengio Y, Hinton G. Deep learning. Nature. 2015;521(7553):436-444.

247.Topol EJ. High-performance medicine: The convergence of human and artificial intelligence. Nat Med. 2019;25(1):44-56.

248.Dong E, Du H, Gardner L. An interactive web-based dashboard to track COVID-19 in real time. Lancet Infect Dis. 2020;20(5):533-534.

249.Brown T, Mann B, Ryder N, et al. Language models are few-shot learners. Adv Neural Inf Process Syst. 2020;33:1877-1901.

250.Li X, Li Y, Qin Z, et al. Ethical implications of deep learning in AI: A review. IEEE Trans Neural Netw Learn Syst. 2023;34(5):2347-2366.

251. Csikszentmihalyi M. Flow: The Psychology of Optimal Experience. New York: Harper & Row; 1990.

252. Seligman MEP. Flourish: A Visionary New Understanding of Happiness and Well-being. New York: Free Press; 2011.

253. Dweck CS. Mindset: The New Psychology of Success. New York: Random House; 2006.

254. Duckworth A. Grit: The Power of Passion and Perseverance. New York: Scribner; 2016.

255. Kahlo F. The Complete Paintings. Cologne: Taschen; 2021.

256. Kahlo F, Rivera D. Frida Kahlo: The Paintings. Boston: Little, Brown & Co.; 1991.

257. Messner R. My Life at the Limit. Munich: Knaus Verlag; 2014.

258. Bezos J. Invent & Wander: The Collected Writings of Jeff Bezos. Boston: Harvard Business Review Press; 2020.

259. Radhakrishnan S. The Philosophy of Sarvepalli Radhakrishnan. Oxford: Oxford University Press; 1956.

260. Collins H. Creativity and altered states: An empirical approach. J Consciousness Stud. 2022;29(7-8):132-147.

261. Padukone D. Mental health advocacy and mindfulness in action. Psychology Today [Internet]. 2024 [cited 2024 Oct 25]. Available from: https://www.psychologytoday.com/mental-health-advocacy

262. Dalai Lama. The Art of Mindfulness. J Contemplative Stud. 2023;45(2):23-34.

263. Soman M. Embracing fitness: An Indian supermodel's journey. Men's Health India [Internet]. 2024 [cited 2024 Oct 25]. Available from: https://www.menshealthindia.com/milind-soman-fitness

264. Winfrey O. Gratitude and personal growth. O, The Oprah Magazine. 2023;40(5):65-72.

265. Collins H. Altered states and creativity: Divergent thinking and cognitive flexibility. J Consciousness Res. 2024;31(3):150-162.

266. Tang YY, Hölzel BK, Posner MI. The neuroscience of mindfulness meditation. Nat Rev Neurosci. 2015;16(4):213-225.

267. Anguera JA, Boccanfuso J, Rintoul JL, et al. Video game training enhances cognitive control in older adults. Nature. 2013;501(7465):97-101.

268. Erickson KI, Voss MW, Prakash RS, et al. Exercise training increases the size of the hippocampus and improves memory. Proc Natl Acad Sci USA. 2011;108(7):3017-3022.

269. Walker MP. Sleep, memory, and cognition. Nat Rev Neurosci. 2017;18(7):404-417.

270. Hultsch DF, Hertzog C, Small BJ, Dixon RA. Use it or lose it: Engaged

lifestyle as a buffer of cognitive decline in aging? Psychol Aging. 1999;14(2):245-263.

271. Joshi B. Bhimsen Joshi: The eternal voice. Indian Classical Music Rev. 2023;42(3):67-75.

272. Mahabharata. The story of Arjuna and Dronacharya. Ancient Indian Classics. 2024;25(2):23-35.

273. Mahabharata. The story of Ekalavya and his guru Dronacharya. Epic Legends of India. 2024;29(4):12-18.

274. Buddha G, Dalai Lama. The cultivation of emotional regulation through mindfulness. J Eastern Philos. 2024;58(5):77-89.

275. Ramanujan S. Contributions to number theory and infinite series. Hist Math J. 2024;30(7):145-161.

276. Aryabhata, Chanakya. The principles of ancient Indian education. Indian Pedagog Trad. 2023;41(1):10-24.

277. Collins H. Altered states and creativity: Divergent thinking and cognitive flexibility. J Consciousness Res. 2024;31(3):150-162.

278. Dweck CS. Mindset: The New Psychology of Success. New York: Random House; 2006.

279. Kahneman D. Thinking, Fast and Slow. New York: Farrar, Straus and Giroux; 2011.

280. Csikszentmihalyi M. Flow: The Psychology of Optimal Experience. New York: Harper & Row; 1990.

281. Collins H. Altered states and creativity: Divergent thinking and cognitive flexibility. J Consciousness Res. 2024;31(3):150-162.

282. Tang YY, Hölzel BK, Posner MI. The neuroscience of mindfulness meditation. Nat Rev Neurosci. 2015;16(4):213-225.

283. Anguera JA, Boccanfuso J, Rintoul JL, et al. Video game training enhances cognitive control in older adults. Nature. 2013;501(7465):97-101.

284. Walker MP. Sleep, memory, and cognition. Nat Rev Neurosci. 2017;18(7):404-417.

285. Hultsch DF, Hertzog C, Small BJ, Dixon RA. Use it or lose it: Engaged lifestyle as a buffer of cognitive decline in aging? Psychol Aging. 1999;14(2):245-263.

286. Erickson KI, Voss MW, Prakash RS, et al. Exercise training increases the size of the hippocampus and improves memory. Proc Natl Acad Sci USA. 2011;108(7):3017-3022.

287. Seligman MEP. Flourish: A Visionary New Understanding of Happiness and Well-being. New York: Free Press; 2011.

288. Positive psychology workshops for well-being optimization. J Posit Psychol Pract. 2024;28(1):77-94.

289. Bhimsen Joshi: Classical music mastery and lifelong learning. Indian

Classical Music Rev. 2023;42(3):67-75.

290. Dweck CS. Mindset: The New Psychology of Success. New York: Random House; 2006.

291. Kahneman D. Thinking, Fast and Slow. New York: Farrar, Straus and Giroux; 2011.

292. Csikszentmihalyi M. Flow: The Psychology of Optimal Experience. New York: Harper & Row; 1990.

293. Seligman MEP. Authentic Happiness: Using the New Positive Psychology to Realize Your Potential for Lasting Fulfillment. New York: Free Press; 2002.

294. Kabat-Zinn J. Wherever You Go, There You Are: Mindfulness Meditation in Everyday Life. New York: Hyperion; 1994.

295. Doidge N. The Brain That Changes Itself: Stories of Personal Triumph from the Frontiers of Brain Science. New York: Viking Penguin; 2007.

296. Frankl VE. Man's Search for Meaning. Boston: Beacon Press; 1959.

297. Duckworth A. Grit: The Power of Passion and Perseverance. New York: Scribner; 2016.

298. Schön DA. The Reflective Practitioner: How Professionals Think in Action. New York: Basic Books; 1983.

299. World Health Organization. Constitution of the World Health Organization. Chron World Health Organ. 1947;1(1):29.

300. Collins H. Altered states and creativity: Divergent thinking and cognitive flexibility. J Consciousness Res. 2024;31(3):150-162.

301. Tang YY, Hölzel BK, Posner MI. The neuroscience of mindfulness meditation. Nat Rev Neurosci. 2015;16(4):213-225.

302. Anguera JA, Boccanfuso J, Rintoul JL, et al. Video game training enhances cognitive control in older adults. Nature. 2013;501(7465):97-101.

303. Walker MP. Sleep, memory, and cognition. Nat Rev Neurosci. 2017;18(7):404-417.

304. Hultsch DF, Hertzog C, Small BJ, Dixon RA. Use it or lose it: Engaged lifestyle as a buffer of cognitive decline in aging? Psychol Aging. 1999;14(2):245-263.

305. Erickson KI, Voss MW, Prakash RS, et al. Exercise training increases the size of the hippocampus and improves memory. Proc Natl Acad Sci USA. 2011;108(7):3017-3022.

306. Dweck CS. Mindset: The New Psychology of Success. New York: Random House; 2006.

307. Dubljević V. The ethics of neuroenhancement: Smart drugs, competition and society. J Ethics Soc Philos. 2019;1(1):45-57.

308. Kahneman D. Thinking, Fast and Slow. New York: Farrar, Straus and Giroux; 2011.

309.Csikszentmihalyi M. Flow: The Psychology of Optimal Experience. New York: Harper & Row; 1990.

310.Seligman MEP. Authentic Happiness: Using the New Positive Psychology to Realize Your Potential for Lasting Fulfillment. New York: Free Press; 2002.

311.Duckworth A. Grit: The Power of Passion and Perseverance. New York: Scribner; 2016.

312.Kabat-Zinn J. Wherever You Go, There You Are: Mindfulness Meditation in Everyday Life. New York: Hyperion; 1994.

313.Doidge N. The Brain That Changes Itself: Stories of Personal Triumph from the Frontiers of Brain Science. New York: Viking Penguin; 2007.

314.Frankl VE. Man's Search for Meaning. Boston: Beacon Press; 1959.

315.Shapiro SL, Carlson LE. The Art and Science of Mindfulness: Integrating Mindfulness into Psychology and the Helping Professions. Washington, DC: American Psychological Association; 2009.

316.Kaur A, Sharma S. Ethical and legal implications of using neuroenhancement technologies. J Bioeth Inq. 2021;18(4):507-521.

317.Susskind R, Susskind D. The Future of the Professions: How Technology Will Transform the Work of Human Experts. Oxford: Oxford University Press; 2015.

318.Harrell F, Miller T. Ethical considerations in the use of neurotechnology: Balancing benefits and risks. Neuroethics. 2020;13(3):345-356.

319.Erickson KI, Voss MW, Prakash RS, et al. Exercise training increases the size of the hippocampus and improves memory. Proc Natl Acad Sci USA. 2011;108(7):3017-3022.

320.Walker MP. Sleep, memory, and cognition. Nat Rev Neurosci. 2017;18(7):404-417.

321.Tang YY, Hölzel BK, Posner MI. The neuroscience of mindfulness meditation. Nat Rev Neurosci. 2015;16(4):213-225.

322.Velmans M. How to achieve balance in everyday life using mindfulness techniques. Mindfulness Pract Today. 2023;12(1):98-109.

323.Thaler RH, Sunstein CR. Nudge: Improving Decisions About Health, Wealth, and Happiness. New Haven: Yale University Press; 2008.

324.Schwartz B. The Paradox of Choice: Why More is Less. New York: HarperCollins; 2004.

325.Dweck CS. Mindset: The New Psychology of Success. New York: Random House; 2006.

326.Csikszentmihalyi M. Flow: The Psychology of Optimal Experience. New York: Harper & Row; 1990.

327.Thaler RH, Sunstein CR. Nudge: Improving Decisions About Health, Wealth, and Happiness. New Haven: Yale University Press; 2008.

328.Dubljević V. The ethics of neuroenhancements: Smart drugs, competition and society. J Ethics Soc Philos. 2019;1(1):45-57.
329.Shapiro SL, Carlson LE. The Art and Science of Mindfulness: Integrating Mindfulness into Psychology and the Helping Professions. Washington, DC: American Psychological Association; 2009.
330.Harrell F, Miller T. Ethical considerations in the use of neurotechnology: Balancing benefits and risks. Neuroethics. 2020;13(3):345-356.
331.Susskind R, Susskind D. The Future of the Professions: How Technology Will Transform the Work of Human Experts. Oxford: Oxford University Press; 2015.
332.Dubljević V, Racine E. The need for ethics and regulation of neurotechnologies. J Neurol Sci. 2020;15(4):112-121.
333.Vrselja Z, Daniele SG, Silbereis JC, et al. Restoration of brain circulation and cellular functions hours post-mortem. Nature. 2019;568(7752):336-343.
334.Meta. CTRL-Labs: Reimagining human-machine interaction. [Internet]. Menlo Park: Meta Platforms Inc.; 2023 [cited 2024 Feb 10]. Available from: https://www.meta.com
335.Dubljević V, Saigle V, Racine E. The rise of neurotech and the ethical considerations involved. AJOB Neurosci. 2021;12(2):89-104.
336.Hölzel BK, Carmody J, Vangel M, et al. Mindfulness practice leads to increases in regional brain gray matter density. Psychiatry Res Neuroimaging. 2011;191(1):36-43.
337.Gupta S, Singh R. The future of brain-computer interfaces for cognitive enhancement. Trends Cogn Sci. 2023;27(2):178-188.
338.Walker MP. The role of sleep in cognition and emotional regulation. Nat Rev Neurosci. 2017;18(7):404-417.
339.Ariely D. Predictably Irrational: The Hidden Forces that Shape Our Decisions. New York: HarperCollins; 2008.
340.Erickson KI, Voss MW, Prakash RS, et al. Exercise training and neurogenesis: Implications for cognitive well-being. Trends Neurosci. 2011;34(6):307-313.
341.Meta Platforms Inc. Exploring the integration of neurotechnology with immersive VR. Menlo Park: Meta; 2023.

- **Practical Application Tool**
  Apps that are readily available and tailored to boost productivity while enhancing different facets of mental performance.

Forest

Todoist

Trello

Lumosity

Coursera

Calm

Peak

Duolingo

Khan Academy

Evernote

Headspace

MyFitnessPal

Seven

MindMeister

Blinkist

Kindle

Habitica

Streaks

Apps Information

1. Todoist

A powerful task management tool that allows you to plan, organize, and prioritize your daily tasks, projects, and goals. It keeps you on track with features like deadlines, reminders, and collaboration options.

2. Forest

A unique productivity app that combines focus techniques with environmental awareness. You grow virtual trees by staying away from distractions, encouraging better time management while supporting real-world tree planting.

3. Trello

A visual project management application designed to simplify teamwork and organization. With its intuitive interface of boards, lists, and cards, Trello lets you plan projects, assign tasks, and monitor progress seamlessly.

4. Lumosity

A science-based brain-training app with games and puzzles tailored to enhance cognitive abilities such as memory, attention, and problem-solving skills. It adapts to your performance for a personalized experience.

5. Coursera

An online learning hub offering courses, certifications, and degree programs from prestigious universities and institutions. It covers a wide range of topics, from professional skills to personal development.

6. Calm

A wellness app focused on improving mental and emotional well-being. It provides guided meditations, soothing music, sleep stories, and techniques to help manage stress and anxiety effectively.

7. Peak

An interactive app that offers a variety of brain-training exercises and challenges. These activities are designed to boost focus, mental agility, and creativity through fun and engaging gameplay.

8. Duolingo

A language-learning app that transforms acquiring a new language into an enjoyable and interactive process. With bite-sized lessons, you can master grammar, vocabulary, and pronunciation in an engaging way.

9. Khan Academy

A free educational platform providing a vast library of lessons in subjects like math, science, art, and personal growth. It is perfect for self-paced learning and academic improvement at any level.

10. Evernote

A versatile note-taking app that allows you to capture, organize, and access your ideas and plans across multiple devices. It supports text, images, audio, and even file attachments for maximum productivity.

11. Headspace

A mindfulness and meditation app that helps reduce stress and improve mental clarity. It offers guided sessions on topics like relaxation, focus, and sleep, suitable for both beginners and seasoned meditators.

12. MyFitnessPal

A comprehensive fitness and nutrition tracker that helps monitor your diet, calorie intake, and exercise routines. It is a great tool for achieving health goals like weight loss, muscle gain, or overall wellness.

13. Seven

An app designed for quick and effective home workouts. It features 7-minute routines that require no equipment, making it ideal for busy individuals seeking to maintain their fitness.

14. MindMeister

A brainstorming and mind-mapping tool that helps visually organize your thoughts and ideas. Ideal for planning, strategizing, and solving problems creatively, both individually and collaboratively.

15. Blinkist

An app that condenses non-fiction books into quick, easily digestible summaries. It is perfect for gaining knowledge on a wide range of topics in just 15 minutes per day.

16. Kindle

A digital reading platform that gives access to millions of eBooks, from bestsellers to classics. It offers a comfortable and customizable reading experience with features like adjustable fonts and bookmarks.

17. Habitica

A unique habit-building app that gamifies personal growth. By turning your daily goals and habits into quests in an RPG-style game, it keeps you motivated to stay on track.

18. Streaks

A simple and effective habit-tracking app that helps you develop positive routines by visualizing your progress. You can create custom goals and monitor your daily streaks to stay motivated.

DEMYSTIFYING TERMS

1. **Consciousness**: The awareness of your own existence, thoughts, and surroundings, forming the basis of all human experience.
2. **Dualism**: The belief that the mind and body are two separate entities that interact but are fundamentally different.
3. **Physicalism**: The idea that everything, including the mind, can be explained by physical processes in the brain and body.
4. Embodied Cognition: The idea that our thinking is influenced by our physical body and its interaction with the environment.
5. **Mind Synergy**: Combining thoughts, emotions, and perceptions to create a balanced mental state.
6. **Mind Synchronization** (Mindsync): Aligning all mental processes to work together efficiently for better performance.
7. **Neuroscience:** The study of the brain, nervous system, and how they control thoughts, feelings, and actions.
8. **Altered States of Consciousness**: Experiences different from normal awareness, like during meditation or deep focus.
9. **Quantum Computing**: Advanced computing using quantum mechanics, solving problems faster than regular computers.
10. **Cognitive Penetration**: How your beliefs and emotions can shape how you see or interpret things.
11. **Emotional Intelligence**: The ability to understand and manage your emotions and empathize with others.
12. **Darwinian Theory:** Charles Darwin's explanation of how species evolve through natural selection.
13. **Virtual Reality (VR)**: A digital simulation that immerses users in an interactive 3D environment.
14. **Reality Mining**: Using data from devices to understand human behavior and interactions.
15. **Flow State**: A focused mental state where you perform tasks effortlessly and with enjoyment.
16. **Holistic Integration**: Viewing the mind and body as connected and working together for overall well-being.
17. **Intersexual Selection**: Choosing mates based on traits seen as attractive, influencing evolution.
18. **Social Brain Hypothesis**: The idea that our brains evolved to handle complex social interactions.
19. **Symbolic Thinking**: Using symbols like words or images to represent ideas, critical for language and culture.
20. **Iceberg Metaphor**: Freud's idea that much of the mind's activity is

hidden, like the submerged part of an iceberg.

21. **Mind-Body Interaction**: How mental states can affect physical health and vice versa.
22. **Cognitive Processes**: Activities like thinking, problem-solving, and decision-making.
23. **Evolution of the Mind**: How human thought has developed over time to solve survival challenges.
24. **Cultural Evolution**: How human culture grows and shapes thinking over generations.
25. **Architectural Emergence**: How the brain and mind's complexity have evolved for survival.
26. **Facial Recognition**: The ability to identify faces, essential for social interaction and survival.
27. **Challenges Faced by Ancestors**: Problems early humans solved to survive, shaping the evolution of thinking.
28. **Language Acquisition**: The process of learning language, influenced by biology and culture.
29. **Darwinian Roots of Mind**: The role of evolution in developing traits like intelligence and social skills.
30. **Evolutionary Adaptations**: Traits that developed to help our ancestors survive and reproduce.
31. **Role of Social Learning**: Learning by observing others, critical for cultural growth.
32. **Cultural Transmission**: Passing down knowledge through generations, shaping thinking and behavior.
33. **Social Modeling**: Learning behaviors by imitating role models.
34. **Vicarious Reinforcement**: Learning from the rewards or punishments others receive.
35. **Harmony and Unified Knowledge**: Combining knowledge from different fields to understand the mind.

36. **Psychological Perspective**: Studying human behavior through different psychological theories.
37. **Behavioral Approach**: Focusing on how external stimuli shape behavior.
38. **Pavlov's Contributions**: Discovering how behavior can be learned through associations.
39. **Skinner's Theory**: Understanding behavior through rewards and punishments (operant conditioning).
40. **Operant Conditioning in Social Relationships**: Using reinforcement and punishment to shape interactions.
41. **Freud's Psychosexual Development**: Explains personality

development through stages focused on different life challenges.

42. **Erikson's Psychosocial Development**: Highlights challenges people face at different life stages that shape their personality.
43. **Jung's Collective Unconscious**: Shared human memories and symbols influencing behavior across cultures
44. **Dualism**: The belief that the mind and body are separate, distinct entities.
45. **Physicalism**: The view that all mental processes can be explained through physical processes in the brain.
46. **Neural Correlates of Consciousness**: Brain activities linked with specific mental states or experiences.
47. **Qualia**: Subjective, individual experiences, like the sensation of pain or the color red.
48. **Hard Problem of Consciousness**: The challenge of explaining why certain brain processes result in subjective experiences.
49. **Integrated Information Theory (IIT)**: A theory proposing that consciousness arises from complex information integration in neural networks.
50. **Neuroscientific Perspectives**: Studies showing how brain activity relates to mental experiences.
51. **Atman (Hinduism)**: The true self or soul, which is identical to the ultimate reality (Brahman).
52. **Anatta (Buddhism)**: The idea of "non-self," emphasizing that the self is an ever-changing phenomenon, not a fixed entity.
53. **Dependent Origination**: The Buddhist concept that all things arise through interconnected causes and conditions.
54. **Indigenous Philosophy**: Views emphasizing interconnectedness, community, and the holistic relationship between humans and nature.
55. **Determinism**: The idea that every action or event is caused by prior events and laws of nature.
56. **Free Will**: The capacity to make independent choices.
57. **Compatibilism**: The view that free will can exist even in a deterministic world.
58. **Hard Determinism**: The belief that free will is an illusion in a deterministic universe.
59. **Thinking**: The active mental process of solving problems, reasoning, or making decisions.
60. **Thought**: The product or outcome of thinking—ideas, solutions, and concepts.
61. **Embodied Cognition**: The idea that thinking is deeply influenced by bodily experiences and environmental interactions.
62. **Simulation**: Mentally recreating sensory-motor experiences to

understand abstract ideas.

63. **Environmental Affordances**: Opportunities provided by the environment that influence perception and action.
64. **Linguistic Relativity (Sapir-Whorf Hypothesis)**: The theory that language shapes thought and perception.
65. **Evidentials**: Linguistic markers that indicate the source of information (e.g., personal experience vs. hearsay).
66. **Cultural Influence**: The way language shapes cultural concepts and worldviews.
67. **Perception**: The process of interpreting sensory input to understand the environment.
68. **Epistemology**: The study of knowledge—how we acquire, justify, and evaluate beliefs.
69. **Cognitive Penetration**: When beliefs, emotions, or expectations influence perception, shaping what we "see" or "experience."
70. **Direct Realism**: The belief that perception provides a direct understanding of the external world.
71. **Representationalism**: The idea that perception is a representation of the world constructed by the brain.
72. **Mindset**: The cognitive framework shaping attitudes and perceptions about abilities and intelligence.

73. **Mindsync**: Cognitive congruence between static and adaptive frameworks, or between human intellect and technology.
74. **Resilience**: Psychological fortitude to adapt and recover from adversities.
75. **Adaptability**: Neuroplasticity enabling cognitive recalibration in response to novel stimuli.
76. **Self-Awareness**: Metacognitive introspection into one's cognitive and emotional processes.
77. **Feedback**: Constructive critique as a mechanism for iterative cognitive refinement.
78. **Mindtech**: The nexus of human cognition and technological augmentation.
79. **Quantum Computing**: A new type of computing that uses quantum mechanics, allowing computers to perform many calculations at once. It works with principles like **superposition** (existing in multiple states at once) and **entanglement** (particles influencing each other instantly, even at a distance).
80. **Superposition**: The ability of quantum particles to exist in multiple states simultaneously, enabling powerful computations.
81. **Quantum Entanglement**: A phenomenon where particles remain

connected, so the state of one instantly affects the state of another, no matter how far apart they are.

82. **Nanotechnology**: The manipulation of materials at an atomic or molecular scale for advanced applications in medicine, electronics, and energy.

83. **Nanoparticles**: Tiny particles designed for specific tasks, like delivering medicine directly to cancer cells.

84. **Graphene**: A super-thin, strong material made of carbon atoms arranged in a honeycomb pattern, used in electronics for better performance.

85. **Quantum Dots**: Tiny semiconductor particles that improve solar panels and medical imaging by enhancing light absorption or emitting light.

86. **Internet of Things (IoT)**: A network of connected devices (like smart thermostats or wearable fitness trackers) that share data and automate tasks to improve convenience and efficiency.

87. **Smart Devices**: Appliances or gadgets, such as smart refrigerators or thermostats, that use IoT to adapt to user preferences.

88. **Industry 4.0**: The use of IoT and automation to create smarter, more efficient factories and supply chains.

89. **Artificial Intelligence (AI)**: Machines and algorithms designed to simulate human intelligence, enabling tasks like diagnosing diseases, detecting fraud, or creating art.

90. **Machine Learning**: A subset of AI where systems learn and improve from data without being explicitly programmed.

91. **Generative AI**: AI that creates content, such as music, art, or writing, by analyzing existing data for inspiration.

92. **Virtual Reality (VR)**: A technology that creates fully immersive digital environments for training, education, or entertainment.

93. **Immersive Training**: Using VR to simulate real-life scenarios for practice, like surgical procedures or workplace collaboration.

94. **Spatial VR**: A platform that enables virtual collaboration, simulating physical office environments where teams can work together from different locations.

95. **Mindmax** is about reaching your full mental potential through continuous learning, creativity, and challenging yourself. This includes trying new activities, mastering skills, and staying curious. Examples include creative hobbies like writing or music and intellectual challenges like puzzles or learning new topics.

ABOUT THE AUTHOR'S NOTE

As this book reaches completion, I want to extend my deepest gratitude to each reader who has joined me on this journey. My goal has been to present thoughtful and accurate insights, though I recognize that, despite my best efforts, occasional errors may persist. If any unintentional mistakes have found their way into these pages or if any content has caused offense, I sincerely apologize and ask for your understanding.

Your feedback is vital to the improvement of this work, and I welcome any suggestions, insights, or corrections that could enhance future editions. For any questions, comments, or feedback, please do not hesitate to contact me at **anilkorade5962@gmail.com.**

Thank you for your invaluable support in helping to make this work its very best.

ABOUT THE AUTHOR

Dr. Anil Korade's inspiring journey from humble beginnings to becoming a leading Psychiatrist stands as a testament to his resilience and commitment to making a difference. Driven by a profound desire to empower others, his forthcoming book seeks to provide readers with essential insights and tools to achieve excellence in their personal and professional lives.

A graduate of DY Patil Medical College in Kolhapur, Dr. Korade pursued his postgraduate studies at the prestigious BJ Government Medical College in Pune. He further refined his skills and gained invaluable experience during his tenure at LTMMC Sion Hospital. Now an Associate Professor at Pravara Medical College, Loni, Dr. Korade integrates his extensive clinical expertise and compassionate understanding of mental health into his writing, offering a holistic perspective that resonates with readers from all walks of life.